THE LEAST OF MY BRETHREN

The Least of My Brethren

Domingo de Soto on Poverty and Property

ERNEST J. WEINRIB

UNIVERSITY OF TORONTO PRESS
Toronto Buffalo London

© University of Toronto Press 2026
Toronto Buffalo London
utppublishing.com
Printed in Canada

ISBN 978-1-0498-0134-6 (cloth)   ISBN 978-1-0498-0136-0 (EPUB)
                                      ISBN 978-1-0498-0135-3 (PDF)

Library and Archives Canada Cataloguing in Publication

Title: The least of my brethren : Domingo de Soto on poverty and property / Ernest J. Weinrib.
Other titles: Domingo de Soto on poverty and property
Names: Weinrib, Ernest J., author | Container of (expression): Soto, Domingo de, 1494–1560.
    Deliberación en la causa de los pobres. English. | Container of (expression): Soto, Domingo de,
    1494–1560. De iustitia et iure. English.
Series: Toronto studies in medieval law.
Description: Series statement: Toronto studies in medieval law | Includes bibliographical references
    and index.
Identifiers: Canadiana (print) 20260125245 | Canadiana (ebook) 20260125326 |
    ISBN 9781049801346 (cloth) | ISBN 9781049801360 (EPUB) | ISBN 9781049801353 (PDF)
Subjects: LCSH: Soto, Domingo de, 1494–1560. Deliberación en la causa de los pobres. | LCSH:
    Soto, Domingo de, 1494–1560. De iustitia et iure. | LCSH: Almshouses – Spain – Early works to
    1800. | LCSH: Poor – Spain – Early works to 1800. | LCSH: Begging – Spain – Early works to
    1800. | LCSH: Poverty – Early works to 1800. | LCSH: Right of property – Early works to 1800.
Classification: LCC HV343.S653 W45 2026 | DDC 362.50946–dc23wWe

Cover design: Alan Jones
Cover image: The Beggars. 1568. Peter Bruegel the Elder, Louvre, Paris. Public Domain.

The manufacturer's authorised representative in the EU for product safety is Mare Nostrum Group
B.V., Doelen 72, 4831 GR Breda, The Netherlands. Email: gpsr@mare-nostrum.co.uk.

We wish to acknowledge the land on which the University of Toronto Press operates. This land is
the traditional territory of the Wendat, the Anishnaabeg, the Haudenosaunee, the Métis, and the
Mississaugas of the Credit First Nation.

This book has been published with the help of a grant from the Federation for the Humanities and
Social Sciences, through the Awards to Scholarly Publications Program, using funds provided by the
Social Sciences and Humanities Research Council of Canada.

University of Toronto Press acknowledges the financial support of the Government of Canada,
the Canada Council for the Arts, and the Ontario Arts Council, an agency of the Government of
Ontario, for its publishing activities.

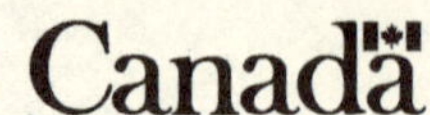

Contents

Preface and Acknowledgments

This book deals with the connection between poverty and property in the thought of Domingo de Soto, a leading theologian and philosopher of Spain's Golden Age. Between his birth in 1494 and his death in 1560 his world underwent momentous transitions that included Spain's conquests in the Americas, the Protestant Reformation, and the Catholic reaction to it. The period also produced social and economic dislocations that aggravated the problem of pauperism, giving rise to new ideas about how to deal with the poor against the background of prevailing conceptions of private property. From his eminent position at Spain's dominant university in Salamanca, Soto was an active participant in the resulting debates. This book offers translations of the relevant texts from Soto's voluminous writings as well as an analysis of his views, especially of their legal dimension.

The book has two principal goals: The first is to expand the resources readily available to legal and political theorists in the English-speaking world by presenting translated texts that academic lawyers and students of political theory may be unable to access in their Latin originals. For example, the theory of property is a vigorous field of legal theory, the modern form of which, for many contemporary scholars, begins with seventeenth-century Dutch legal philosopher Hugo Grotius. The texts presented in this book and discussed in its introductory essay facilitate both a re-assessment of the connection between Grotius and his scholastic predecessors, and an appreciation of the relationship between the medieval and modern conceptions of property.

The second, is to provide in its introductory essay a detailed treatment of the juridical significance of Soto's reflections on poverty and property. Soto's discussions of begging and of the relationship between private property and the needs of the indigent are legally grounded and jurisprudentially complex. Although Soto's ideas on poverty have in recent decades been investigated by very fine intellectual historians,[1] in this book his thinking receives additional jurisprudential analysis at a very granular level. For instance, one of Soto's most striking claims is that the proposed restrictions on begging were inconsistent with the right to beg. The existing literature on Soto considers this obscure right only in very general terms, without elucidating the detailed legal reasoning that supports it. The book aims to fill this and other gaps. Similarly, although the scholastic triad that consists of common possession, private property, and extreme necessity is well-known, the book suggests a juridical structure of thinking that integrates and reconciles the triad's apparently incompatible components. It then traces the implications of this structure into the analysis of the right of extreme necessity and the entitlement to restitution for what has been taken in the exercise of that right. Throughout the introductory essay, Soto's views on poverty are presented in the light of the opinions of the other scholastic thinkers on whom he drew, or with whom he disagreed, or who subsequently elucidated his ideas.

I am happy to acknowledge my gratitude to those who read and commented on earlier drafts of the introductory essay: Shmulick Baron, Peter Benson, Abraham Drassinower, Jim Gordley, Chris Essert, Larissa Katz, Dennis Klimchuk, Malcom Thorburn, Arthur Ripstein, David Sandomierski, Jacob Weinrib, and Lorraine Weinrib. I am particularly indebted to Jacob and Lorraine for their comments regarding the invocation of proportionality in section VIII of the essay.

Parts of sections VIII–X were incorporated into my lecture entitled "Theology in *Vincent v Lake Erie*" delivered at Berkeley Law to the North American Workshop on Private Law Theory on receiving the 2025 John G. Fleming Memorial Prize for Torts Scholarship. I very much appreciate the comments made by Workshop participants in the aftermath of the lecture.

Toronto
April 2025

---

1 Notable examples in English are Andreas Blank, "Domingo de Soto on Justice to the Poor" (discussing the principal themes of Soto's *Deliberatio*); Annabel S. Brett, *Changes of State: Nature and the Limits of the City in Early Modern Natural Law*, 10–36 (on the distinctive conception of political space emerging from Soto's treatment of natural law and the *ius gentium* in his discussion of begging); and Daniel Schwartz, *The Political Morality of the Late Scholastics*, 58–77 (on Soto's conception of the poor as belonging within a body politic).

THE LEAST OF MY BRETHREN

Domingo de Soto on Poverty and Property

I The Crisis of Pauperism: Tavera's Law

Today's welfare state embodies the idea that the state uses its power for the benefit of those who most particularly need its assistance. In modern praxis, the execution of this idea is sophisticated and ramified. It encompasses a variety of programs that address different kinds of needs, the financing of these programs through taxation, the establishment of a network of specialized administrative bodies, the determination of criteria of eligibility, and the formulation of appropriate procedures for accessing the assistance. These arrangements are executed through the exercise of public authority using public power to distribute benefits in the public interest through public institutions. Such state activity is categorically different from the generosity of charitable institutions or private individuals who act out of piety, conscience, or social expectations.

The contemporary conceptualization of the welfare state owes much to liberalism's expansive development based on the notion of equal citizenship, and to the social democratic effort to address the needs of workers and other disadvantaged groups.[1] However, controversy about the role of state institutions in alleviating poverty goes back at least to the sixteenth century, predating liberalism and other modern ideologies. At that time new ideas emerged in support of enlisting public authority in the treatment of indigence.[2] These ideas connected the relief of poverty to innovative state and municipal mechanisms that would supplement or supplant personal benevolence, the incentives of religious salvation, and the uncoordinated work of charitable foundations, hospices, confraternities, and other lay organizations.

---

1 Moon, "The Idea of the Welfare State," 660.

2 An earlier adumbration can be found in fourteenth-century Nuremberg; see Grimm, "Luther's Contributions to Sixteenth-Century Organization of Poor Relief," 223.

Domingo de Soto's *In Causa Pauperum Deliberatio* (1545) is a central document within this development. Soto championed the older vision of interpersonal charity over the newer proposals for the deployment of state and municipal authority in the distribution of poor relief. In the *Deliberatio*, Soto critically reviewed government plans to regulate and restrict the begging of paupers. As a member of the mendicant Dominican order, Soto was alive to the spiritual dimension of begging. In defending the right of the poor to public and itinerant begging, he was affirming an essential and characteristic practice of his religious order. Soto was also familiar, as a practical matter, with the efficacy of the beggars' personal impact in face-to-face encounters. "We religious mendicants," he remarked in the *Deliberatio*, "are obligated to go to the assistance of mendicant paupers."[3] Moreover, in the famine that attended the drought of 1539, Soto had, in his capacity as prior of the monastery of San Estaban, actively engaged in securing food for students in Salamanca, even to the extent of begging at the doors of the wealthy.[4] His *Deliberatio* reflects and responds to the shifting attitudes characterizing the transition between the medieval and the modern worlds, when the demands of piety were being overlain and even superseded by imperatives of organized and efficient public administration.

Then almost fifty years old, Soto was already a theologian of considerable stature.[5] He was a close associate of Francisco de Vitoria, his teacher and mentor, who was a leader of the sixteenth-century Thomist revival and who famously applied Thomist ideas to the new problems arising from the Spanish conquests in America. Vitoria, along with Soto and other disciples, transformed the University of Salamanca into Spain's most prestigious academic institution. At the time of the *Deliberatio*, Soto was holding the second-ranking chair in theology (the *catedra de visperas*) at the University of Salamanca. He would subsequently go on to become the confessor of Charles V, the emperor's representative at the Council of Trent, an assessor at the debate in Valladolid on the treatment of the Americas' Indigenous peoples, and the holder of the first-ranking chair in theology (the *catedra prima*) at the University of Salamanca, a position that has been termed "the most important professorship in the Spanish kingdom."[6] His intellectual interests were wide-ranging, and his achievements included contributions to theology, natural philosophy, logic, economics, and the philosophy of law. So admired was Soto's learning that it was said of him that if you knew Soto you knew everything (*Qui scit Sotum, scit totum*). A decade after the *Deliberatio*, he

---

3 Soto, *Deliberatio*, Chapter XI. Translations of Latin passages are, unless otherwise noted, those of the author of this introductory essay.

4 Hubeñak, "Domingo de Soto en el contexto de su época," 24; Jaime Brufau Prats, "Introducción," in Soto, *Relecciones y Opusculos* I, 192.

5 Doyle, "Soto, Domingo de (1494–1560)," 37.

6 Izbicki and Kaufmann, "The School of Salamanca."

created with his magisterial *De Iustitia et Iure* a new form of jurisprudential literature, in which the notions of law and right – which had been treated separately by Aquinas – were elaborated into a single, continuous, and systematic exposition. This work became a model and a standard point of reference for generations of writers on natural law.[7]

In the sixteenth century a significant increase in the number of beggars occasioned a re-evaluation of welfare policy throughout Europe. This increase was the result of many causes: population growth, the urbanization that attended incipient commercial capitalism, economic insecurity as feudalism gave way to wage labour, famine resulting from crop failures, the recurrence of old diseases such as the bubonic plague and the outbreak of new ones such as the great pox, and (as the century wore on) inflation fed by gold and silver from the new world. As a result, the large number of persons who could no longer support themselves, as well as their movement from countryside to city and from town to town, severely strained the traditional haphazard mechanisms of poor relief.

In these circumstances beggars were seen in an ambiguous light. On the one hand, they were the embodiments of the poverty that Christ had chosen and thereby sanctified. Non-responsiveness to the beggar as the living image of the suffering Christ would imperil one's soul at the final judgment. Beggars and persons of means existed in a social and theological symbiosis. God's providence in allowing a world of severe material inequality presupposed that wealth should be used to alleviate need. The presence of the poor enabled persons of means to cultivate the virtues of generosity and compassion and to perform the good works necessary for salvation. Correspondingly, poverty called for the poor to exhibit the virtues of resignation and humility, and to offer grateful prayers – including at funerals where charity was ritually staged[8] – for the souls of those who had assisted them.

On the other hand, beggars (especially the deracinated and mobile vagabonds who wandered about unconstrained by the norms of settled social life and unintegrated into the community structures that inculcated Christian virtues) were thought to pose a threat to the social order. They were considered to spread disease, engage in immoral behaviour, and idly subsist on the labours of others. Some were thought to have mutilated themselves or their children in order to render themselves more pitiable. Particularly reprehensible were the phoney beggars, who feigned an inability to work, thus defrauding donors by their pathetic self-presentations, and diluting the benefits available to more worthy recipients.

By the first decades of the sixteenth century towns in Europe (and eventually wider state authorities) responded to the crisis of widespread pauperism by

---

7 Scattola, "Natural Law Part I: The Catholic Tradition," 561.
8 On the "ritual enactment of charity" at funerals, see Flynn, *Sacred Charity*, 75–8.

adopting measures addressing poverty as a social issue rather than solely as an occasion for individualized charity. Exemplary and influential (and mentioned by Soto) was the reform in 1525 of the provision of poor relief in Ypres in Flanders, then under Spanish rule. The municipality established a common fund for support of the poor that consolidated the revenues of existing charitable institutions, delegated the distribution of assistance and general oversight of the poor to municipal appointees, required children of the poor to be schooled or apprenticed at the expense of the common fund, prohibited public begging on pain of imprisonment, restricted the time that foreigners could reside in hospices, and expelled all vagabonds.[9] When challenged, the scheme was referred to the theologians of the University of Paris, who gave their approbation by ruling that, subject to certain qualifications, its provisions were "pious and salutary."[10]

Two intellectual developments provided additional impetus or confirmation for this growing municipal role in the centralization of poverty relief. The first was the influence of Martin Luther's doctrines and activities.[11] Insisting on justification through faith alone, Luther repudiated the notion that good works, such as the giving of alms, would figure on the Day of Judgment as credits in God's salvific ledger. He construed assistance to the poor not as a modality for securing salvation but as the obligatory expression of love for one's neighbour within a Christian community of believers. This led to his active involvement in the early 1520s in formulating new welfare ordinances for German towns. Drawing on existent but sporadic German practices, Luther supported establishment of a common chest for poor relief, funded out of discontinued religious endowments that were supplemented by compulsory levies. Communal representatives from different sections of the population were to be chosen to administer the fund. They would provide not only for direct relief to the poor, but also for the storage of food against future famines, the provision of training or schooling to orphans and other impoverished children, the supply of dowries to poor women, and assistance in the transition to a new trade. The administrators' familiarity with the local population would prevent the diversion of resources to the fraudulent or undeserving poor. Begging would be prohibited because disbursements from the common chest would make it unnecessary. Those who were not truly indigent would be compelled to either work or leave. The idea of a common chest responded to the new evangelical theology by replacing the vagaries of begging and interpersonal charity with organized municipal mechanisms of social welfare. This arrangement spread quickly to many German cities.

---

9 J. Nolf, *La Réforme*, xxvii–xxviii.

10 Nolf, *La Réforme*, lix.

11 Chung-Kim, *Economics of Faith*, 27–51; Grimm, "Luther's Contribution"; Lindberg, "Reformation Initiatives for Social Welfare," 79.

The second development was roughly simultaneous with, and perhaps influenced by, the first, but lacked Luther's theological premises. In 1526 Juan Luis Vives published his *De Subventione Pauperum sive de Humanis Necessitatibus* (On the relief of the poor or On human necessities), written at the invitation of the mayor of the town of Bruges,[12] and subsequently much translated and widely read. Vives, born in Spain to a family of Jewish origin, educated in Paris, active as a teacher in Oxford and at the English court, and living much of his adult life in Flanders, was a versatile and prolific Catholic humanist, and a friend of Thomas More and Desiderius Erasmus. The book affirmed that care for the poor was a public responsibility derived from the magistrate's obligation to take care of the community in its entirety, just as a physician must attend to the body as a whole. Otherwise, the poor would be forced into a life of crime and immorality. Accordingly, the vices of the indigent – sickness, theft, prostitution, disorderliness, indifference to religious practice – should be attributed not to the poor themselves, but to the government's failure to fulfil its function of producing good citizens. To deal with poverty, Vives proposed a number of measures: municipal officials should inspect hospitals that house the poor, and should make a record of the denizens and their reasons for being there; foreign able-bodied beggars should be sent back to the towns or villages from which they came; the native able-bodied poor should be required to work in accordance with their capacities, and should be assigned work if they cannot find it on their own; children of the poor should be educated in public schools to learn literacy and good behaviour; officials should be appointed to keep track of the life and prospects of the poor, so that no-one would be allowed to live in idleness; annual accounts should be made of the income of hospitals, which would be administered by wardens appointed by and accountable to the government; money left to the church or donated to collection boxes should be administered by municipal appointees and promptly distributed to the poor. These measures would result in the disappearance of public begging, the reduction of crime, the safeguarding of the morals of poor, and the promotion of social harmony.

Illustrative of the attitude towards begging among Vives's humanist associates was Erasmus's droll colloquy "Beggar Talk" published in 1524.[13] This work featured an imagined conversation between a beggar and a former beggar, both of whom Erasmus presents as charlatans. The former beggar now supports himself by inveigling people into buying the recipe for a powder that turns metal into silver or gold. After revealing the mechanics of the scam, he tries to persuade his friend to give up begging and to join him. The beggar refuses, insisting that he is

---

12 A translation is found in Spicker, *The Origins of Modern Welfare.* On the circumstances of its composition and on its significance, see Fantazzi, "Vives and the *emarginati.*"
13 Erasmus, *Collected Works,* 564–8.

as free as a king, able to do what he pleases. He points out that beggars are free from military service, taxation, and inspection, are not worth arresting for crime, can strike another without fear of reprisal, and benefit from the superstition of being under God's protection. Far from desiring the alchemist's finery, the beggar regards his rags as the source of true happiness. The alchemist then points out that this happiness will not long endure, because "citizens are already muttering that beggars shouldn't be allowed to roam about at will, but that each city should support its own beggars and all the able-bodied ones will be forced to work." When the beggar replies that this will never happen, he is told, "Sooner than you'd like, perhaps."

This prediction was quickly realized. Within a few years several of the towns in the Low Countries followed the example of Ypres, instituting the very reforms of which the alchemist had warned. Then in 1531 Charles V of Spain, the ruler of the Low Countries, reinforced this movement towards reform. He issued an express approval of the Ypres ordinance on the terms formulated by the theologians of Paris;[14] and using Ypres as a model, he promulgated an imperial edict that called on the towns of the Low Countries to prohibit begging except in specified cases and to consolidate charitable revenues into a municipal common fund administered by local officials.[15]

Thus, the sixteenth century in Europe was a period of ferment about the treatment of the poor, especially the mendicant poor. Personalized charity began to give way to publicly organized regulation. The new arrangements drew on a standard repertory of features that included the centralization of assistance through a common purse, an increased role for municipal institutions and municipal appointees, the prohibition of begging, the identification of fraudulent beggars, the coercion of the poor to work, and the control of the mobility of beggars.

The crisis of pauperism affected staunchly Catholic Spain as well. There pauperism was aggravated by a series of factors: natural disasters and poor harvests, the expense of European wars, the proliferation of non-productive nobility, the accumulation of land in ecclesiastical and lay hands, rampant inflation, and the migration of rural poor from the countryside in the wake of royal privileges given to the sheep farming guild.[16] The conditions stimulated an alarming growth of "that gaunt army, the beggars, whose battalions never seem to leave the roads of Spain."[17] Municipal authorities repeatedly petitioned the king to deal with the deleterious effects of vagabondage and massive begging. They requested that beggars be confined to their native territories or that phoney beggars be ferreted out

---

14 Nolf, *La Réforme*, Document XIX.

15 Steinbicker, *Poor Relief in the Sixteenth Century*, 245–8.

16 Alonso Seco, *Juan de Robles*, 166–75.

17 Grice-Hutchinson, *School of Salamanca*, 1.

by a licensing procedure. The king, however, either failed to respond or responded ineffectively.

The drought of 1539 and the resulting famine spurred a new wave of indigent migration from the countryside to the cities. Consequently, at the initiative of Cardinal Tavera of Toledo acting as the king's regent in Spain, the Crown comprehensively addressed the question of poor relief. In 1540 a royal decree, subsequently known as Tavera's law, listed and confirmed the poor laws of the previous century and a half. These had imposed penalties on able-bodied idlers, confined beggars to their native territories, required the placing of beggars in hospices, and subjected begging children to work training. The decree also recited the social detriments of begging outside one's native territory, where the true material situation of the beggars was unknown, where they led dissolute and irreligious lives, and where they diverted alms from the genuine poor of the locality. Most importantly, the decree gave notice to the local governments of a new set of instructions concerning begging issued by the royal notary.[18] In the *Deliberatio* Soto critically examined several of these instructions.

In his description of the pertinent events in Chapter II of the *Deliberatio*, Soto summed up the instructions that he regarded as contentious:

> First of all, it is provided that no one is permitted to beg before his poverty undergoes an examination for its legitimacy. Second, that it be permissible even for a legitimate beggar to beg only within the fixed limits of his own homeland, except in time of extreme famine or some other great calamity. Third, that no one may beg without a certificate of the priest or the person to whom this job has been delegated. Fourth, that such certificates for begging be granted only to those who have first made confession in church. Fifth, pilgrims to Santiago are forbidden to tarry long on the road or to deviate from the direct route more than twelve miles, which we Spaniards call four leagues.

Soto observed that the remaining instructions, which he did not enumerate, were "most justly enacted and are uncontroversial." These included permission for foreign beggars who had fallen ill to beg or to be received into a hospital, provision for the children of beggars, permission to the blind to beg without licences in their native territories, a prohibition on begging during High Mass, permission to students to beg with the consent of academic or Church officials, and an instruction to find ways to support the poor who were ashamed to beg.

The most notable article – *omnium celeberrimus* in Soto's characterization[19] – was a sixth article appended to the others. Soto summarized this article as requiring that "the diocesan and city authorities, according to their respective abilities,

---

18 The text of the king's 1540 reforms is found in Soto, *Relecciones y Opúsculos*, II2375–8, 380–4.
19 Soto, *Deliberatio*, Chapter VII, first paragraph.

should occupy themselves in refurbishing the hospitals and should exact endowments for them from their debtors and patrons; in this way they would take care, if possible, that the poor would be sustained in their own territory, so that no necessity would compel them to wander about."

This article pointed in a new direction. Whereas the other provisions in this set of instructions subjected begging to regulation and control, the final article held out the prospect of doing away with begging. It expressly declared that the aim of state policy was to sustain the poor without their having to beg at all. This could be achieved, it suggested, if the existing institutions for dealing with the poor were properly attentive to generating and distributing their revenues. It therefore encouraged local ecclesiastical and municipal authorities to replace individual begging with the institutional distribution of alms. Only if this approach to maintaining the poor were not possible would the articles that regulated begging be applicable. Soto interpreted this article as disallowing begging in the streets and from door to door.[20]

For these instructions to be effective, local authorities had to establish the mechanisms of inspection, licensing, enforcement, collection, and distribution. Accordingly, towns began to enact ordinances that set out specific arrangements for dealing with the poor. Zamora formulated the most influential of these.[21] Zamora's ordinance established fixed amounts of money to be given weekly to those who could not work, with the express aim of ensuring that no truly poor person needed to beg publicly. This money was to be raised either by voluntary public subscription or by private contribution to charity boxes located in churches. The money would not be given to persons capable of working; instead, local officials would compel them to work. Nor, except in cases of extreme need, would it be available to moral or religious delinquents. Special provision would be made for assistance to be discreetly given to the unhospitalized sick and to the poor who were ashamed to beg. Young orphans and foundlings would be sheltered and given religious instruction until they could be placed in suitable crafts. Paupers who died would be given a decent burial. Finally, an administrator would be elected semi-annually to hold, distribute, and be accountable for the money; and constables would be assigned to assist travellers and to prevent those who were being maintained from begging.

Domingo de Soto's *Deliberatio* was written in reaction to certain aspects of these developments, especially to the restrictions on begging and on the movement of beggars. The Zamora ordinance had provoked such controversy that it was referred to the theologians of Salamanca. Soto responded that he was willing

---

20 Soto, *Deliberatio*, Chapter VII, first paragraph.

21 The details of the Zamora ordinance are provided in Juan de Robles, *De la orden que en algunos pueblos de España se ha puesto en la limnosa para remedio de la verdaderos pobres* (1545); a text of this work is available in the appendix to Alonso Seco, *Juan de Robles*.

to endorse the ordinance provided that certain changes were made. As he sheepishly recounts in the *Deliberatio*, when a document was produced for his signature a few days later, he wrongly assumed that the text had been modified to meet his objections, and he signed without reading it. In a subsequent interview with Cardinal Tavera, Soto again expressed his reservations and was embarrassed to be confronted with his signature on the document. The *Deliberatio* was written in the aftermath of this incident as a discursive presentation of his fully considered views

Soto published the *Deliberatio* in January 1545 in parallel Latin and Spanish versions. The reason for issuing a Spanish version was that, although the work was formulated as an appeal to Prince Phillip, who was then the regent of Spain, it was also intended for the broad popular audience that was then keenly interested in the issue of pauperism. As Soto observed, the *Deliberatio* was not a work of scholastic disputation featuring accurate and succinct definitions. Its purpose, rather, was to move the readers to a sympathetic appreciation of the plight of the poor by drawing attention to the rights to which the genuine poor were entitled, the ends that public policy regarding the poor must serve, and the suitability or non-suitability of the reforming measures as means to those ends. It has been said, perhaps too extravagantly, that the *Deliberatio* belongs to the realm of social-political journalism, closely related in form, language, and content to Vives's book without in any way being influenced by it.[22] Be that as it may, it is (like Vives's book) the sixteenth-century analogue to a modern position paper that discusses and assesses a set of prescriptions for dealing with a current social issue.[23] For Soto, the framework for evaluating those prescriptions is his understanding of scripture and the Church Fathers, and a conception of natural law reflecting the requirements of compassionate, rightful, and fair treatment of the poor.

In his preface to the Venetian edition in 1547, Soto asserted that he had originally composed the work in twelve days without consulting any of the literature presenting a different view of the subject.[24] The speed of composition indicates that his views were fully formed before he began to write. This is presumably because during the 1542–3 academic year he had given a lecture, described as outstanding by his eminent Salamanca colleague Melchor Cano, dealing with the new measures concerning the poor.[25] And three years previous to that, he had written a commentary on Saint Thomas Aquinas's foundational discussion of almsgiving.

Soto's views did not go unchallenged. Within two months Juan de Robles, the Benedictine abbot whose preaching had promoted the Zamora ordinance,

---

22 Deuringer, *Probleme der Caritas in der Schule von Salamanca*, 44–5.

23 On Vives's *De Subventione Pauperum* as a one of the earliest studies of social policy, see Spicker, *Origins of Modern Welfare*, 5.

24 Deuringer, *Probleme der Caritas*, 43n18.

25 Deuringer, *Probleme der Caritas*, 43n18. This lecture has apparently not survived.

published a response at the prompting of Cardinal Tavera.[26] Robles countered Soto's appeal to the traditional practices of almsgiving by asserting the value of systematic and efficient administration of poor relief. Although they shared their hostility to the fraudulent poor, Soto and Robles had opposing views on other issues. Whereas for Soto the interaction of donor and beggar held intrinsic spiritual value and most effectively generated assistance for the poor, Robles favoured a prohibition on public begging and proposed that public power should support the truly poor through an organized and systematic program for collecting and distributing alms. Whereas Soto sharply distinguished between the virtues of mercy and justice, so that almsgiving, which was a manifestation of mercy, should not be used for purposes of social discipline, Robles held that the two were intertwined, so that alms could be withheld from social and religious delinquents. Most fundamentally, Soto thought that the freedom of beggars directly to solicit alms from others was a right that could be limited only when beggars received an equivalent benefit. Robles, in contrast, believed that like other freedoms, the freedom to beg could be abridged for the sake of the common good, which he claimed was forwarded by eliminating begging; as Robles put it, although a freedom was being taken from the poor without their fault, it was not being taken without cause.[27] On this point, the dispute between Soto and Robles reflected the distinction between an activity that has the status of a right, the infringement of which is compensable, and an activity that can be subject to regulation, the exercise of which is within the regulator's public authority without compensation.

Robles's criticism made no impression on Soto. In his 1547 preface,[28] Soto wrote that in the time since the original edition he had carefully read the works of those who disagreed with him, but he found in them nothing to which he felt he needed to reply. He reissued the text largely unchanged.

The following sections of this essay discuss Soto's *Deliberatio*, as well as related texts of his that deal with poverty and with the place of the poor within a system of private property. The essay addresses three large issues that emerge from Soto's writings. The first issue (section II) deals with the obligation to give alms. The scope of that obligation comprised the minimal level of assistance to the poor that was incumbent on persons of means – that is, on persons who had some surplus over what they needed to sustain themselves and their families in their present social positions – if they were to avoid calamity on the Day of Judgment. Scholastic thinkers specified that scope in different ways. Soto favoured an expansive view that made compliance with the obligation a challenging prospect. For Soto, the obligation to give alms formed the indispensable background for considering the

---

26 Robles, *De la orden*.
27 Alonso Seco, *Juan de Robles*, Anexo, 90.
28 Deuringer, *Probleme der Caritas*, 44–5.

problem of begging, for it contradicted the notion that one could use one's wealth as one pleased. The second issue (sections III to VII) refers to Soto's reasons for opposing restrictions on begging. Those reasons had inescapable legal dimensions that included the use of roads and public spaces, the right of hospitality, and especially the notion that genuine paupers had a right to beg that the state could not impair without compensation. But how was this right to be understood, and how did it fit both within the standard array and operation of rights held by individuals and within the idea of *ius* understood as the ensemble of legal arrangements that is objectively expressive of rightfulness? The third issue (sections VIII to X) concerns the conceptual relationship between three diverse ideas: the natural right of common possession, the private property into which the external world was divided as a matter of positive right, and the permissibility of taking another's property if one was confronted by extreme necessity. How do these seemingly contradictory ideas fit within a rational and ordered account of the role of external things in legal relationships among persons?

II   The Precept of Almsgiving

In Chapter VII of the *Deliberatio* Soto observes that the purpose animating public policy toward the poor should be to increase rather than decrease the assistance given to them. The poor occupy a divinely favoured position that will be recognized on the Day of Judgment. Christ identified himself with the poor: "what you have done to one of the least of my brethren, you have done to me" (Matthew 25:40). His preaching and the practice of his apostles honoured poverty, considering it more worthy than abundant riches. Accordingly, no measures concerning the allocation of alms should be undertaken out of disgust at the behaviour or appearance of beggars, nor should the mendicant poor be subjected to treatment that implicitly denigrates them. Conversely, proposals that diminish what the poor receive, instead of being responsive to Christian obligation, give rise to the suspicion of being motivated by revulsion and self-interest. A prohibition on public begging, therefore, cannot properly rest on a fastidious desire to avoid the discomfort occasioned by personal interaction with genuinely poor beggars. Similarly, the justification for disqualifying fraudulent beggars cannot properly lie in the resulting reduction in the burden on persons of means. Because the goal should be to increase rather than decrease the assistance to the poor, the money saved by weeding out fraudulent beggars should be redirected to the support of the genuine poor.

The primacy that Soto ascribes to increasing the assistance to the poor leads him to forestall a possible objection. The wealthy might claim that what they choose to give to the poor is their own affair, that they are entitled to be assiduous in holding on to what they have, and that they commit no injustice provided they do not encroach on what belongs to others. Soto's riposte is that the wealthy do not give alms out of the goods they own (*ex propriis bonis*).[29] By saying this Soto does not mean to repudiate the notion of proprietary entitlement – indeed, a few years earlier Soto had published a lecture affirming the power of owners to use what is owned in any way not prohibited by law.[30] Rather, his point is that what one owns is encumbered with an obligation, more extensive than is popularly realized, to support the poor. In Chapter VIII of the *Deliberatio* Soto outlines the character of this obligation.

Soto suggests that the very disparity that God allows between the resources of rich and poor can be consistent with God's providence only if wealth that is superfluous to the rich flows to the poor. Unless one were to consider that God was not a father solicitous for the welfare of all his human children, wealth must be regarded as something given to the wealthy in trust so that it could be transferred to the indigent. Breach of this trust renders wealth a calamity to its possessor on the Day of Judgment. The consequence of God's providence was, in an act of profound deliberation, to bind the human race into a relationship of mutually sustaining love by requiring the rich to relieve the miseries of the poor.

Reinforcing this very general idea is a complex set of detailed arguments about the nature and scope of the obligation to give alms. Because he is offering this work to the regent and to a wide popular readership rather than engaging in scholastic debate, Soto in the *Deliberatio* merely gestures toward these arguments. He had treated them more exhaustively in his commentary on Aquinas's discussion of almsgiving in *Summa Theologica* II-II, q. 32.[31] Only in the light of that earlier work by Soto can one appreciate the conclusions that he sets out in Chapter VIII of the *Deliberatio* on the extensiveness of the Christian obligation to give alms. That obligation serves as the minimal baseline of what almsgivers should make available over their whole lives to the beggars who approach them.

Soto begins his commentary with a statement he says is unanimously accepted among theologians, that almsgiving is a matter of precept and not of counsel; almsgiving is, therefore, obligatory rather than something that one has the discretion to choose to do or not do. Almsgiving is included in the biblical precept that one must love one's neighbour as oneself, because love implies an exterior action and not merely an interior condition. The status of almsgiving as a precept is also shown by Jesus's reference to the omission to give alms as a mortal sin, for which the penalty is eternal damnation. Anticipating his comments in the *Deliberatio*, Soto asserts that in a world of unequal wealth, only a precept to assist the needy is consistent with God's providence toward all his children.

---

29 Soto, *Deliberatio*, Chapter VIII.

30 Soto, *De Dominio*, s. 4 (1535), in Soto, *Relecciones y Opúsculos* I, 110.

31 The text of Soto's commentary is found in Deuringer, *Probleme der Caritas*, 143–58. Subsequent reference is to the section numbers of this commentary.

The precept to give alms, like all precepts, is a component of natural right. Following Aquinas, Soto holds that natural right is composed of three levels of norms: (i) general principles so self-evident that they are imprinted on natural reason even without being specifically posited (for example, "do evil to no-one"); (ii) more determinate norms, such as the commandments of the Decalogue, that even the unschooled can readily derive from those general principles; and (iii) additional biblical norms that the exegesis of the wise can trace back to a commandment of the Decalogue.[32] The obligation of almsgiving falls into this third category, through its relationship to the commandment in the Decalogue to honour one's parents. That commandment is considered to be merely the most obvious and undeniable example of a broader principle of beneficence that extends to honouring the aged and being kind toward the poor.

Moreover, the obligation to give alms belongs to natural right because it is a surviving residue of the original possession in common of all things that characterized the state of innocence in the Garden of Eden. Even after private property was instituted in the wake of the Fall, the natural right of common possession remains valid in circumstances of necessity, because "the right of nations in dividing goods could not prejudice natural right."[33] The obligation to give alms applies as a matter of natural right in favour of persons who find themselves in a condition of necessity.

But what is the relevant condition of necessity? This was one of the central issues in the controversy that arose about this obligation. Whereas theologians agreed on the existence of the obligation to give alms, they held radically different views regarding its scope. Soto's teacher Francisco de Vitoria had earlier, in his own commentary on Aquinas, characterized the controversy as a "serious and difficult dispute among scholars."[34] The root of the problem was that although the conceptual categories that governed the relationship between the givers and the recipients of alms had more or less agreed meanings (within a certain latitude), the contending viewpoints deployed these categories differently in relation to one another.

These conceptual categories came in two sets. The first set dealt with the giver's aggregate material condition. The chief distinction was between what was necessary for givers to carry on their lives and what was superfluous (literally, the overflow). The latter, comprised of everything that was not included among the necessaries, was subject to the obligation to give alms, on the ground that (as Soto was to put it in Chapter VIII of the *Deliberatio*), God "provided that the wealthy

---

32 Soto, Commentary, s. 5; compare Aquinas, *Summa Theologiae*, I-II, q. 100, a. 3 and a. 11.

33 Soto, Commentary, s. 5. On the underlying theory of property, see below, section IX.

34 Deuringer, *Probleme der Caritas*, 169: *gravis et difficilis disputatio inter doctores*.

abound in goods not so that the goods would overflow, but so that the excess would flow out to the poor and needy."

Within this first set, a further distinction was made between necessities of nature and necessities of status. Necessities of nature include everything that is necessary physically to sustain oneself and one's family. Being necessary "always and absolutely,"[35] these never have to be sacrificed to support the poor no matter how desperate their situation.

Necessities of status, in contrast, are what is necessary to respectably maintain the person's (and the family's) social position and standard of living. Whereas necessities of nature are what one needs to live, necessities of status are what one needs to live suitably.[36] They are "conditionally" necessary,[37] as they are relative to the person's particular social standing. Among such necessaries might be the resources to keep a horse, or to provide for the dowries of daughters, or to have the prospect of suitably respectable marriages for children, or to practise the liberality appropriate to a person's station, or to have a reserve against the contingencies of sickness and famine.[38] Necessities of status were not, however, exclusively concerned with preserving what one had. Because the amelioration of one's social standing was permissible, necessities of status also included acquiring and retaining the resources to rise to a higher social status, provided that that status was reasonably attainable in the near future.[39] Necessities of status had a more uncertain significance than necessities of nature: whereas necessities of nature were never encumbered by the obligation to give alms, one of the issues under dispute was whether one was obligated to give alms at the expense of one's necessities of status.

The second set of categories dealt with the recipient's predicament. Was the person who would receive the assistance in a situation of "extreme necessity" (*necessitas extrema*), or was it a less dangerous situation of "grave necessity" (*necessitas gravis*)? Necessity is extreme when someone is in danger of death or crippling injury. What matters is the probability, not the imminence, of the injury; even if one can anticipate that the injury will not materialize until far in the future, the necessity becomes extreme from the moment that the probable injury can be avoided through the assistance of another person. Extreme necessity thus refers not to the immediacy or the inevitability of injury, but to the possibility of preventing it. As Vitoria put it, "one need not wait until he gasps."[40]

---

35 Soto, Commentary, s. 16.

36 Vásquez, *Tractatus de Eleemosyna*, Caput Primum, dub. III (1617), para. 9 (*non ut quis simpliciter vivat, sed ut vivat commode*).

37 Soto, Commentary, s. 16.

38 Instances of necessities of status are collected in Lugo, *De Iustitia et Iure*, Disp. XVI, Sec. VII, para. 137 (1642).

39 Soto, Commentary, s. 44.

40 Deuringer, *Probleme der Caritas* 147: *Non opus est expectare a que boquee.*

Extreme necessity was especially salient in the conceptualization of the relationship between rich and poor. The category was not only pertinent to the eleemosynary duty of the rich, but it also had a notable legal consequence. When they found themselves in a situation of extreme necessity, poor persons were allowed to seize the property of another in order to survive. Such seizure was not considered theft; rather, the pauper's emergency occasioned a resumption of the equal availability of all things that supposedly preceded the instituting of private property. The nature of this licence to seize what belonged to another and its connection to the duty to give alms were also matters of controversy, as will become evident later.[41]

In comparison with extreme necessity, grave necessity involves a less drastic danger. It refers the existence or imminence of a condition that, although not life threatening, significantly disrupts the way one lives. This includes such misfortunes as a serious illness, unjust captivity, the serious besmirching of one's honour or reputation, or the inability to carry on respectably in one's social station.[42] A grave necessity is an adversity that falls short of posing a probable danger to one's life, but yet rises above the quotidian tribulations – such as the horrors of unemployment or unprovided old age – routinely endured by the poor.[43]

The theologians' dispute about the scope of the obligation to give alms concerned the interaction of these categories. The issue was simultaneously a theological and an interpretive problem that converged on a foundational passage in Aquinas's treatment of almsgiving:

> We should take into consideration something on the part of the giver, and something on the part of the recipient. On the part of the giver, we should consider that he should give what is superfluous to him as alms … By superfluous I mean not only with reference to himself, that is, what is over and above what he needs as an individual, but also with reference to those whose care is in his charge … Each one must first provide for himself and for those whose care is in his charge, and afterwards relieve the needs of others with what remains …
>
> On the part of the recipient, he is required to be in need; otherwise, there would be no reason to give him alms. But since it is not possible for one person to relieve the needs of all, it is not every need that obligates us under precept, but only that without which the person who suffers the need could not be sustained. That is the case in which what Ambrose said applies: "Feed the person who is dying of hunger;

---

41 See below, section IX.

42 Lugo, *De Iustitia et Iure*, Disp. XVI, Sec. VII, para. 136, 154 provides a catalogue of the instances of grave necessity.

43 In the brief characterization subsequently formulated by Vásquez, *Tractatus de Eleemosyna*, Caput Primum, dub. III, para. 9, "*alia vero dicitur gravis cum aliquod dicitur notabile incommodum, alia vero dicitur communis, cum multi communiter patiuntur pauperes.*"

if you have not fed him, you have killed him." Accordingly, to give alms from what is superfluous is a matter of precept; as well as to give alms to one who is in extreme necessity. But otherwise, almsgiving is a matter of counsel.[44]

From this material emerged three conceptions of the scope of the obligation to give alms. The narrowest, ascribed by Soto to the canonists, was that the considerations Aquinas enumerated as pertaining to the giver and the recipient had to be jointly present for the obligation to arise. Only when the giver had a superfluity over and above the necessities of nature and status, *and* only when the recipient was in a situation of extreme necessity, was there an obligation to give alms: "Neither part in itself makes a precept."[45] The obligation's scope was restricted to the combined categories of the recipient's most extreme need and the giver's most prosperous material condition. It did not extend to a situation in which the giver's superfluity could alleviate a need of the recipient that was grave but less than extreme, or in which the giver could save another's life by an expense that would diminish his own status. Almsgiving in those situations was a matter of counsel only.

The second conception, while also treating extreme necessity as the exclusive marker on the recipient's side, posited a more expansive scope for obligation on the giver's side. Soto calls this conception an "intermediate opinion,"[46] and he tells us that it was "the opinion of all the moderns."[47] Presumably the argument for it followed from Ambrose's sharp comment, much cited by the proponents of this view, about the person who is dying of hunger: "If you have not fed him, you have killed him." However, a person so indigent that assisting another would have endangered his own life could not plausibly be regarded as a murderer. Accordingly, the omission to assist someone in extreme necessity did not breach the precept if the sacrifice had to come from the giver's necessities of nature. The same, however, could not be said about necessities of status. Consequently, the obligation on the giver included expenditure not only from one's superfluity but also from the resources comprising the necessities of one's status. The result was that one was obligated to diminish one's status even to a considerable extent in order to relieve another's extreme necessity. Decisive for this conception was the peremptory character of extreme necessity. As in the first conception, assisting someone who was in a situation of grave – as opposed to extreme – necessity was not obligatory; it was a matter merely of counsel and not of precept.

The third conception – the one favoured by Soto – was the most expansive. While accepting that one had to sacrifice necessities of status to relieve another's extreme necessity (as in the "intermediate opinion"), the third conception

---

44 Aquinas, *Summa Theologiae*, II-II, q. 32, a. 5.
45 Soto, Commentary, s. 8.
46 Soto, Commentary, s. 9.
47 Soto, Commentary, s. 10.

in addition departed from the assumption that the obligation to give alms was restricted to situations of extreme necessity. As formulated by Soto's much older contemporary, the distinguished theologian Thomas Cajetan, the third conception denied that the considerations Aquinas attributed to the giver's side and to the recipient's side operated only jointly.[48] Instead, the giver's superfluity and the recipient's extreme necessity were mutually independent markers of the giver's obligation. This was taken to be both the theologically correct position and the appropriate reading of Aquinas, whom Soto in the *Deliberatio* then cited as authority for the position.

Two conclusions followed from adopting this conception. First, the very fact of having a superfluity beyond the necessities of nature and status obligated one to distribute that superfluity to the poor. Second, because the obligation attaching to the giver's superfluity was no longer tied to a recipient's extreme necessity, sufferers from less urgent necessity qualified as beneficiaries of that obligation. Indeed, Cajetan's original presentation took this idea to its logical extreme: because the existence of superfluity was an independent basis of the obligation, the necessity to be relieved did not even have to be grave but could be a pauper's routine need. Cajetan's subsequent opinion – which Soto and others followed – resiled from the notion that omitting to relieve a necessity that was less than grave was a mortal rather than merely a venial sin.[49] The precept was held to prioritize extreme necessity over grave necessity and grave necessity over superfluity. Hence, Soto in the *Deliberatio*[50] expressed (and ascribed to Aquinas) the view that from one's superfluity one was obligated to relieve another's grave (and not only extreme) necessity. Soto, accordingly, summed up the entire structure of the obligation that emerges from the categories of the giver's material condition and the recipient's predicament in a single sentence: "Just as we are obligated to value the life of another more than our status, so we are obligated to value the status of another more than our superfluities."[51]

In comparison with the first two conceptions, the third conception radically transformed the scope of the obligation to give alms. Discharge of this obligation was no longer restricted to responding to a specific emergency threatening another with death or serious injury. The obligation was now, in a world of significant disparities of wealth, simply concomitant to the possession of resources over and above what was necessary for the maintenance of the giver's social position and standard of living. Moreover, the class of possible recipients was now a large and amorphous collection of sufferers from a variety of conditions that,

---

48 Soto, Commentary, s. 11.
49 On Cajetan's opinions, see Vásquez, *Tractatus de Eleemosyna*, Caput Primum, dub. III, paras. 19–20.
50 Soto, *Deliberatio*, Chapter IV, Chapter VIII.
51 Soto, Commentary, s. 40.

although not life threatening, seriously affected one's health, reputation, or social standing. The modality of performing the obligation was also different: in a situation of extreme necessity the giver was obligated to assist the specific person at risk, whereas in the case of grave necessity "no-one is necessarily bound to give to a particular person or at a particular time, but it is enough if someone contributes from his superfluity to some needy persons at some time."[52]

Proponents of the "intermediate opinion" objected that if the precept about almsgiving were interpreted so broadly, compliance with it would be so difficult that scarcely any of the rich would be saved. They thought that determining what is damnable as a mortal sin should rest only on the most explicit scriptural authority. In the absence of that authority, true charity required that the burden of so broad an obligation not be imposed.[53]

In claiming that the obligation to give alms was more extensive than was popularly realized, Soto was taking aim at the "intermediate opinion." This opinion he dismissed as a contrivance for erecting doctrinal barriers against almsgiving so as to avoid terrifying the rich. In line with this claim, he insisted that neither scripture nor the writings of the Church Fathers nor reason limited the precept about almsgiving to situations of extreme necessity.

In addition, Soto suggested, in exercising their judgment about when, what, and to whom assistance should be given, persons of means should not stintingly apply the relevant categories. The third conception – already expansive in its own terms – should operate expansively in practice. The obligation to use one's superfluity to relieve another's grave necessity would be undermined if in practice the wealthy assumed a self-interestedly exaggerated standard of what constitutes superfluity or grave necessity. If that were done, wealth supposedly exposed to the obligation to give, or the predicaments supposedly requiring relief, would be diminished inconsistently with the precept to give alms. Superfluity is not the equivalent of luxury; it is merely the excess of what one has over what is needed to maintain life and status. Anyone who is not a pauper has something that can be given without prejudice to the giver's household. Similarly, a necessity not alleviated because a prospective giver considers it insufficiently grave may turn out on the Day of Judgment to have been precisely the one for which relief was obligatory. Thus, not only the set of categories but also the operation of those categories in specific situations should be attuned to the broad scope of the obligation to give alms. The mercy mandated by that obligation was inconsistent with the inclination of the rich toward avarice and stinginess.[54]

---

52 Soto, *Deliberatio*, Chapter IV.
53 Gabriel Biel, *Collectorium Sententiarum*, Lib. 4, Dis. 16, q. 4, concl. 5 (1501).
54 Soto, *Deliberatio*, Chapter VIII.

III   Roads and Hospitality

The organizing distinction of the *Deliberatio*, announced at the beginning of Chapter III of that work, is that one determines first what measures are legally permissible, and then which of the permissible measures is most beneficial. These two tasks each make use of a different criterion. The former requires reference to the law – including not only the positive law of a particular jurisdiction but also the divine law, the natural law, and the law of nations – because a legally prohibited act does not allow for further deliberation. In contrast, the latter requires wise deliberation about what is fair and good in order to assess the permissible alternatives and choose among them.

Falling under the first of these tasks are the related issues of whether to distinguish between fraudulent beggars ("vagabonds") and legitimate ones, and whether to restrict the movement of legitimate beggars. Although he was sensitive to the diverse circumstances (including variations in health, in the physical capacity to work, and in the availability of jobs) that made the distinction difficult to apply,[55] Soto unequivocally supported the suppression of fraudulent beggars as a dictate of divine law, natural law, and positive law. The divine law was evident in the injunction on being expelled from the Garden of Eden that man should eat bread by the sweat of his brow. The avoidance of productive labour by the able-bodied also contravened natural law and natural reason, because it was inconsistent with the teleology of a world populated by both the rich and the poor, within which the rich were charged with governance and the poor with providing the means for sustaining human life. Moreover, the idleness of the fraudulent beggars was the portal to iniquity, as was recognized by classical and religious authorities and by all the great lawgivers. Finally, fraudulent begging was punishable under a succession of laws going back to the Roman emperors and subsequently elaborated by Spanish monarchs.

Once one disqualifies fraudulent beggars, the remaining question is the legal permissibility of restricting the activities and movements of non-fraudulent beggars. Tavera's law aimed to prevent beggars from begging except in their own homelands and to work toward the elimination of begging in the streets and from door to door. In response Soto asserted that genuine beggars could not be excluded from any part of the kingdom. He adduced a number of considerations for supposing that Tavera's law contemplated restrictions, especially on travel, that were not legally permissible.

First, in accordance with the learning of his time[56] Soto asserted that by the right of nature and nations (*iure naturali et gentium*) roads and cities were open to

---

55 Salamanca, "Domingo de Soto and Itinerant Poverty," 33–4.
56 Schwartz, *Political Morality of the Late Scholastics*, 65–6.

everyone except those who commit crimes or shameful acts. Accordingly, restrictions could apply to the movements only of fraudulent beggars. It followed that legitimate beggars could stay in any town they wished for as long as they wished. Considered against this baseline, the exclusion of legitimate beggars from any town was a form of exile that violated one's right to stay where one wished.

Evincing a realization that this might not be his strongest argument, Soto immediately adduced a second consideration described as "perhaps more evident." He might have been uneasy about claiming that sending beggars back to their native lands is a form of exile. Although asserting that the penalty might be harsh (citing Roman law that exile is the closest thing to capital punishment), Soto admitted that its application in these circumstances might not be. Or perhaps he thought that a stronger consideration would relate specifically to beggars, rather than travellers generally.

With its reference to the right of nature and nations, Soto's first argument invokes the scholastic notion that the institution of property developed in stages. At the first stage everything was held in common as a matter of natural right. Subsequently, to prevent free-riding and to provide an incentive for the productive employment of resources, the things of the world were divided under the right of nations into private holdings. In limited circumstances where the rationale for privatizing possession does not hold, the original idea of common property remains or is revived. In his later work *De Iustitia et Iure* Soto enumerated roads and the state as instances of things that the right of nations could not disperse into private holdings, as well as air and water, shores and harbours, and fish and wild animals.[57] The status of roads and public spaces belongs, as the *Deliberatio* puts it, to "the right of nature and nations," because roads and public spaces continue to be held in common in accordance with the right of nature even after private property was established under the right of nations. Thus, the inapplicability of private ownership to roads and public spaces allowed Soto to treat them as the ongoing residue of natural right's original common possession. From this he concluded that beggars who did no wrong could not be excluded from them.

In making this claim about roads and public spaces, Soto explicitly drew on Roman law but flattened the nuances that the Roman jurists recognized. The very section of Justinian's *Institutes* that Soto adduced[58] enumerated different categories of non-private holdings. Some things were capable of being privately owned but were available to all because they had not yet been acquired by anyone, such as fish and wild animals. Other things were incapable of being privately owned. In this latter group the Roman jurists distinguished between things that were common

---

57 Soto, *De Iustitia et Iure*, IV, q. 3, a. 1 (p. 298).

58 Justinian, *Institutes*, 2, 1; see also Justinian, *Digest* I, 8, both in Krueger and Mommsen, eds., *Corpus Juris Civilis*.

to all by natural right (such as air and water) and things that were corporately held by a community rather than by individuals (such as theatres, stadiums, and other public spaces). This distinction vanishes in Soto's treatment, leaving an undifferentiated aggregate of things that the right of nations could not privatize and that, therefore, had to be kept open to all, including legitimate beggars. This homogenizing of non-private property allowed Soto to ignore the difference between property common to all and a community's public property, namely, that the right to use the latter belongs not to everyone but only to members of the specific community. The consequence of this distinction is that the exclusion of foreign beggars from public spaces seems no longer to be legally impermissible. Soto avoids this unpalatable conclusion by treating a community's roads and public spaces as areas common to all.

Soto derived his second and "more evident" argument from the right of hospitality (*ius hospitalitatis*), which provides an urgent benefit to those who come from elsewhere. As Soto noted, both the pagan antiquity of Greece and Rome and the Jewish and Christian biblical texts celebrated and cultivated the exercise of hospitality towards travellers and foreigners. For example, Cicero approvingly referred to the praise of hospitality by the Greek philosopher Theophrastus. Moreover, under the name of Jupiter Hospitalis, the greatest god in the pagan pantheon was regarded as the judge and avenger of violations of the rights of guests. Similarly, on the biblical side, Soto mentions the paradigmatically hospitable figures of the Bible (Abraham, Lot, and Rahab), the scriptural injunctions of kindness to strangers, and Jesus's inclusion of hospitality among the required acts of mercy. Repeatedly underlining that hospitality is a duty (*officium*), Soto concluded that if foreign beggars were confined to their homelands, one could not perform this duty by acts that benefit the poor, as Jesus intended. Instead, hospitality would be nothing but the interaction of the rich and illustrious with their visiting social equals.

One might wonder how these considerations about hospitality confirm the point at issue, that banning foreign beggars is *legally* impermissible. In repeatedly characterizing such hospitality as a duty (*officium*), Soto used the Latin word that referred not to a bond between obligor and obligee as a matter of law, but more generally to an action appropriate to the role that one has in the kind of social relationship in which one finds oneself.[59] Accordingly, in Soto's presentation of hospitality the sole unambiguous point of contact with the idea of law was his initial use of the phrase *ius hospitalitatis*, which treats hospitality as belonging to right in some way.

Soto's deployment of the right of hospitality as a legal concept in the *Deliberatio* emerged from within the intellectual activity of the Salamanca school under the

---

59 Dyck, *Commentary on Cicero, De Officiis*, 5–8.

leadership of Soto's mentor and colleague, Francisco de Vitoria. Six years before the *Deliberatio*, in his 1539 *Lectures on the American Indians*, Vitoria had associated hospitality with the cluster of entitlements that reflect humanity's natural partnership and communication. These entitlements include the right of Spaniards to travel to, dwell among, and trade with the Indigenous peoples of America provided they do them no harm. In Vitoria's words, "Amongst all nations it is considered inhuman to treat strangers and travellers badly without some special cause, humane and dutiful to behave hospitably to strangers."[60] Vitoria argued that if the Indigenous peoples had offended against these rights – which he affirmed was not the case – Spain could justifiably have waged war against them and subjected them to Spanish rule. In Vitoria's view the rights existed by virtue of the law of nations (*ius gentium*), which Roman law had defined as the kind of law (*ius*) observed equally by all nations on the basis of "what natural reason has established among all men."[61] Vitoria's argument was that everyone's right to travel wherever one wanted had existed when everything had been held in common, and that the subsequent instituting of separate properties and jurisdictions under the *ius gentium* was never intended to prevent free mutual intercourse. Introduced in this way into the law of nations, the notion of hospitality subsequently reverberated with refinements and qualifications through the major European writers on law, including Grotius, Vattel, and Pufendorf, until it achieved an honoured and influential place two and a half centuries later as the centerpiece of Kant's cosmopolitan right.[62]

Soto's claim that restricting the movement of legitimate beggars is inconsistent with the demands of legality inherent in the right of hospitality draws on Vitoria's placement of that right within the *ius gentium*. In his later work *De Iustitia et Iure* Soto described the *ius gentium* as a body of positive law that was ordered toward a certain end under certain circumstances.[63] The distinctive feature of this body of law was that the circumstances were such that what is suitable to a given end can be inferred by any rational individual; for that reason it is common to all peoples. Although unmentioned in this later treatment by Soto, hospitality can be seen as belonging to the *ius gentium* on the ground that any rational person can realize that as purposive mobile beings we desire to receive hospitality *from* others, and that therefore we should show it *to* others.[64] Moreover, the very reciprocity of hospitality so conceived conforms to the most fundamental characteristic of *ius*, that as the object of justice it is expressive of equality.[65]

---

60 Vitoria, *Political Writings*, 278.

61 Vitoria, *Political Writings*, 278; Justinian, *Institutes* 1, 2, 1.

62 Cavallar, *Rights of Strangers*.

63 Soto, *De Iustitia et Iure*, III, q. 1, a. 3 (p. 196).

64 Aquinas, *Epiphany and Ante-Lenten Homilies*, Homily 3. Aquinas gives this as a reason for regarding the law of hospitality as part of the natural law.

65 Soto, *De Iustitia et Iure* III, q. 1, a. 2 (p. 194).

What sort of right is the *ius hospitalitatis* that Soto invokes? Presumably, what Soto had in mind was not that each person in need of lodging had an entitlement to such lodging enforceable at law against an indefinite set of defendants. Thematic for the *Deliberatio* is that beggars do not have rights to particular benefits from particular persons; they merely have a right to solicit such benefits. Accordingly, rather than entitling any given person to lodging, the right of hospitality refers more generally to the ensemble of norms pertinent to the relationship between potential hosts and guests. The *ius* in question is like the *ius positivum* or the *ius gentium*: a set of norms of rightful conduct that governs a sphere of human interaction. In the language of later legal theorists, the right of hospitality has an objective rather than a subjective meaning. That would account for Soto's repeated formulation of the *ius hospitalitatis* not as an entitlement exigible by the traveller but as an *officium* befitting those whose circumstances are such that they can provide the needed shelter.

Although Soto takes the phrase *ius hospitalitatis* from Roman literature and buttresses its invocation by referring to Cicero, he has in mind a more extensive arrangement than the Romans contemplated. Soto uses the term to indicate the rightfulness of providing for the needs of strangers and travellers generally. In contrast, the Roman *ius hospitalitatis* or *iura hospitii* referred to a set of extra-legal social norms of mutual assistance (such as supplying provisions, lodging, and protection) between antecedently connected members of different communities when they were in each other's localities.[66] Though hospitality was favoured in ancient society, the set of norms belonging to the *ius hospitalitatis* pertained to particular and already existing relationships into which the parties or their forebears had entered. It was not general, and it did not have the force of law. Its maintenance depended, rather, on the continuing goodwill of the parties, the reputational effects of violating these norms, and the supposed divine oversight of Jupiter Hospitalis. Moreover, it presupposed a relationship between approximate social equals, especially among the elites of their communities.[67] Thus, it was not suitable for describing a general juridical duty to itinerant beggars. Indeed, in the very passage that Soto cites, Cicero goes on to say that what is honourable about hospitality is that the homes of illustrious men are available to illustrious guests[68] – precisely what Soto deemed an inadequate version of Christian hospitality, and what earlier Christian writing found objectionable in this very text of Cicero.[69]

---

66 Nicols, "Hospitality among the Romans," 422.

67 Badian, *Foreign Clientelae*, 11.

68 Cicero, *De Officiis*, 2, 18, 64: *est enim, ut mihi quidem videtur, valde decorum patere domos hominum illustrium hospitibus illustribus.*

69 For example, Lactantius, *Divine Institutes* 6, 12.

More than a millennium earlier Ambrose had written that supplying lodging to a foreigner was the public appearance of humanity.[70] Vitoria's and Soto's invocations of hospitality as a legally significant idea expands the old Roman *iura hospitii* from the social norms of particular relationships to an overarching legal norm that expresses the general shared humanity of hosts and guests. Whereas Vitoria had deployed this aspect of the *ius gentium* in discussing Spanish imperialism against foreign peoples in distant regions, Soto used it to discourage interference with the free movement of beggars within Spain. Soto thereby manifested "confidence in the uniformity of the rational order of being, an order that does not know of significant normative fractures between the internal and the external relations of states."[71]

IV *Ius*

Aside from these two arguments for the legal impermissibility of restricting beggars' movements – the status of roads and other public spaces, and the right of hospitality – Soto offers a third that goes to the very heart of his thinking about the poor. Soto asserts that beggars, whom he defines as persons in such need that they must live off the contributions of others,[72] have a *right* to beg (*ius mendicandi*). This right can be restricted as envisaged by Tavera's law, Soto claims, only if the poor receive the equivalent of what they would probably have gotten by exercising it. Unlike the other two arguments, this one is geared specifically to beggars, rather than to those who travel the roads or need lodging. It ascribes to the activity of begging the legal protection inherent in the holding of a right (*ius*).

Soto asserts the existence of this right without offering much elaboration. Indeed, the conclusion that begging is a right that cannot be restricted without providing for the beggars in a different way is in his view "too obvious to need much testimony."[73] He is also explicit that the right to beg extends to everyone who is in need, even to those who are not under extreme or grave necessity. Accordingly, the right is not coterminous with anyone's obligation to relieve another's extreme or grave necessity, even under the expansive version of that obligation that Soto favoured (as set out above in section III). In Soto's presentation, a given beggar may not be owed alms, either because the beggar's necessity is grave rather than extreme (and so does not obligate almsgiving at a particular time or to a particular person), or because the beggar's need does not amount to grave necessity (and so does not create any obligation at all and is a matter of counsel rather than precept). However, Soto contends that even beggars to whom alms are not owed

---

70 Ambrose, *De Officiis*, 2, 21, 103: *est pubica species humanitatis ut pregrinus hospitio non egeat.*
71 Coccoli, "Il conflitto sulla mobilità alle soglie dell'età moderna," 53.
72 Soto, *Deliberatio*, Chapter XII.
73 Soto, *Deliberatio*, Chapter XI.

have a right to ask for them. The result, he points out, is that although giving to beggars is a matter of mercy rather than justice, depriving beggars of the right to beg without providing them with an equivalent would be unjust.[74]

By postulating that the needy – presumably each of them individually – have a right to beg, Soto was referring to a term, *ius*, that had a tangled history in medieval legal and philosophical thought.[75] In his later work *De Iustitia et Iure* Soto discussed *ius* in detail, drawing upon and elaborating Aquinas's treatment from almost three centuries earlier. In his exposition of *ius* in this work Soto's main focus is on the set of legal arrangements that are expressive of rightfulness as an objectively understood idea, rather than on entitlements such as the right to beg held by particular persons.

In setting out this objective idea, Soto emphasized that the noun "*ius*" is used in two principal ways.[76] Both relate *ius* to the equality or fairness (*aequitas*) that is the defining characteristic of justice, but they do so from complementary standpoints. First, *ius* may refer to law, which Soto (following Aquinas) defines as an ordering and prescription of reason for the common good, promulgated by the person who has charge of the state.[77] That the law can be regarded as *ius* in some sense is evident from such phrases as *ius positivum* (positive law) and *ius gentium* (the law of nations). Law provides the authoritative framework that creates just arrangements through the operation of practical reason and endows them with legal character. *Ius* in this sense stands for "the rule of reason and the dictate of prudence through which we measure the equality of justice; the laws fit that description."[78] As the "rule of practical reason established by prudence, and therefore the idea for what is just (*ratio iusti*)," law is "what makes and establishes what is just (*factiva et constitutiva iusti*)."[79]

Second, *ius* may refer to justice's characteristic equality as manifested in concrete juridical relationships among persons. *Ius* is the distinctive kind of social reality that pertains to law as an ensemble of dictates of practical reason. It is the same as *iustum* ("what is just"); that is, it is what justice – "the virtue of the will that establishes what is just in things in accordance with the law"[80] – strives to achieve. Understood as "what is just *in things*," *ius* marks the juridical character of the actual human interactions that take place in the world. Regarded as the arrangements of human interaction that conform to the equality that is justice's regnant idea, *ius* is the object of justice.

---

74 Soto, *Deliberatio*, Chapter XI.
75 Brett, *Liberty, Right and Nature*; Tierney, *Idea of Natural Rights*; Tuck, *Natural Rights Theories*.
76 Soto, *De Iustitia et Iure, Prooemium*; III, q. 1, a. 1 (p. 191).
77 Soto, *De Iustitia et Iure*, I, q. 1, a. 1 (p. 6).
78 Soto, *De Iustutia et Iure*, III, q. 1, a. 1 (p. 191).
79 Soto, *De Iustitia et Iure*, III, q. 1, a. 1 (p. 193).
80 Soto, *De Iustitia at Iure*, III, q. 1, a. 1 (p. 193).

The kind of object that justice has follows from the contrast between justice and the other virtues. Although every other virtue aims at achieving a result that is distinctive of that virtue (temperance, for instance, aims at the proper use of what is pleasurable to the touch), the merit of other kinds of virtuous actions lies in their ordering the agent toward the agent's own good. Justice is different; it is an ordering of the agent toward someone else. This is why the motive of the agent is crucial to the exercise of the other virtues, whereas for just action what matters is the performance of the just act regardless of motive. For example, justice requires the repaying of a debt even if the debtor is basely motivated by the expectation that the repayment will stimulate the creditor's profligacy. Consequently, Soto argues, the other virtues work on certain subject matters (for example, bravery works on the dangers of war, temperance on tactile pleasures), but *qua* virtues they have no objects separate from their exercise. In contrast, because equality is a relationship between at least two things, justice has the distinctive object of producing the equality toward which it is oriented. *Ius*, which signifies and is etymologically related to what is just (*iustum*), is the noun that refers to the object of justice. That object consists in the working of equality in particular relationships.[81]

The two principal senses of *ius* that Soto highlights fit into each other. The first sense signifies the role of law in framing and ordering relations among persons in accordance with practical reason. The second sense denotes the character of *ius* as the product of an idea of equality. For example, it is a matter of right, reflected in the equivalence of what is borrowed and what is repaid, that borrowers should repay their debts to their creditors. The first meaning of *ius* focusses on the law that recognizes the legal character of the relationship between borrower and lender, and that therefore enables the lender to insist on and enforce such repayment. The second meaning of *ius* focusses on the loan transaction as the site of a certain kind of equality, namely, the arithmetic equivalence that characterizes commutative justice, rather than the proportional equivalence that characterizes distributive justice.[82]

Soto's exposition of the twofold significance of *ius* is a gloss on the famous statement by Aquinas that "law is not right itself (*ius ipsum*), properly speaking, but is a certain idea of right (*quaedam ratio iuris*).[83] In its context Aquinas's statement is the conclusion of an analogy drawn between law and the Aristotelian notion of craftsmanship. "Just as there pre-exists in the mind of the craftsman a certain idea (*quaedam ratio*) that is said to be the rule of the craft," Aquinas writes, "so also for a particular just work determined by the idea (*quod ratio determinat*) there also pre-exists in the mind a certain idea (*quaedam ratio*) as a kind of rule

---

81 Soto, *De Iustitia et Iure*, III. q. 1, a. 1 (p. 192).
82 Soto, *De Iustitia et Iure*, III, q. 5, a. 2 (p. 243).
83 Aquinas, *Summa Theologiae*, II-II, q. 57, a. 1, ad 2.

of prudence." In all crafts the craftsman produces an artefact in accordance with the pre-existing idea (*ratio*) kept in the mind's eye as the work is being executed. That idea implies a rule for acting in a certain way to fashion the artefact. Aquinas calls this "the rule of the craft (*regula artis*)," that is, the rule that the craftsman must observe if he is to produce the artefact in question by executing the idea. Similarly, a law (defined as a prescription of practical reason promulgated by the ruler for the common good) articulates a rule for acting in a certain way; because this rule reflects practical reason, Aquinas calls it a "rule of prudence" (*regula prudentiae*). In Aquinas's analogy, the "rule of prudence" is the form taken by the "rule of the craft," when the craft in question aims to produce the doing of what is just (in Aquinas's formulation, the performance of a "particular just work"). Just as the pre-existing image in the craftsman's mind is the idea (*ratio*) for producing the artefact, so the law is the pre-existing idea in the actor's mind for acting in accordance with *ius*, understood as the object of justice. Because *ius* rather than law is the object of justice, the law is not strictly speaking *ius* itself. Nonetheless, in the production of acts that conform to *ius*, the law indicates to the actor what *ius* requires. In this sense, law is the idea for *ius* (*ratio iuris*).In calling law the idea for what is just (*ratio iusti*), Soto followed in Aquinas's tracks. Although he treated this conception of law as one of the two principal meanings of *ius*, Soto noted that law was not its primary meaning. Turning the analogy to craftsmanship in another direction, Soto focused on the evolution of the different significations of the word *ius* as a matter of linguistic usage:

> [T]he law itself is called just, because it establishes what is just in things. But just as the words for manufactured and crafted things are transferred to signify the skills as well, and just as the word for medicine, which is a thing put together by skill, is adapted to the skill itself, so the word *ius* undergoes derivation, first to signifying the art of knowing what is just, and from this in turn to signifying the law. You should take care not to think that the art of what is good and fair is the same as law. Art is not a dictate but rather is the kind of moral knowledge that jurists have to investigate what is fair for law to ordain. Law, however, is a rule of prudence, or a practical dictate established from it, for example "Do" or "Don't do."[84]

Starting with his thematic point that the law establishes what is just in concrete human interactions, Soto in this passage goes on to sketch the process of linguistic derivation by which the term *ius* came to be attached to the law. First, a word referring to what is produced is often transferred to the skill that produces it. "Medicine," for instance, was originally the word for a product generated by the physician's skill but was then applied to the skill itself. Similarly, the word *ius*,

---

84 Soto, *De Iustitia at Iure*, III, q. 1, a. 1 (p. 193).

originally used to denote what the law establishes as just in human interactions, is transferred to the skill of jurists (as is indicated by the Latin word by which Soto refers to them, *iurisconsulti*). *Ius* in this extended sense is not a social reality "in things"; rather it is an intellectual virtue that consists in knowing how to investigate and determine what effect the law should justly have. The paradigmatic example of this sense of *ius* is found in the Roman jurist Celsus's definition of *ius* as "the art of what is fair and good."[85] Soto understands this art as Aristotelian *epieikiea*, that is, as the non-application of a law to circumstances in which its strict application would unjustly produce a result contrary to the legislator's intention. From *ius* as the jurists' skill in applying their knowledge, *ius* then becomes identified with the content of that knowledge is, that is, with the law itself. One can, accordingly, distinguish between the primary meaning of *ius* as the object of justice – which Soto, like Aquinas refers to as *ius ipsum* (*ius* itself) – and a derivative meaning of *ius* as law. Soto's extended discussion lands up by a different route in exactly the same place as Aquinas's more epigrammatic statement that law is not *ius* itself but a certain idea of *ius*.

To sum up Soto's portrayal: Law is one of the principal meanings of *ius* because, as the set of norms elaborated through the exercise of practical reason and enacted for the common good though the ruler's authority, law (in Soto's words) "makes and establishes" what is just. *Ius* in its other (and original) principal meaning is the object of justice, that is, the ensemble of concrete juridical relationships expressive of the notion of equality or fairness. In Soto's account both justice and law "make" *ius*, though they make it in different ways. Justice makes *ius* by establishing the other-directed character of juridical norms, so that *ius* counts as the object of justice rather than being associated with some other virtue. Law makes *ius* by making those norms effective as the expression of practical reason promulgated for the common good. Accordingly, on the one hand concrete juridical relations can be consonant with the practical reason that is law's ordering principle under Soto's first meaning of *ius*; and on the other hand, law's ordering can be discerned in the human relationships that compose it under his second meaning of *ius*.[86] Right is thus the totality of concrete equal relationships that belong to law as an exercise in practical reason.

V   Subjective Rights

Soto's account of *ius* in his *De Iustitia et Iure* explicated the roles of law and equality in establishing what is right; it did not directly deal with the rights exercised by an individual. In the terminology of later legal theory,[87] his treatment concerned

---

85 Justinian, *Digest*, 1, 1, pr.

86 Scattola, "La virtud de la justicia en la doctrina de Domingo de Soto," 339.

87 This terminology was introduced in the eighteenth century and became established when adopted by Bernhard Windscheid a century later; see Fouto, "Revisiting 'Subjectivity' in Right Theories," 1111–12.

itself with the objective sense of right rather than with subjective rights (such as the right to beg mentioned in the *Deliberatio*). In the *De Iustitia et Iure*, Soto offered no parallel account of the concept of a right held and exercised by individuals. He contented himself with skimpy remarks to the effect that *ius* is the object of justice and that rights are conducive to what is fair and just.[88] Such remarks gesture toward, but hardly explicate, the relationship between *ius* as an objective idea and *ius* as an individual entitlement. At any rate, by Soto's time individual rights had for several generations received the attention of Christian thinkers, who had developed the idea that a right was a power (*potestas*) or a capability (*facultas*) to act.[89]

The notion of *dominium* formed the context within which both Soto and his mentor Vitoria considered *ius* as a right of the individual. *Dominium* was an omnibus term that included not only the proprietary ownership found in Roman law but other forms of legitimate control ranging from control over one's own actions to the ruler's political control. The question that exercised Vitoria and Soto concerned the relationship between *dominium* and *ius*. A few decades earlier, the Tübingen theologian Conrad Summenhart had asserted that *dominium* should be expansively understood as interchangeable with *ius*: "whoever has a *ius* in something can be said to be the *dominus* of it, and therefore *ius* is the same as *dominium*."[90] If *dominium* were limited to legal ownership, Summenhart argued, it would be puzzling why the holder of a lesser interest in a thing could bring an action for theft, which Roman law had defined as the taking of something against the will of its *dominus*. Summenhart's specific claim about *dominium*, which was more acceptable to Vitoria than to Soto, prompted the two Salamancan professors to comment more generally on the individual right that *dominium* put into play.

Vitoria's approach was direct and explicit.[91] In discussing restitution – that is, reparation for injury – as an act of commutative justice that restores the equivalent of what was wrongfully taken, Vitoria raised the issue of how *ius* is related to *dominium*. Because he supposed that all *dominium* was based on right (*nullum est dominium quod non in iure fundetur*), and that all restitution was based on *dominium* (*omnis restitutio fundatur in dominio*), Vitoria viewed *dominium* as the paradigmatic individual right for the infringement of which compensation was due. He accordingly asked the straightforward question: What is a right? Although his response is not completely new, it is organized in a distinctive way along two tracks comprising a nominal definition and a real definition. These two kinds of definition reflect the difference between what a name signifies and what the named thing really is.[92]

---

88 Soto, *De Iustitia et Iure*, IV, q. 1, a. 1 (p. 279).

89 Varkemaa, *Conrad Summenhart's Theory of Individual Rights*.

90 Varkemaa, *Conrad Summenhart's Theory of Individual Rights*, 79.

91 Vitoria, *De Iustitia/Über die Gerechtigkeit, Teil 2*, Q. 62, a. 1, paras. 5-8 (pp. 4–14).

92 Aristotle, *Posterior Analytics* II, 7: "to define is to prove either a thing's essential nature or the meaning of its name."

Vitoria first presented what he calls the "nominal" definition of a right, that is, a definition that brings out the meaning of the word *ius* as it appears in our speech. Referring to Aquinas's statement (quoted above with reference to objective right)[93] that law is a certain idea of right, Vitoria insisted that rights operate within the framework of the law. He concluded that a right is that by virtue of which some action is legally permitted. Accordingly, when we say that I do or do not have the right to do something, what we mean is that my action is or is not permitted. This notion of a right draws attention to a particular aspect of the modalities in play within a legal system, namely, that law includes not only dictates of what must or must not be done, but also permissions of what may be done.

By calling this definition "nominal" rather than "real," Vitoria signalled his belief that although it usefully distinguishes actions that the law permits from actions that the law prohibits or requires, the definition does not capture the essence of the idea of a right. One may surmise that the definition's deficiency lies in its understating a right's normative significance. To be sure, permission is inseparable from a right, because to the extent that one has a right to something, one is permitted to use it. However, when defined as a permission, a right refers merely to the status of an action that one is not under a duty not to perform; it does not necessarily signify that others have a duty not to interfere with that action. For example, with reference to *dominium* (Vitoria's central concern in this context), owners have more than a legal permission to use what is owned; in addition to the owners' being under no duty to others to abstain from such use, others are under a duty to owners not to interfere with what is owned. This duty is essential to *dominium,* but as it is not implied by the permission alone, it finds no place in Vitoria's nominal definition. In Hohfeldian terms,[94] a right viewed only as a permission is a liberty, not a claim-right; a principal point of the Hohfeldian analysis is that one person's liberty is not correlative to another's duty. From his definition Vitoria drew the reasonable conclusion that having a right means that an action in accordance with that right is permitted. However, by characterizing the definition as nominal and not real, he evinced an awareness that this conclusion, although it may faithfully represent our linguistic usage, does not adequately disclose what a right is.

Now one might object that Vitoria had no reason to be familiar with the Hohfeldian analysis, which he antedated by four centuries. This objection would be misguided. Of course, Vitoria was ignorant of Hohfeld. He was, however, cognizant of this aspect of the Hohfeldian analysis, for it was implicit in the well-known

---

93 Aquinas, *Summa Theologiae,* II-II, q. 57, a. 1, ad 2.
94 Hohfeld, "Some Fundamental Legal Conceptions as Applied in Judicial Reasoning," 16. Contemporary legal theorists generally use the term "liberty" instead of Hohfeld's "privilege." Adams, "Hohfeld on Rights and Privileges," 89, suggests that the best interpretation is to read Hohfeld's "privilege" as "permission."

contention by the Franciscans that, consistent with their vow of poverty, their consumption of things (such as the food they ate and the clothes they wore) was permissible and did not amount to an assertion of *dominium* over them.[95] Indeed, about the very time that Vitoria was proposing his nominal definition, his colleague Domingo de Soto was discussing the Franciscan issue in almost Hohfeldian terms. Soto observed that the Franciscans

> have use but not *dominium*. By use I mean a rightful liberty (*iusta licentia*) or a right to eat and drink, which can certainly be called a use as of right (*usus iuris*) with respect to that act … Here one must note that the ability to consume something does not suffice for true *dominium*. What is required for this is that one can alienate it, vindicate it in court, and so on, which the Franciscans cannot do … All they have is a limited liberty (*licentia*) to eat and drink and clothe themselves.[96]

After giving the nominal definition, Vitoria moved to what he called the "real" definition of a right. This involves formulating the essence of what is being defined rather than the way we speak about it. The definition that he proposed is that "a right is a power or faculty appropriate to someone in accordance with the laws … Whoever has a faculty according to the laws has a right."[97] This definition echoes the one that had been suggested by Summenhart, who had explained that power and faculty were words denoting activity; a faculty or a power is "a potency in a condition of activity, that is, a potency of doing something with respect to something."[98] To have a faculty or power over a thing, then, is to be so situated with respect to that thing that it is continually available for the exercise of one's activity. Accordingly, a faculty (or power) not only permits the right-holder to act, but it also requires others to abstain from interfering with the ongoing availability of the right-holder's activity with respect to the object of the right. An interference with that availability would be a violation of the right. In other words, a faculty so understood can constitute a Hohfeldian claim-right.

In adopting Summenhart's definition, Vitoria introduces an important innovation. Instead of tying the faculty to right reason (as Summenhart had done), Vitoria ties it to the laws, thereby underlining its dependence on the specific legal configurations contained in the positive law.[99] Viewed as a power or faculty, a right

---

95 Tierney, "Hohfeld on Ockham," 365.

96 Soto, *De Dominio*, para. 7.

97 Vitoria, *De Iustitia*, Q. 62, a. 1, para. 5.

98 Varkemaa, *Conrad Summenhart's Theory of Individual Rights*, 73n28; *Nam facultas significat potentiam active se habentem, id est potentiam aliquid agenda circa aliquid. Similiter et potestas si proprie capiatur significat tamen potentiam active se habentem.*

99 On Vitoria's alteration of the definitions of Conrad Summenhart and Jean Gerson, see Tierney, *Idea of Natural Rights*, 260.

endows a particular person with a capability consequential upon the existence and application of the laws. For instance, ownership authorizes owners to do what they will with their property, and legal configurations short of ownership generate more limited faculties: *usus* authorizes the use of another's property; *usufructus* authorizes the derivation of profit from another's property; tenancy authorizes the possession of another's property, and so on. Vitoria's own example is the protest voiced by the buyers and sellers in the Temple as Jesus was expelling them:[100] they demanded to know what right he had to do this and on what authority (*quo iure illud faceret et unde liceat*). They were questioning the legal authenticity of the capability that Jesus was supposedly exercising through his actions.

In the real definition the notion of a faculty captures the essence of what an individual's right is by ascribing to a particular person the capability of using something in accordance with the law. The faculty is something that the actor "has" under law in such a way that an injury to it is a legal wrong for which compensation is due. When the faculty is engaged through the exercisability of a specific right, the actor has whatever sphere of activity is legally authorized for that faculty. Accordingly, an injury to a right is a derogation from a faculty that the right-holder has – that is, from the capability of using the object of the right in the legally authorized way; consequently, the injurer is required to restore what the right-holder has lost. As Vitoria explains in his treatment of *dominium*:

> Because if we take something from someone who has *dominium*, we thereby deprive him of the faculty of using the thing, and therefore we are obligated to make restitution. For me to be obligated to make restitution, it is enough that I do an injury to someone with respect to something in which he has any faculty whatsoever. That is, no matter the faculty, if I do it injury, I am obligated to make restitution.[101]

Right so understood refers not to an objective idea of what makes for justice within the legal system considered as a whole, but to a faculty attributed to individuals, who accordingly may say "I use my right, and you use yours."[102]

In Vitoria's account the subjective and objective senses of right, although analytically different, are connected within the operation of a legal system. Objective right provides the framework for the subjective rights, so that both forms of right are aspects of a single ensemble of norms that govern just relationships. What links the two forms of right – and what occasioned Vitoria's treatment of subjective right – is the role of restitution in restoring to an injured party the equivalent of the injury. On the one hand, because it manifested the equality of what was

---

100 Luke 20:2.
101 Vitoria, *De Iustitia*, Q. 62, a. 1, para. 8.
102 Vitoria, *De Iustitia*, Q. 62, a. 1, para. 5.

taken and restored, restitution belonged to commutative justice, and thus to objective right. On the other hand, restitution presupposed a baseline for the operation of this equality. One might ask: What was the reason for requiring restitution, and what was restitution supposed to accomplish? Reference to subjective rights supplied the answer: restitution was due because the injurer had interfered with an individual's right by depriving that individual of the faculty of using something, and restitution vindicated that right by undoing the deprivation. Without subjective rights commutative justice could not work; and without the objective right of commutative justice, subjective rights could not participate in justice. The existence of subjective rights was thus a feature of the architecture of legal relations.[103]

When we move from Vitoria to Soto, his colleague at Salamanca, we again find the notion of a faculty at the centre of the relationship between *ius* and *dominium*. Unlike Vitoria, Soto does not directly ask what a right is; instead, his treatment of *facultas* is intertwined in his account of *dominium*. Soto defines *dominium* as "any person's own faculty and right (*propria cuisque facultas et ius*) in anything at all that he can use for his own benefit with any use whatsoever permitted by law."[104] Rejecting Summenhart's conclusion that right and *dominium* are identical, Soto asserts that *facultas* is the genus of which *dominium* is the species. Soto then elaborates the notion of *facultas* in a succinct gloss on Summenhart (and his predecessors), from which one can disentangle three threads.

The first concerns the etymology of the word *"facultas."* Summenhart had accepted the view that *facultas* is derived from *fas* ("it is allowed") and signified a permitted power to act on a thing. Soto rejected this, insisting instead that the word comes from *facilis* ("easy" or, more accurately, "doable"), and is synonymous with facility or easiness and the contrary of difficulty. Elsewhere Soto affirmed that etymologies are illuminating: because words are indicators of concepts, the founders of languages, acting on the model of Adam in the Garden of Eden, take care to endow things with names that are explicatory of their nature.[105] Accordingly, the derivation of *facultas* from *facilis* is a significant clue to its meaning.

In the legal context, a faculty denotes something doable with ease, because the right-holder alone determines how the right is exercised. In Soto's words, "a person is said to have a facility in a horse, because he can use it easily, that is, without the permission of someone else."[106] Thus, in refusing to identify a faculty with a permission, Soto treats etymologically what Vitoria had assigned to different modes of definition. For Soto, the origin of the word *"facultas"* points not to the permissibility of the right-holder's exercise of the right, but to the irrelevance of the permission of others. From this incapacity on the part of others to determine

---

103 Spindler, "Vernunft, Gesetz und Recht bei Francisco de Vitoria," 41.
104 Soto, *De Iustitia et Iure*, IV, q. 1, a. 1 (p. 280).
105 Soto, *De Iustitia et Iure*, IV, q. 3, a. 1 (p. 328).
106 Soto, *De Dominio*, para. 2.

the right-holder's use of the object of the right, it is but a short step to the notion that an interference with that use is a wrong that others have a duty not to commit.

Second, Soto notes that *facultas* carries a specifically moral meaning that is less inclusive than the broader and morally neutral term *potestas* ("power"). Summenhart had considered, but not definitively resolved, the question of whether *facultas* and *potestas* were synonymous, or whether *potestas* lacked the moral valence that that *facultas* had.[107] Soto adopted the latter view. His conclusion was that the robber has the *potestas* but not the *facultas* to use what belongs to another.[108] Similarly, a tyrant has the *potestas* to make use of the property of citizens for his own good, but he lacks the "*facultas,* that is, the facility" to do so. The goods of citizens are subject to the faculty of their owners who may use what they own without securing anyone else's permission, whereas the tyrant acts "without the owner's permission and faculty or a just intervening cause."[109] *Facultas* is thus a term that is specifically appropriate to the legal relationship between the holder of the right and others (like the robber and the tyrant), who act unjustly if they subject to their power what is within another's right.

Third, Soto thinks that part of the meaning of *facultas* is the right-holder's *immediate* capability to act on the object of the right. Summenhart had accepted the view that *dominium* was a "proximate (*propinqua*) power or faculty" of taking things into one's licit use.[110] By "proximate" as opposed to "remote" Summenhart meant that the power did not require a further activating event in order to become operative. (Summenhart's example of a remote power was the power of a person in deadly sin to merit beatitude if, and only if, he undergoes a transition from not having to having God's love.)[111] Soto considered the reference to this additional element of proximity to be superfluous, because it is already contained within the meaning of the word *facultas*. To him the very idea of a remote power made no sense.[112] If one had a *facultas* to use something, the power to use it must already have been operative, so that describing it as proximate was redundant. Conversely, if one described the power as remote because it needed the activation of a further event, then it could not be functioning as a faculty; the very remoteness of the power would show that the thing in question was not one's own. In Soto's curt

---

107 Varkemaa, *Conrad Summenhart's Theory of Individual Rights,* 70.

108 Soto, *De Dominio,* para. 2.

109 Soto, *De Iustitia et Iure,* IV, q. 1, a. 1 (p. 280).

110 Varkemaa, *Conrad Summenhart's Theory of Individual Rights,* 71–4.

111 Varkemaa, *Conrad Summenhart's Theory of Individual Rights,* 71–2.

112 "Nor is there need to add 'proximate,' because physically a remote power is not said to be a power, just as cold water is not said to have the power of getting hot." Soto, *De Dominio,* para. 2. The point of the reference to water is that cold water does not become hot without the occurrence of an event or act that heats it up.

formulation, "a remote power to use something that belongs to another is not a faculty."[113]

In sum, then, for Soto right as the object of justice is concretized in an ensemble of individual rights, including the paradigmatic right of *dominium*, that generically are capabilities (*facultates*) of the person.[114] A *facultas*, in turn, morally demarcates a juridical space within which the right-holder can directly act without requiring the permission of others.

VI The Right to Beg

Against this general background of Soto's understanding of right in both its objective and subjective senses, one can now consider more specifically the right to beg that Soto postulates.

The right to beg differs in a significant respect from the right of *dominium* that provided the context for Soto's explication of the notion of an individual right in his *De Iustitia et Iure*. Central to a person's right of *dominium* is the object over which dominion is asserted. The right to beg, in contrast, concerns itself not with an object but solely with the activity in which the right-holder engages.

To explain: In Soto's view *dominium* was the specific kind of right that we have in anything that we use as we wish for our own utility.[115] The object of the right is that through which the *dominus* is related through the capability of using or enjoying it for any legally permissible end. Anything that stands in this juridical relation between the *dominus* and his use or enjoyment – whether one's body, the external goods that one owns or is owed, or one's honour and reputation[116] – can count as the object of a right. In the event of an injury, the effect on the object of the right provides the measure of the restitution that the injurer must make.

In contrast, a right that consists solely in the right-holder's engagement in an activity has no object. In the typical instance, the activity is carried out by virtue of an office or an officially authorized procedure where restitution is not usually in issue. In Roman times, for instance, magistrates with imperium had the right to command (*ius imperandi*), citizens facing punishment had the right to appeal to the people (*ius provocationis*), and litigants had the right to sue (*ius persequendi*). Similarly, under canon law bishops had rights to preach (*ius praedicandi*), to judge (*ius iudicandi*), and to administer (*ius administrandi*). For members of the

---

113 Soto, *De Iustutia et Iure*, IV, a. 1 q. 1 (p. 280): *Potestas siquidem remota utendi aliena re non est facultas.*

114 Folgado, *Evolucion Historica del Concepto del Derecho Subjectivo*, 196.

115 Soto, *De Iustitia et Iure*, IV, q. 1, a. 1 (p. 279): (*Dominium autem non quodcumque ius et potestatem significat, sed certe illam quae est in rem qua uti libito nostro possumus in nostram propriam utilitatem*).

116 Soto, *De Iustitia et Iure*, IV, q. 6, a. 3 (p. 334).

Franciscan and other mendicant orders, the solicitation of alms was a practice authorized by the order's Rule and affirmed by the pope.[117] Soto mentions rights that pertain to specific relationships, such as the right of fathers to act for the benefit of their children, or the right of children to be cared for by their parents.[118] Compared to these, the right to beg that Soto invoked differed in two respects. First, the right to beg was not tied to an office or a procedure or a relationship between two specific parties, but it was available at large to everyone legitimately in need and could be exercised with reference to all superfluities of wealth. Second, the right to beg produced an obligation of restitution on the part of anyone who interfered with it.

A structural contrast exists between the right of *dominium* and the right to beg: in the case of *dominium*, the action of the *dominus* occurs within the framework of his relationship to the object of the right. It is because of this relationship that the *dominus* has the legal capability of acting with respect to the object. Thus, actions in exercise of the right flow from the person's entitlement to the object of the right, which is conceptually prior to the specific actions authorized by the *dominus*'s relationship to it. The right to beg is different. No anterior relationship to an object governs the activity undertaken by the right-holder pursuant to that right. The exercise of the right consists simply in the performance of the act of begging itself, without reference to something conceptually prior.

A generation after Soto's *Deliberatio*, the eminent theologian Luis de Molina deployed the right to beg in a radical explication of the distinction between a right to an object and a right to engage in an action:

> One is said to have a right to something in two ways. One way is because something is in some way owed to him or is his. We divided right understood in this way into right *in re* and right *ad rem*. The other way one is said to have a right to something is not because something is owed to him, but because he has a *facultas* for something, the contravention of which wrongs him. In this way we say that one has a right of using one's own things, such as eating one's own food, so that if he is impeded, a wrong and injustice is done to him. We even say that a pauper has the right to ask for alms, that a labourer has a right to hire out his services, that one has a right to hunt and fish where it is not prohibited, so that if any of these persons is impeded in those matters, wrong and injustice are done to him, with restitution due for what the interference precluded him from gaining, even though no one owed it to him.[119]

---

117 E.g., *Solet Annuere*, Bull of Pope Honorius III on the Rule of the Friars Minor, Caput VI (1221), in *Gli Scritti di S. Francesco D'Assisi*, 462.

118 Soto, *De Dominio*, s. 2; Soto, *De Iustitia et Iure*, IV, q. 1, a. 1 (p. 279).

119 Molina, *De Iustitia et Iure, Tomus Tertius* (*De Restitutione*), Tract. II, Disp. DCCXXVII, 1 (p. 540).

What makes this explication radical is that for Molina a *facultas* is always about action and never about an object. This is, of course, the case when the *facultas* refers to free-standing action unattached to an object (as in the right to beg). Molina insists, however, that a *facultas* is also a right to an action and not to an object when the entitlement to act is a consequence of owning something or being owed something (for example, eating one's own food). Even when rights to perform actions with respect to something are derived from owning what one is acting on, the rights to act are analytically different from the ownership, which is not itself a right but is the cause of rights to act in a certain way.

The immediate context for this assertion by Molina is his discussion of whether a person was obligated to make restitution for "impeding another's pursuit of some good thing that he could licitly attain." Molina noted that restitution is due to a prospective donee from a person who by force or fraud prevented the gift from being given, even though the gift was neither owned by nor owed to the prospective donee. (This is an issue that we will consider more fully in the next section.) Just as the beggar, the labourer, and the hunter are entitled to restitution for being deprived of what they do not yet own, so too is the disappointed donee. To be sure, receiving a gift is a "passive faculty" (as Molina calls it), whereas begging, labouring, and hunting are activities performed by the right-holder. However, the underlying principle that one has a compensable right to a benefit that one does not yet own applies equally to all of them.

Molina's view on ownership cuts both ways: not only does the lack of *dominium* not preclude having a right, but *dominium* itself is not a right except as a figure of speech. Although in the quoted passage Molina says that *dominium* is called a right in one sense, he did not in fact consider *dominium* to have the status of a right "formally and essentially."[120] This is because *dominium* did not share the characteristics of a *facultas* but was something antecedent to it that was called a right by metonymy from its consequences. Presumably, Molina took seriously Soto's derivation of *facultas* from *facilis* ("easy"); easiness is more readily attributed to actions than to objects.

Molina gave several reasons for distinguishing *dominium* from *facultas*. One of these reasons is that something owned can be subject to several different rights (the right to sell, the right to use, and so on), whereas the nature of *dominium* in a single thing is itself singular and uniform. Another is that the owner can confer some of the rights to what is owned to another, while still retaining his ownership over the object. Nor did this mean that ownership was merely a bundle of rights; ownership is not derived from its *iura* – that is, from the different actions that ownership makes legally possible – any more than a person is the result of his capacities. As he graphically put it, a person is not an owner of something because

---

120 Molina, *De Iustitia et Iure*, II, Disp. 3.

he has the capability of disposing of it, but rather he has that capability because he is the owner, just as someone is not a person because he has the capability of laughing, but has the capability of laughing because he is a person. One might say that *dominium* is a concept that triggers and unifies the various rights to which it gives rise.

On the relation between *dominium* and *ius*, Soto is situated between his predecessor Summenhart and his successor Molina. Summenhart had identified *dominium* and *ius*. Both Soto and Molina rejected this identification, but to different effect. Molina's conclusion was directly opposite to Summenhart's. Molina treated the two as necessarily distinct, thereby differentiating the ownership of an object from the *iura* that consisted in what the owner could do with the owned object.[121] Soto, on the other hand, regarded *dominium* as a species within the genus *ius*. This was both inconsistent with Summenhart and vigorously denied by Molina.[122] Of course, Soto's assertion that *dominium* is a species of *ius* implicitly leaves room for other kinds of rights, such as the right to beg or engage in other activities.

Every right establishes a connection between the holder of the right and the actions of others. In the case of rights that have an object, the juridical positions of the parties reflect their correlative connections to each other through that object. The object of the right is, so to speak, the fulcrum on which the legal relationship pivots. The function of legal analysis is to identify the object and to determine its scope and legal effects. If the object is something that the right-holder owns, everyone else is bound not to interfere with that object. If the object is something that the right-holder is owed, the obligees are the debtors who must discharge the debt in accordance with its terms. And if the right is infringed, the damage to the object of the right and the interference with how the right-holder would use that object are the bases for establishing the compensation to which the right-holder is entitled.

In the case of the right to beg – a right to engage in an activity – the scope of the right and the consequences of its breach have to be worked out despite the absence of an object around which the right is organized. In contrast to *dominium*, the right to beg does not entitle beggars to anything. It merely authorizes paupers to present themselves to potential almsgivers; how those potential almsgivers react is up to them. The right gives paupers nothing more than the opportunity to realize the possibility of receiving an indeterminate something from an indeterminate someone.

Soto gives some shape to this relatively amorphous right by situating it in the relationship between persons in need and those in whom a superfluity of resources

---

121 Kant made the same distinction, but with a significant difference in terminology; see Weinrib, *Reciprocal Freedom*, 33–41.
122 Contrast Soto, *De Iustitia et Iure*, IV, q. 1, a. 1 ("*ius* is posited as the higher genus in the definition of *dominium*") and Molina, *De Iustitia et Iure*, II, Disp. 3 ("although it is commonly said that *ius* is the true genus of *dominium*, the opposite seems to me to be more true").

created the responsibility for acts of loving-kindness toward the less fortunate in accordance with the biblical injunction to love one's neighbour as oneself. Confining beggars to a particular place was inconsistent with the right to beg, because it impeded both the satisfaction of the needs of the poor and the exercise of compassion by the rich. Soto adduced considerations, both individual and systemic, that elucidated the right to beg in a way that precluded restrictions on the movement of beggars. The individual considerations included the variability in the habits of compassion or avarice among the populations of different regions, the benefit to sick paupers of being in a more salubrious climate, and the need of beggars who have become an annoyance or have run afoul of the law in one region to move on. The systemic considerations arose from Soto's theological and ethical construction of the bonds of sociability that link persons beyond their original locations and that give them reason to plead for assistance from others or to be receptive to such pleas. In the *Deliberatio* Soto traces an ever-expanding circle for the exercise of compassion. This circle is constituted by a series of progressively more inclusive unities that tie persons to one another, from its narrowest version in the nexus between rich and poor as members of the same city or bishopric, to the wider unity of all cities and bishoprics as members of the same kingdom, and to the still wider unity of all Christians within the body of Christ. In the Latin (but not the Spanish) version, the series culminates in the striking idea, drawn from Stoic cosmopolitanism, that "humankind is by its own nature joined in so tight a bond … that even mendicant infidels cannot be expelled."[123] These various unities indicate the broad social and moral bonds between beggars and those who should be compassionately responsive to their appeals. The underlying theme is that the diversity of wealth among persons and across regions is intelligible as part of God's plan only if the resources of the wealthy contribute to alleviating the condition of the poor. The instrumentality through which this alleviation takes place is the right of the poor to solicit the assistance of their more prosperous fellow townsfolk, fellow Spaniards, fellow Christians, and fellow human beings. What is important is the responsiveness to the need, not the location of the needy.

In Soto's argument the significance of treating the begging by paupers as a right is that one cannot legitimately impair a right without compensating the right-holder for the loss caused by that impairment. If one impairs the right to beg by restricting the movements of beggars, one owes them such assistance as would replace what they would have gotten had their right remained intact. The unavailability of this assistance undercuts the legitimacy of the proposed restrictions.

Accordingly, Soto argued that from the existence of a right to beg, one could readily infer the illegitimacy of confining beggars to their native towns or preventing them from begging door to door. Beggars moved from place to place to exercise

---

123 Soto, *Deliberatio*, Chapter IV.

their right to beg because they had difficulty satisfying their needs in their places of origin. Such movement was not in itself a wrong that beggars could be prohibited from committing but was rather a step in the exercise of their right. Conversely, if they were prevented from moving, they would be exposed to the very deprivation that the right to beg was supposed to relieve. Accordingly, a restriction on their movements would be legitimate only if it was accompanied by the law's assurance of assistance that would minister to their needs in their homelands. But no such assistance had been or could feasibly be instituted in the Spain of that day. Soto asserted that without it beggars would not be bound by a restriction on their movements, and they would be entitled to exercise their right to beg anywhere.

This conclusion lies at the junction of what Soto calls three "fundamental points."[124] The first fundamental point is that neither precept nor law prescribes the scope of almsgiving in any particular situation. Left unspecified is the proportion of one's wealth one should donate, the number of persons one should support, and the necessities one should relieve. As observed above in section II, only under circumstances of extreme necessity does precept mandate the provision of assistance to a specific pauper. Under the less severe circumstances of grave necessity, almsgiving is required, but the almsgiver has the freedom to decide about the specific recipient and the specific occasion. The right to beg, however, goes beyond these kinds of necessity. All who are genuinely in need have the right to implore the compassion of others. Thus, both in the case of grave necessity, where precept obligates, and in situations of the more routine tribulations of poverty, where almsgiving is a matter of counsel only, the poor have the right to beg without the almsgiver being specifically directed about what to give or how much or to whom. Indeed, this indefiniteness is an aspect of the spirituality of almsgiving, embodying not the rigidity of rules but the flexibility of loving one's neighbour as oneself to the extent of one's ability.

The second fundamental point is the obverse of the first: because the requirement of almsgiving does not specify particular givers or particular gifts, what one donates to the poor is (aside from circumstances of extreme necessity) a matter of one's personal choice. Moreover, the primacy of an almsgiver's personal choice limits the law's role in relieving poverty. The law has no basis for imposing, on pain of penalty, obligations about almsgiving that exceed what the gospel lays down as a matter of precept. The most that Soto is willing to countenance is that the state might compel alms by threat of penalty when the necessity is extreme. For other situations, Soto in his second edition quotes Paul's statement that "each person should do as he has decided in his heart, not sadly or under compulsion, for God loves a cheerful giver."[125] The result is that avarice and insufficient generosity cause

---

124 Soto, *Deliberatio,* Chapter XI; see also Chapter IV.
125 2 Corinthians 9:7.

the alms donated to fall far short of the needs that they are supposed to satisfy, without the law's being able to exercise compulsion to make up the deficit.

The third fundamental point adds the crucial juridical consideration: anyone who injures the rights of others is obligated to make good their losses. Thus, the status of begging as an activity to which paupers have a right becomes the determining factor for the consequence that should accompany the curtailment of that activity. Soto explains this in a passage that he especially wants the supporters of the proposed restrictions to bear in mind:

> Whoever deprives the beggars (or causes them to be deprived) of the right to solicit thereby owes them relief from their misfortune and assistance with their needs, or at least with those that morally speaking, as they say, they likely could have provided for by soliciting. For example, assume the city has a hundred or a thousand legitimate paupers, whose needs could not be sufficiently provided for with less than two hundred ducats, which they likely could have gotten if they had been permitted to beg door to door. I then understand this fundamental point in this way: although helping those who are permitted to solicit is not an obligation of justice but only a matter of mercy, nonetheless the state or the person who prevented soliciting would as a matter of justice be obligated to pay those who were so prevented the entire two hundred ducats. This is certainly obvious. The beggars have the right to seek alms, and whoever deprives a person of his right is liable for the loss according to the well-known principle that whoever is the cause of loss is looked upon as having inflicted the loss.[126]

Two paragraphs later Soto restates the point more succinctly:

> When they are permitted to beg, no one is obligated to bestow mercy except for extreme or perhaps grave necessity. But when they are forbidden to beg, what was mercy becomes justice. For as I just said, a person who deprives a pauper of his right becomes his debtor for all that the pauper could have acquired by begging.[127]

In these passages Soto sets out the transformative consequence of understanding begging as a right. Although the process of begging is a matter of mercy rather than justice, an interference with that process is nonetheless an injustice. Potential almsgivers can respond to the beggar's solicitations as they wish, but by preventing beggars from moving between regions or from begging door to door the state incurs a duty to replace the assistance that beggars would have received. Although the restrictions limit the activity of eliciting acts of compassion that are not legally

---

126 Soto, *Deliberatio,* Chapter XI.
127 Soto, *Deliberatio,* Chapter XI.

owed, beggars nonetheless have a right to engage in that activity. They are, accordingly, entitled to be made whole if their right to do so is impaired.

In Soto's view, the fatal difficulty with the proposal to restrict begging now arises, because the first two fundamental points inevitably place compliance with the third one beyond reach. The first of these fundamental points denies the determinability of the amount of assistance or of the number of persons to be assisted; the second affirms that all are free to contribute alms as they wish. Taken together these points render impossible the provision of the alms that justice requires: "For if neither the paupers nor what they need is determined in any certain number or manner … and citizens cannot be compelled to give alms, how, I ask, can the state discharge the debt that it incurred by prohibiting begging?"[128] The underlying assumption is that the conduct from which the beggars will be barred under the proposed reforms – moving to a more prosperous region rather than being supported in their poorer homelands, or making a personal appeal with their desperate misery evident rather than receiving alms collected and distributed by respectable municipal agents – will be more productive for them than the new arrangements. Consequently, the beggars would not be fully indemnified for being deprived of what they would otherwise have received. From this Soto concluded that in injuring the beggars' rights the reform would burden the state with an indebtedness to them that it could not discharge.

Soto adduces this argument as support for his claim that the proposed restrictions on begging are not legally permissible. To what kind of legal defect is he pointing?

The obvious response is that the measures preventing beggars from moving between regions or from begging door to door fall under the legal category of delict. As developed in modern law, a delict is "an infringement of an individual's rights (but is not exclusively a breach of contract)" leading to a sanction "the purpose of [which] is normally to compensate the injured party."[129] Conforming to this characterization of delict is Soto's statement that because beggars have a right to seek alms, "whoever deprives a person of his right is liable for the loss that follows." Accordingly, beggars are owed the assistance that would make up for the loss of what they would have secured by unrestricted begging. As is standard in delict, by infringing another's right – in this case, the right to beg – one commits a wrong against the right-holder, and this wrong is remedied by compensating for the losses that flow from it.

The modern conception of delict, evident in outline in Soto's argument, emerged by a lengthy process from its antecedents in Roman law. Reaching its most influential formulation in the account of delict given by Hugo Grotius eight

---

128 Soto, *Deliberatio,* Chapter XI.
129 Nicholas, *Introduction to Roman Law,* 208.

decades after the *Deliberatio*,[130] this process yielded a general conception that connected the wrongdoer's fault, the damage to the victim's rights, and the wrongdoer's obligation to repair that damage. The point of departure for much of this development was the Roman law of Aquilian liability for wrongfully inflicted damage (*damnum iniuria datum*),[131] which remained a constant reference.

In his treatment of the right to beg, Soto diverged from that basis of liability in two relevant respects that reflected modifications in Aquilian liability that took hold in the medieval period.[132] First, the basic assumption of Roman jurisprudence (adjusted only under anomalous circumstances) was that damage was not actionable unless done to something that the victim owned.[133] Translating this into the discourse of rights, one may say that Aquilian liability dealt with damage to rights that had an object, not to rights (like the right to beg) that referred solely to the right-holder's activity. In contrast to the approach of classical Roman law, Soto shared the assumption of medieval jurisprudence that the plaintiff could recover for pure economic loss – in Soto's case, the loss of future alms – even in the absence of damage to or deprivation of something that the plaintiff owned.

Second, Aquilian liability did not recognize damage that was indirectly caused. In their interpretation of Aquilian liability, the Roman jurists distinguished between slaying another and furnishing the cause of another's death[134] and held that damage had to be inflicted by the defendant's own bodily force (*corpore suo*).[135] Indirect damage they handled by discretionary extensions by analogy rather than as a matter of core Aquilian liability. In this way Roman law, while recognizing that the causation of harm was indispensable to delictual liability, expressed its reluctance – shared by other legal systems – to trace the consequences for which one was responsible through an open-ended causal chain.[136] The Roman jurists would have ascribed some significance to the fact that the restrictions on begging did not directly deprive beggars of whatever resources they had, but instead diminished the assistance that donors would otherwise have provided. It would have mattered that although this loss was causally traceable to the restrictions, the restrictions did not themselves inflict it. By Soto's time these niceties of Roman law had come

---

130 Grotius, *De Jure Belli Ac Pacis*, II, 2, 17; see Sampson, *Historical Foundations of Grotius' Analysis of Delict*.

131 Birks, *Roman Law of Obligations*, 192.

132 On these modifications, see Zimmermann, *Law of Obligations*, 1022–4.

133 Zimmermann, *Law of Obligations*, 197; an example of an anomalous circumstance is damage done to an inheritance in the interval between the death of the decedent and the heir's acceptance of the inheritance, when the inherited property is technically not owned by anyone (Justinian, *Digest* 9, 2, 13, 2; *Digest* 9, 2, 43).

134 Justinian, *Digest* 9, 2, 6.

135 Justinian, *Institutes* 4, 2, 16; see Birks, *The Roman Law of Obligations*, 198–202.

136 The definitive discussion of this point in the context of Anglo-American law is Holmes, *Common Law*, Lecture III.

to be ignored. Soto, accordingly, referred in the quoted passage to the "certainly obvious" connection between the impairment of the beggars' rights and the consequent loss, curtly appealing to the principle encapsulating the medieval approach, that "whoever causes the loss is looked upon as having inflicted the loss."

In both of these respects – the allowance of claims for pure economic loss and the erasure of the difference between direct and indirect causation – Soto's argument is intelligible only against the background of a significant expansion of the scope of Aquilian liability from its more limited Roman form.

VII   *Lucrum Cessans*

This issue of the causal connection to the loss suggests a further question: Did the lessening of alms that would result from the restrictions constitute a legally cognizable loss at all? The problem is that the proposed restrictions deprived beggars of alms that they had not yet been given. Can they be said to have lost what they never had?

This too is a question with a history. In dealing with Aquilian liability for damage to property, the Roman jurists had made the owner's interest in the property, and not merely the value of the property on its own (or the amount of damage that it suffered), the measure of the owner's recovery. This allowed owners to claim the gain that this damage prevented them from realizing. In the medieval period this measure of recovery became known as *lucrum cessans* (foregone profit) in contrast to *damnum emergens* (loss that came to light). Restitution that included *lucrum cessans* compensated for the loss of something that the owner never had. For instance, the Roman jurists held that if the damage consisted in the death of a slave who had been instituted as someone's heir, the owner would be awarded the value of the inheritance that would now never accrue to him. The limiting case was a gain that was too uncertain. For example, a fisherman whose net was wrongfully damaged could not recover the profit he would have made from the fish that he was prevented from catching.[137]

In the sixteenth century a frequently discussed variant on this theme was a scenario that, at least structurally, was closely related to the impairment of the right to beg. The discussion elaborated on observations that Aquinas had earlier made concerning what one may call the case of the disappointed prospective prebendary.[138] Suppose that someone interfered with a bishop's plan to appoint a particular person to a clerical benefice; was the intervenor obliged to make restitution to the person whose appointment he had frustrated? This situation presented a complex instance of the more general issue of what the consequences were of

---

137 Lawson and Markesinis, *Tortious Liability*, 35.
138 Aquinas, *Summa Theologiae*, II-II, q. 62, a. 2, ad 4.

preventing someone from attaining some good thing (*impedit aliquem ab aliquo bono consequendo*), such as a legacy or a gift. The complexity resided in what Grotius, following his scholastic predecessors, was later to call the concurrence of distributive justice and commutative justice:[139] choosing a suitable appointee was a matter of distributive justice, which was to be determined by the person with the authority to make the appointment, but intervening to frustrate a particular appointment raised an issue of commutative justice between the person interfering and the disappointed candidate. Even if the candidate has no right to an appointment that lies within the discretion of the appointing authority, does he have a right as against the intermeddler for frustrating his prospects?

Soto's criticism of the restrictions on begging shares with Aquinas's case of the prebendary a structure in which an intervenor (in Soto's case, the state) acts to prevent the bestowers of a benefit (the almsgivers) from conferring it on prospective beneficiaries (the beggars). Just as the prospective prebendary had no right to an appointment, so the beggars had no right to alms from any particular person. Nonetheless, both the prospective prebendary and the beggar had a right to be considered for their respective benefits without being subjected to the intervenor's wrongful conduct. In his own treatment of the prebendary case in his *De Iustutia et Iure*, Soto explicitly noted the parallel with the situation of the beggars:

> It seems that one who prevents another from something that was not yet his right but depends on another's pure will does not become liable to him for restitution. I say this is false. For even if it is within the prelate's discretion to give the benefice to this person or that person, nonetheless the intervenor deprives him of his particular right to seek the appointment. Just as with the person who by force or fraud prevents a pauper from seeking alms, he is liable to make restitution to him. For although they bestow it upon him at their will, he nevertheless has the right to seek it.[140]

In the prebendary case Aquinas treated the purpose of the intervenor's action and the firmness of the bestower's intention as the decisive considerations. The intervenor was not liable to compensate the disappointed would-be prebendary if he acted for the purpose of securing the appointment of a more qualified candidate. However, the result would be different if, out of personal animosity or spitefulness, he acted for the purpose of harming a suitable candidate. The amount of the compensation would then depend on the firmness of the appointer's intention. If the intention was not firm, the intervenor would be under a qualified obligation to compensate; that is, he would be required to make not *full* compensation for

---

139 Grotius, *De Jure Belli*, II, 2, 17, 3; see especially Soto, *De Iustitia et Iure*, IV, q. 6, a. 3
     (pp. 347–8); Covarrubias y Leyva, *Regulae, Peccatum* II, 7, 8.
140 Soto, *De Iustitia et Iure*, IV, q. 6, a. 3 (p. 348).

the lost benefice (given that for many reasons the appointment in the end might not have come to pass) but rather *some* compensation in accordance with a wise person's judgment of the worthiness of the candidate and the propinquity of his appointment. If, however, the intervention caused the appointer to go back on a firm decision, the intervenor was obligated to make full compensation if he had the means. Upsetting a firm decision was considered tantamount to depriving the candidate of what was already his.

In his discussion of this issue Soto (as well as other sixteenth-century thinkers) changed Aquinas's criteria but not his general approach. Soto offered both a negative and a positive amendment to Aquinas's formulation. On the negative side, in Soto's view the intervenor's motive could not be a decisive determinant of restitution. The obligation to make restitution arises only on the commission of injustice, whereas motivation pertains to the virtue of charity, not to justice. As Soto succinctly put it, what matters for restitution "is not with what intention you act but by what right."[141] Acting even from animosity or spitefulness in itself imposes no burden of restitution. The base motive is at most a sign that indicates but does not constitute a failure to act according to one's right. On the positive side, Soto asserted that the criterion for restitution was that the intervenor had exercised force or practised fraud in frustrating the appointment. One could not engage in such conduct by right. The intervenor could legitimately entreat the person bestowing the benefit to change his mind, but he could not distort the operation of the bestower's will by applying force or fraud. If he did, the intervenor would be liable to make restitution in whole or in part, in accordance with the beneficiary's propinquity to the realization of the benefit.

The major opponent of Aquinas's approach was Cardinal Cajetan, Soto's much older contemporary and the great commentator on Aquinas.[142] In Cajetan's view the insuperable objection to Aquinas's approach was that Aquinas's view required the intervenor to compensate the disappointed beneficiary for something to which the beneficiary never had a right. Even if the intervenor acted out of malevolence toward the prospective beneficiary, the obligation to make restitution would be out of place, because the point of restitution is to repair the loss arising from the violation of a right. In this situation the beneficiary's right to the prospective benefit had not yet been established, as is evident from the still existing power of the bestower to change his mind without committing an injustice. Using a graphic expression from Roman law,[143] Cajetan notes that the will of the bestower was still "ambulatory."

---

141 Soto, *De Iustitia et Iure*, IV, q. 6, a. 3 (p. 349): *Videndum ergo est quantum ad restitutionem res attinet non quo animo id facias sed quo iure.*

142 Cajetan, *Commentaria ad Aquinas, Summa Theologiae*, II-II, q. 62, a. 2 and a. 4.

143 Justinian, *Digest* 34, 4, 4 ("*ambulatoria enim est voluntas defuncti usque ad vitae supremum exitum*").

Nor could it be claimed that the prospective beneficiary had a right as a matter of hope (*ius in spe*). A right as a matter of hope, Cajetan insisted, is not a right, just as being rich as a matter of hope is not the same as being rich. To be sure, in situations of *lucrum cessans* one was compensated for the loss of what one hoped for. The paradigmatic case, mentioned by Aquinas, featured the wrongful destruction of a crop before it matured, where the assessment of compensation includes the prospect of the crop maturing and being harvested.[144] In that case, however, the owner at least owned the object through which the hope would be realized, and he could sell that object at a price that would include the value of the hope. In contrast, the disappointed prospective prebendary had a free-standing hope that did not rest on an existing right. In Cajetan's opinion, if no right of his was violated, there was nothing for which he should be compensated. One can add that if Cajetan's view was correct, Soto's beggars would also not be entitled to compensation for the reduction in their alms.

Soto (and other leading thinkers of the time)[145] rejected Cajetan's analysis. While accepting the premise of Cajetan's position, that compensation presupposed the violation of a right, Soto asserted that the requisite right was present. Cajetan, he argued, had confused two different claims: Cajetan wrongly attributed to Aquinas the notion that the intervenor should be liable for inflicting a loss that came close to being compensable due to the propinquity of the anticipated appointment. That would be nonsensical, like saying that a person who almost murdered someone should be punished for murder. Aquinas's true position was that the intervenor should be liable for inflicting compensable damage in a matter (that is, being appointed as a prebendary) that came close to occurring. The root of the liability was not that the prospective prebendary almost had a right to the future appointment, but that, because of the state of the bestower's deliberation about the appointment, the loss was already compensable when the interference took place. What was at stake was not a right to the appointment – at no time did the candidate have that – but a right to seek the appointment. This antecedent right was the one with reference to which the intervenor inflicted a compensable loss.

Understood in this way, the case of the prebendary was an instance of *lucrum cessans*, no different in principle from the crop wrongfully destroyed before it matures. The prospective loss of the mature crop or of the prebend goes to the assessment of the damage done, respectively, to the underlying right to the crop or to the right to seek the appointment. In his treatment of *lucrum cessans*, Aquinas had distinguished between two modes of loss: the deprivation of what a person has actually, and the deprivation of what a person has potentially and is on the way to obtaining by virtue of what he has actually.[146] The latter mode of loss is

---

144 Aquinas, *Summa Theologiae*, II-II, q. 62, a. 4.
145 Gordley, *Jurists*, 87–9.
146 Aquinas, *Summa Theologiae*, II-II q. 62, a. 4.

compensable in accordance with the circumstances, considering that the potential profit can be frustrated in many ways. Accordingly, the owner of the immature crop has the harvest not actually but potentially, so that if the crop is wrongfully destroyed, the compensation should reflect the loss of that potentiality. Similarly, in the case of the prebend, the intervenor caused the loss of a potentiality that was contained in a right that the prospective prebendary already had, and that was on the way to maturing into a benefice through the decision of the bestower.

Soto's remarks allow for a more detailed reconstruction of the interference with the prospective beneficiary's right. The wrong has two conceptual components that relate the prospective beneficiary to the bestower of the benefit in a way that makes the intervention an injustice to the beneficiary. The first component is that the conferral of benefits is within the prerogative of the bestowers, who are free not to confer benefits or to confer them on anyone they wish or consider worthy. The intervenor who causes the bestower to go back on his decision through an interference with that freedom acts wrongfully. The intervenor can legitimately entreat the bestower to change his mind, because entreaty is an appeal to the bestower's will to which the bestower can choose to accede or not. However, force or fraud signify constraints or impositions on the bestower's will and are therefore wrongful.

The second component is the freedom of the beneficiary to accept the benefit and thereby to include it among the things to which he has a right. Even though the force or fraud are applied to the bestower (and *a fortiori* if applied to the beneficiary), they are directed against and affect the prospective beneficiary by preventing him from having the opportunity to accept. This makes the interference a wrong against the potential beneficiary, and not something that might count as a wrong against the bestower. Using Aquinas's categorization of the different modes of harm, one might say that the beneficiary has an actual right to seek the benefit and a potential right to accept it if the bestower's deliberations put him on the way to obtaining it. The right to seek contains the potentiality of the right to accept. Referring to the example of the frustrated legacy, Soto summed up his view of this complex three-party situation:

> If you apply force or fraud to prevent the testator who is prepared to leave his goods to Peter from carrying that out, you are obligated to make restitution. For although the testator leaves his goods to whomever he wishes, you nonetheless wrongfully deprived Peter of his right to accept (*ius quod habebat recipiendi*), and that is a faculty and a capacity and a proximate suitability (*facultatem et capacitatem et proximam aptitudinem*). If, however, you neither applied force nor created a fraud, you are not obligated to make restitution, even if you accomplished it through entreaties.[147]

---

147 Soto, *De Iustitia et Iure*, IV, q. 6, a. 3 (p. 350).

Decades later Grotius, drawing on Soto, expressed this conclusion more succinctly: "the capacity for a legacy is a kind of right, and it has the consequence that impeding the freedom of the testator in this matter is a wrong."[148]

The contrast between the views of Cajetan and those of his opponents, including Soto, underlines the centrality of the difference between rights in objects and rights to an activity. Cajetan held that until the object of the right was acquired, the prospective right-holder had no grounds in justice for complaining about being prevented from deriving the benefit anticipated from it. In contrast, the rights to an activity that were articulated by Soto, such as the right to seek a prebend or to beg, had a different juridical orientation, in which the central element was not injury to an object, but freedom from conduct that wrongfully interfered with what one was permitted to do.

Rights of the latter sort originated in the *actio iniuriarum* of Roman law. This delictual action assigned liability in a wide range of circumstances for wilfully outrageous behaviour that was injurious to another's person, dignity, honour, or reputation. Relevant to the present discussion is that under this delict one could be liable for such conduct as interfering with another's maritime fishing or sailing, preventing another from bathing in a public bath, barring another from sitting in a public theatre or walking in a public space, and obstructing another's use of his own property.[149] In all these instances the contumelious behaviour was an affront to the other's honour, in that it insultingly interfered with an activity in which the other was lawfully at liberty to engage. In its own way, the delict reflected a Roman version of the ethos of equal respect.[150]

The scholastics inherited this form of liability and adapted its underlying principle to the treatment of pre-empted benefits. As was mentioned in the previous section. Molina formulated the issue as whether a person was liable to make restitution for "impeding another's pursuit of some good thing *that he could licitly attain.*" In their treatment of this issue, the principle of non-interference with another's permissible activity included not only the other's active pursuit of the good thing in question, as in the case of the beggar, but also the receipt of a gift or legacy (Molina's "passive faculty," mentioned above). The scholastics also reformulated the vague notion of contumelious behaviour into more specific concepts of improper purpose (the spitefulness or personal animosity mentioned by Aquinas) or improper means (Soto's force or fraud). Moreover, they integrated the elements of the wrongful pre-emption of benefits into their taxonomy of distributive and commutative justice, allocating to the former the authority to choose the beneficiary and determine the benefit, and to the latter the wrongfulness of the interference. Most importantly, by Soto's day when the operation of commutative justice

---

148 Grotius, *De Iure Belli ac Pacis,* II, 2, 17, 3: *nam capacitas legati ius quoddam est, cui est consequens, ut libertatem testatoris in eo impedire iniuria sit.*

149 Justinian, *Digest* 43, 8, 2, 9; 47, 10, 13, 7.

150 Birks, *Roman Law of Obligations,* 222.

presupposed the existence of subjective rights – an idea solidified by Vitoria (see above, section V) – they shifted the juridical centre of gravity from *iniuria* to *ius*, that is, from the wrongfulness of the interference to the right to be free of such interference. Thus emerged a subjective right that consisted not in one's legal power over an acquired object but rather in one's entitlement not to be subjected to an egregious wrong while carrying on a permissible activity. This, in turn, allowed the remedy for interference to be of the value of the unattained benefit rather than, as was the case in the Roman *actio iniuriarum*, a monetary penalty that would provide appropriate solace for the contumelious offence to one's honour.[151] As a result, the scholastics postulated the existence of a right to seek a benefit that was in the gift of someone else and of an entitlement to compensation from a third party who wrongfully prevented the realization of the benefit. Accordingly, whereas Cajetan denied that a merely prospective benefit could ground a right, Soto insisted that the right in play was of a kind that eluded Cajetan's argument.

However, even if Soto was correct regarding the disappointed prebendary's right, begging raised an additional problem. If the right protects the permissibility of an activity, what prevents the law from rendering the activity in question impermissible? Recall that Molina subsequently grouped the right to beg with the right to hunt and fish "where it is not prohibited," presumably referring to such considerations as the impermissibility of hunting in certain locations, the restriction of the kind of nets that fishermen could use, and the reservation of the activity of hunting to nobles or licensees. On what basis did Soto think that the law could not legitimately impose on begging restrictions analogous to these?

The answer lies in the connection of begging to natural right. In this vein, some have suggested that the right to beg can be seen as an immediate consequence of one's right to existence.[152] That suggestion may not tell the whole story, because the right to beg was available even to those whose need was not life-threatening. But one can perhaps point to a related line of enquiry that traces the right to beg back to the situation before the institution of private property.

An additional basis for the immunity of the pauper's right from the legal restrictions proposed in Tavera's law may rest on Soto's belief that the obligation to assist the poor was the residue of the common possession that preceded private property.[153] This belief followed through on Aquinas's assertion that exterior things

---

151 Nicholas, *Introduction to Roman Law,* 217; on the history of this transition in Grotius and on his indebtedness to "the late scholastic Spanish model," see du Bois, "Punishment, Reparation and the Evolution of Private Law," 245.

152 Deuringer, *Probleme der Caritas* 65; Brett, *Changes of State,* 27.

153 Soto, in Commentary, s. 5, treats almsgiving as a matter of right that is derived from the right of nature regarding common possession; see also Soto, *De Iustitia et Iure,* IV, q. 3, a. 1 (p. 297); V, q. 3, a. 4 (p. 428): "The natural right in common continues to the extent that whoever has too much ought to be beneficent to the to the indigent."

belong to human beings under the aspect not only of ownership but also of use, so that a denizen of the postlapsarian world holds things as common (*communes*), that is, as readily sharing (*communicet*) the use of them with others.[154] In this way (as Aquinas's commentator Cajetan strikingly put it) relations between rich and poor "are without the unfair inequality (*absque iniqua inaequalitate*) of external things."[155] The right to beg postulated by Soto can then be seen as the transformed continuation of the arrangement that had existed under primordial common possession, when anyone could use anything. Although the availability of everything to everyone had been ousted by private property, it survived – a mere shadow of its former self – as a right to ask the owner for some of the superfluities that he owned. Thus, the primordial right of each person to use what came to hand was succeeded by the right of any needy person to attempt to access the things of the world, which were now privately owned, through the exercise of begging. In the postlapsarian world no other individualized procedure for funnelling superfluities from the wealthy to the indigent was conceivable. Understood in this way, begging was the social mechanism for instigating the acts of sharing that reflected the primordial communality of goods. Because it could be traced back to the natural right of common possession, begging could not legitimately be restricted; positive law had to remain consistent with this attenuated residue of natural right. Accordingly, although acceding to the beggar's petition was an act of compassion, the beggar made that petition as a matter of right that positive law could not eliminate or restrict.

From this emerges a relational conception of the legal architecture through which assistance to the poor becomes operative as the expression of the divinely mandated love of one's neighbour as oneself. Although the obligation to give alms is one of charity and not justice, its execution presupposes a set of legal mechanics. The solicitation of alms is the point at which the almsgiver's ownership of superfluities intersects with the pauper's right to beg. Of course, the beggar's right is not to the superfluities themselves, but to a mode of accessing them by presenting oneself to their owner and inducing a benefit. In accordance with the severity of the beggar's need, owners who in their turn allowed themselves to be induced either avoid damnation by fulfilling an obligation incumbent on them as a matter of precept or contribute to their own salvation by meritoriously assisting the poor as a matter of counsel.

In this relationship of owner and beggar, the two do not stand toward each other merely as prospective donor and donee. Rather, because one has superfluities of which he should divest himself and the other has needs for the satisfaction of which he is entitled to petition, the two parties are intertwined in the charitable

---

154 Aquinas, *Summa Theologiae*, II-II, q. 66, a. 2.
155 Cajetan ad Aquinas, *Summa Theologiae*, II-II, q. 66, a. 2.

relationship that arises when private property supplants common possession. The owner's legal position is that he has a proprietary right that places the charitable deployment of his superfluities within his discretion. The beggar's legal position is that he has a parallel right to influence the owner's exercise of that discretion. Their respective legal positions reflect the potential assistance that one should wish to give and the other is entitled to solicit when superfluity and need coexist once private property has been instituted.

Accordingly, when begging is characterized as a right, the beggar is not conceived as the entirely passive recipient of another's largess. Instead, despite the horrific material inequality between them, the beggar and owner interact as juridical equals on the basis of their respective rights. Because the beggar's right is exercised by the petitioning of a specific person, it is consonant with the traditional view that – in contrast with the administrative arrangements of the proposed reform – almsgiving is meritorious only when the benefit is handed out personally and non-anonymously.[156] Matching this juridical equality is the mutuality at the theological level of salvific good works that consist in the owner's relieving the needs of the pauper, and the pauper's praying for the owner's soul.[157] Through the right to beg the law signals that the beggar has the dignity of a person with agency, who is entitled to press for at least some of what owners should give to people like him. As mentioned above in the previous section, this right exists by virtue of his humanity, and not of his nationality, religion, or location,

One can now return to Soto's observations about the comparable legal positions of the prebendary and the begging pauper concerning the right to seek a benefit that depends on someone else's decision. Soto seems to believe that the parallel between pauper and prospective prebendary suffices for his conclusion in the *Deliberatio* that the proposed restrictions on begging called for compensation. This conclusion is questionable. Although the right to beg is structurally similar to the right to seek the prebend, the circumstances in which the right to beg operates in the *Deliberatio* are quite different. The right of the prospective prebendary points to a set of identifiable particular parties and actions: *this* candidate seeking *this* prebend, *this* bishop with *this* intention regarding *this* prebend, and *this* intervenor practising *this* violence or fraud to prevent the execution of *this* intention. In contrast, in the violation of mendicant rights alleged in Tavera's law, the beggar is any (and every) legitimate beggar, the bestower is any person of means, and the benefit is whatever that person decides to give. The elements are too amorphous to establish a set of viable legal relationships; and the possible benefits are too variegated

---

156 Kahl, "Religious Roots of Modern Poverty Policy," 99, 108.

157 "Prayers from the poor were the most effective way of ensuring entrance to heaven in a world oriented towards the afterlife. *Pauper* and *potens* thus engaged in a reciprocal – and for both sides essential – commitment: the *potens* passes out the alms, and, in return, the *pauper* prayed for the donor's soul." Kahl, "Religious Roots of Modern Poverty Policy," 96.

to allow an estimate of what any bestower was on the way toward giving and what any beggar lost. The prospects for alms under these circumstances are even more indefinite than the predicament of the fisherman with the wrongfully damaged net who, according to the Roman jurists, could not be compensated for fish he was prevented from catching. In contrast to the begging discussed in the *Deliberatio*, the passage from the *De Iustitia et Iure* noting the parallel of the would-be prebendary and the beggar (quoted above) envisaged a specific and individual instance of the prevention of almsgiving, not the application of a political policy to all the assorted encounters over time with beggars throughout the entire kingdom.

The point can be formulated as follows. On the basis of past practice one can perhaps work out what all the beggars have historically received in aggregate over a certain period of time and then estimate the total loss that the new arrangements would bring to beggars as a class. Whether feasible or not, this is at least an intelligible way of approaching the issue. Indeed, Soto himself seems to be thinking along these lines in the example, quoted above, of the city that would have produced two hundred ducats for beggars going door to door.[158] However, one cannot trace the requirements of liability applicable to the prebendary case into all the individualized transactions through which the right to beg is carried out. Soto's problem of the shortfall in assistance to the poor requires attention to the totality of losses by beggars, not a judgment about the congruence with the prebendary case of particular interactions between beggars and prospective almsgivers. Formulated in modern terms, the problem is one for public law, not private law.

Moreover, in the case of Tavera's law, what is it that makes restrictions on begging wrongful? The criteria for wrongfulness set out in the case of the prebend are the application of force or the practice of fraud. The interference with almsgiving in Tavera's law is clearly not the latter and only problematically the former. To be sure, the laws of the kingdom are backed up by the state's control of coercion, but that does not mean that conformity to a law (which Soto regarded as an ordering of reason for the common good) must be conceived as nothing more than the submission to force. Furthermore, the threat of official violence to enforce the law has a legitimacy absent from the threat of private violence, with which Soto is concerned in the prebendary case. This legitimacy makes it implausible to regard what the law requires as a wrongful constraint on the wills of almsgivers. Nor is the state's prevention of begging in certain locations readily interpretable as an interference with the more or less fixed will of potential almsgivers to accede to the pleas of beggars that they will no longer hear. Accordingly, in connection with the significance of wrongfulness also, the public dimension of the state's action is hard to fit into the private-law model of interference that Soto assumes.

---

158 Soto, *Deliberatio*, Chapter XI.

Finally, Soto has inverted the relationship between the impairment of the right and the correction of that impairment. One usually thinks of the former as a wrong and the latter (including the compensation due for the wrongful injury) as the remedy that repairs the wrong to the extent possible. This nexus of right, wrong, and remedy readily fits into Soto's account of individual rights in his later work *De Iustitia et Iure*. As explained above, Soto regards a right as a faculty that demarcates a moral space within which the right-holder is directly free to act without needing the permission of others.[159] Corresponding to this, a wrong may be said to be an intrusion into that space against the will of the right-holder, which the wrongdoer can repair by restoring what the right-holder would have had but for the intrusion. In undoing the effects of the wrong, compensation does not transform a wrongful act into a rightful one. Rather, the remedy presupposes and preserves the normative quality of the wrongfulness to which it responds. Its function is to correct the wrong, rather than to make it permissible. For if the provision of compensation were conceived as a retrospective legitimation of the wrong, then the right would not be exercisable independently of the will of others, as Soto supposes, but would be subject to an involuntary sale to anyone prepared to compensate for infringing it.

However, this emphasis on the primacy of the right is not the way the argument goes in the *Deliberatio*. Soto ties the illegitimacy of the restrictions on begging to the absence of compensation for those restrictions rather than to their impairment of the right to beg in the first place. If only the first two fundamental points had been different, so that the beggars could have been compensated for having their movements restricted, then Soto's objection to the proposed reform on this score would have fallen away, despite the effect on their right to beg. Instead of demarcating a moral space for the right-holder's autonomy, the right would merely set the price for expropriation by others.

Even if Soto was not consciously thinking of expropriation, the power of the state to expropriate by virtue of what Grotius later called its eminent domain[160] is indeed the phenomenon that most closely (although not perfectly) fits Soto's treatment of the right to beg in the *Deliberatio*. As subsequently expounded by the jurist Fernando Vasquez of Menchaca (Soto's sometime colleague at Salamanca), the state has the authority to take what belongs to a private citizen if the taking is for the public benefit and if the state compensates the owner for what was taken.[161] In these circumstances, what would otherwise be a wrongful infringement of a person's right becomes a permissible state act. As is the case with the impairment of the right to beg in the *Deliberatio*, expropriation treats compensation as

---

159 Above, section V.
160 Grotius, *De Iure Belli*, III, 20, 7, 1.
161 Vasquius Menchacensis, *Controversiae*, Liber I, Caput V, 1, 1.

the condition that legitimates the causing of injury, rather than as its remedy. The unlawfulness of the state's act lies not in the infliction of loss but in leaving the loss uncompensated.

The idea that the state can exercise its power to expropriate only when it is for the public benefit encapsulates the complexity of Soto's position. In Vasquez's account, the public benefit of the taking was itself the basis of the requirement of compensation, on the principle that the inconveniences and expense of a taking should be borne by the party that benefits from it. Whether impairing the right to beg was for the public benefit would have been an awkward issue for Soto. On the one hand, Soto criticized the legitimacy of restricting the right to beg. On the other hand, he might have been understandably reluctant to characterize as wrongful a reform regarding a pressing social issue that the government has proposed with the best of intentions. His focus on the inadequacy of the compensation rather than on the wrongful quality of the restrictions on begging allowed him to occupy an ambiguous middle ground.

From Soto's perspective this focus makes all the more sense in view of the consequence that he ascribes to the failure to compensate. Soto suggests that this failure would absolve the beggars from the obligation to comply with the law's restrictions. Speaking of the proposed constraints on the beggars' mobility, Soto remarks that the uncompensated paupers "would then be free of the edict and would be able to go wherever they wanted to beg."[162] Why would this be so? The reason that Soto gives – that the law cannot prohibit what is otherwise neither a crime nor a wrong – cannot be the complete story, because it does not explain why a law that purported to enact such a prohibition would result in the freedom not to comply with it. Presumably, Soto's unspoken premise is the traditional scholastic view that unjust laws – this includes laws that exceed the legislator's jurisdiction and laws that are substantively unjust – do not create obligations. Later, in his *De Iustitia et Iure*, Soto expressed this view clearly: "An unjust human law does not obligate in the forum of conscience … for since an unjust law is not correct (*recta*), it cannot be a rule (*regula*), and therefore neither can it be a law. But whatever is not a law obligates no one."[163]

If warranted non-compliance with the law by paupers is the consequence to which Soto wants to alert his readers, then the injustice relevant to that consequence consists in the failure to compensate and not merely in the initial infringement of the paupers' right to beg. As Soto indicates, an unjust law cannot obligate because "it cannot be a rule," that is, the injustice of the law disqualifies the law from being regulative of human conduct. Injustice can have this effect only if it is current when action is contemplated. The disqualification comes from

---

162 Soto, *Deliberatio*, Chapter IV.
163 Soto, *De Iustitia et Iure*, I, q. 6, a. 4 (pp. 50–1).

the continuing injustice of the law, not from its history. Even if the restrictions had breached the beggars' rights, the injustice of the law would be continuous to the present only in the absence of compensation. Conversely, if compensation had been provided, the injustice which had occurred in the past would have been remedied to the extent possible, so that non-compliance with the law would no longer be justified by an ongoing injustice. To be sure, compensation does not eliminate the wrong that the requirement of compensation itself presupposes. However, it prevents the wrong, to the extent that the legal system can, from festering on as a matter of continuing injustice. Thus, when injustice is enacted through a law, compensation does not eliminate the breach of rights that was done by the law, but it does eliminate the reason for regarding the law as not binding in conscience. The failure to compensate for the breach of the paupers' rights, and not the breach itself, is the decisive ground for the non-compliance that it justifies.

VIII   Common Possession and Private Property

Soto's ruminations about begging are situated within a larger intellectual context informed by the medieval Christian conception of property and of its relationship to poverty. His formulation of that conception is the subject matter of the following sections.

Soto's elucidation of the development of private property follows a tradition of enquiry that rests on three ideas concerning the significance of the Fall for the history of law.

The first of these ideas is the communality of goods that prevailed when the first humans inhabited the Garden of Eden, regarded as a paradigm of perfection and innocence that stood in stark contrast to the harsh and corrupted realities of the fallen world. The idea of an original communality of goods was anchored in the influential statement in Gratian's *Decretum*, the authoritative twelfth-century compilation of canon law, that "by the right of nature all things are common to everyone."[164] That statement had drawn on the much earlier patristic literature. Augustine, for instance, had argued that assertions of private property ("This is my villa, this is my house, this is my slave") were the results of human law, and that by divine law the earth and its fullness were God's and were granted to a humanity whose members were all created from the same soil.[165] Similarly, Ambrose had pointedly declared that when God made the world "nature created right in common, but usurpation made right private."[166]

---

164 Gratian, *Decretum*, D. 8, c. 1.
165 Augustine, *Homilies on the Gospel of John 6*, 25.
166 Ambrose, *De Officiis*, 1, 28; see Swift, "*Iustitia* and *Ius Privatum*," 176.

Perhaps because the assumption of an Edenic world of common possession was so well established in his own day, Soto does not dwell at length on what justified it or how it operated. In summary he tells us that, in contrast to the postlapsarian problems that the introduction of private property was supposed to solve, in Eden "there were no disputes, and everyone diligently did what pertained to the common good."[167] As this statement indicates, one can reconstruct the situation in the Garden of Eden by working back from Soto's explanation in the *De Iustitia et Iure* of what ensued after humanity's expulsion from it. When this process of reconstruction is combined with pioneering earlier accounts of the original common use of things,[168] the following rough picture of the Garden of Eden emerges. In the Garden of Eden both the natural world and human psychology differed from their present condition. Unlike the fallen world in which humans must sustain themselves by the sweat of their brows, Eden spontaneously produced an abundance sufficient for everyone's needs with minimal human labour. Moreover, human beings were not subject to the competitiveness and cupidity that later characterized postlapsarian society. As a result, everything could be treated (as air is presently) as immediately available, so that persons could make use of whatever they came across. Given the moral innocence and perfection of mankind, no one coveted what someone else needed, nor was anyone inclined to snatch away what someone else was using. The abundance of the world and the uprightness of mankind ensured that, through the communality of everything to everyone, things were being used "in a way that conduces to peaceful dealings in society and to meeting people's needs."[169] Under these happy circumstances, when "mine" and "thine" were not words that answered to an existing social reality, private property was neither desirable nor necessary nor even intelligible.

In contrast to this first idea, the second idea was the instituting of private property in the aftermath of mankind's Fall and removal from the Garden of Eden. The consequences of the sin of eating from the forbidden tree were transformative both for the earth and for mankind. In response to mankind's mutiny against God, the earth mutinied against mankind, producing the thorns and thistles that made mankind's sustenance a laborious task.[170] At the same time mankind, having eaten what was prohibited, became subject to limitless desires and insatiable avarice. Under these changed conditions, the original communality of goods encouraged indolence and facilitated free-riding on another's labour, as everyone attempted to take advantage of everyone else by gaining the most while doing

---

167 Soto, *De Dominio*, s. 19.

168 Duns Scotus, *Ordinatio* IV, d. 15, q. 2, n. 81, in *Selected Writings on Ethics*, 273; Bonagratia of Bergamo, quoted in Geltner, "Eden Regained," 74.

169 These were the criteria set out by Duns Scotus, *Ordinatio* IV, d. 15, q. 2, n. 81, in *Selected Writings on Ethics*, 273.

170 Genesis 3:17.

the least. Moreover, disputes about how the common goods should be managed and used were endemic. (An example was the dispute between Abraham and Lot that led to a paradigmatic division of what they had previously shared.)[171] Communality of goods, therefore, no longer met human needs or conduced to peaceful interactions. In this way Soto, like his predecessors in this line of thought,[172] reproduced and transposed into the biblical context the criticism that Aristotle levelled against Plato's notion of common possession.[173]

The solution to the problems that beset mankind in this changed world was the division of the earth into private holdings. This provided owners with an attachment to what each owned, with the incentive to make what they owned productive, and with the stable and demarcated control that minimized disputes and promoted social peace. The creation of private property also had additional advantages: it protected the state by enabling the differentiation of the various social roles that contributed to the functioning and the preservation of society; and it established the material basis for practising the virtue of liberality.

The consequence of instituting private ownership was to create a world in which some were rich and others were poor. In the Garden of Eden when nature was intact, poverty was unknown. Everyone was endowed in body and disposition with the perfection of innocence, and all had equal access to the earth's resources. Conversely, in the postlapsarian world humans were avaricious. The existence of private property enabled some people to accumulate resources beyond their needs, while others were left destitute. Even after private property was instituted, the governing principle of the Garden of Eden, that all things were in common, remained applicable to the extent that those who had too much were under an obligation to be beneficent to the poor. In Soto's view, however, that obligation could not be enforced because it was "not of justice but of charity, to which no one can unwillingly be compelled."[174] The existence of private property and the presence of multitudes of indigent persons in different locations and at different times combined to place within the discretion of property owners the decision about when, where, and to whom they were to distribute their superfluous holdings.

The one exception to this was found in the third of the three ideas concerning the transition from the Garden of Eden. Persons who found themselves in a condition of extreme necessity – that is, confronting the probability of serious injury or death – had the right to save themselves by using what belonged to another. Unlike the more general situations of need, a person of means had a specific obligation to assist someone suffering extreme necessity, but in Soto's view it remained an obligation of charity and not of justice. However, the decision to assist under

---

171 Genesis 13:5–13.
172 For example, Duns Scotus.
173 Aristotle, *Politics* II, 5.
174 Soto, *De Iustitia et Iure*, V, q. 3, a. 4 (p. 428).

these circumstances was not within the sole discretion of the property holder. Desperate persons could help themselves to what they needed to stay alive or to avoid serious injury: "So innate in man is the right to save himself that everything else yields to it."[175] Such takings did not count as theft, as their permissibility was a continuation in the postlapsarian world of the universal right to use in accordance with the original communality of goods.

Given the relevance to the late medieval conception of property of these three ideas – the original communality of goods, the institution of private property, and the taking of another's things to relieve one's extreme necessity – how is one to conceive of the relationship between them within a system of natural law? This question has two aspects. One aspect concerns itself with the relationship between the first and second ideas; the other aspect deals with the relationship between these two ideas and the third idea.

With respect to the first two of these ideas, the significant point is that they belong to different orders of right. The communality of everything to everyone (which underlies a paradigm of perfection that no longer applies) is a matter of natural right, whereas private property (which is present in the world that we now have) is the product of posited right. More specifically, private property is the product of the *ius gentium*, that is, of the body of norms that emerge from the consensus of all humans in the exercise of their rationality, in order to achieve a particular end under particular circumstances.[176] Because of the role of humans in its creation, Soto regarded the *ius gentium* as a category of positive right. The focus in the *ius gentium* on the rational evaluation of ends is what differentiates it from the *ius naturale*, which involves the immediate apprehension of what is non-contingently adequate to something's nature. Indeed, Soto treats private property as paradigmatic of the *ius gentium*:

> That this plot of land should be possessed by this private owner, rather than that everything should be possessed in common, is not something that is required by the nature of things considered absolutely. And yet, if one considers this field as something to be cultivated for bearing its produce and to be possessed in peace, in the condition of corrupted nature in which men are more sluggish in expending their own personal efforts on tasks destined for the common good, and are covetous of what others have, reason at once concludes that that it is completely advantageous that possessions be divided.[177]

Aside from its role in the Garden of Eden, Soto does not spell out in detail the reason for considering possession in common a tenet of natural right. Presumably, because right connotes a conception of equality, the availability of everything to

---

175 Soto, *De Iustitia et Iure*, V, q. 3, a. 4 (p. 428).
176 Soto, *De Iustitia et Iure*, III, q. 1, a. 3 (pp. 196–7).
177 Soto, *De Iustitia et Iure*, III, q. 1, a. 3 (p. 196).

everyone is immediately apprehended as an embodiment of equality among persons with respect to their use of the things of the world. Possession in common thus represents what Soto calls "*aequitas naturalis*" – the term that Grotius later also used in his parallel account of these very matters.[178]

The problem that then arises is this: axiomatic within a system of natural law is the primacy of natural right over positive right. "If the human will establishes something that is contrary to the right of nature," remarks Soto following a long line of Christian thinking, "it will never obtain the force of law."[179] The natural-right idea that all things are common to everyone and the positive-right idea of private property seem indeed to be contraries. Nonetheless, private property rather than the communality of goods turned out to be the regnant principle for juridical relationships among humans with reference to the external world. If private property is repugnant to natural right, how can this be?

Some indeed thought that it cannot be. Aquinas,[180] citing Augustine, referred to a group of early Christians, the Apostolici, who claimed that holders of private property had no hope of salvation. Accordingly, they refused to admit into their communion persons who possessed something as their own. In their view the incompatibility of possession in common and private property entailed the illegitimacy of the latter. In contrast, Aquinas considered the heretical status of this group to be evidence of the legitimacy of private property. Similarly, Aquinas thought that the patristic rhetoric hostile to private property was not aimed at the legitimacy of ownership, but at the tendency to keep what one owned for oneself without responding to the imperative of sharing with the needy.

In the thirteenth century John Duns Scotus suggested ("cleverly" as Soto says before revealing his respectful opposition) a different approach to the contradiction between common possession and private property.[181] Duns Scotus claimed that the precept of natural right that everything was in common was revoked after the Fall for precisely the reasons that justified instituting private property (facilitating peaceful dealings and the satisfaction of needs). This revocation made it permissible to appropriate what had hitherto been in common. In the circumstances of the fallen world, the incompatibility of possession in common and private property entailed the revocation of the former in the face of the desirability of the latter. Accordingly, although private property was inconsistent with the Edenic principle of the communality of goods, that principle was no longer valid

---

178 Soto, *De Iustitia et Iure*, III, q. 1, a. 3 (p. 196); Grotius, *De Iure Belli*, II, 2, 6, and 11. On the role of natural equity in Grotius's account, see Klimchuk, "Grotius on Property and the Right of Necessity," 239.

179 Soto, *De Iustitia et Iure* III, q. 1, a. 2.

180 Aquinas, *Summa Theologiae*, II-II, q. 66, a. 2.

181 Soto, *De Iustitia et Iure*, IV, q. 3. a. 1 (p. 299); Duns Scotus, *Ordinatio* IV, d. 15, q. 2, nn. 82–7.

when private property became legitimate. After the Fall no contradiction between private property and natural right existed, because the Edenic principle itself had vanished.

The notion that a precept of natural right had been revoked did not gain acceptance, as it was inconsistent with the supposed immutability of natural law. The standard position, formulated by Aquinas and repeated by Soto,[182] was that while positive law could add to the norms of natural law by specifying legal particulars that were consistent with them, it could not subtract from them. Natural law was a combination of self-evident general principles of practical reason (for example, "Do good and avoid evil") and more detailed secondary precepts derived from them (such as, "a deposit should be returned"). Although these secondary precepts were immutably valid, impediments arising from changing human circumstances might occasionally make them inapplicable under specific conditions. The stock example, drawn from antiquity,[183] was that one did not have to return a sword that the owner was going to use to harm himself or others. In such cases, "the change occurs not in the law itself but in the circumstances."[184] This is no different from withholding food, which is generally beneficial, from a person suffering from a fever.

Duns Scotus's suggestion proceeded from the seemingly obvious assumption that private property contradicted the precept of common possession. Hence, the legitimacy of private property entailed the revocation of the precept. If common possession and private property are contradictory, they cannot both be valid at the same time. This leaves no choice but to affirm one of them and to deny the other. Both Duns Scotus and the Apostolici did this, though they chose to deny different things.

Instead, for the preferred solution that emerged, the assumption of contradiction was discarded. The communality of goods continued to be valid after the Fall, but in a way that allowed for its co-existence with private property. Crucial to this solution was a reconsideration of the normative significance of the communality of goods. Aquinas took the position that although the communality of goods belonged to natural right, it did not (as Duns Scotus later supposed) have the status of a precept dictating that everything should be held in common. Goods were in common only in the sense that they were not privately owned,[185] so that common possession signified merely that private property existed by virtue of positive right

---

182 Aquinas, *Summa Theologiae,* I-II, q. 94, a. 5, II-II, q. 66, a. 2; Soto, *De Iustitia et Iure,* I, q. 4, a. 5 (p. 36).

183 Plato, *Republic* 331c.

184 Soto, *De Iustitia et Iure,* I, q. 4, a. 5 (p. 36): *mutatio haec non tam in lege fit quam in rebus ipsis.*

185 Compare Grotius's statement that "with reference to that early age, the term 'common' is nothing more nor less that the simple antonym of 'private.'" Grotius, *Commentary on the Law of Prize and Booty,* 315.

and not of natural right. That is to say, common possession belonged to natural right not in the affirmative sense that natural right prohibited private property, but in the negative sense that natural right did not require private property.[186] This allowed common possession to prevail in the ideal conditions of the Garden of Eden, while leaving the positive law free to institute private property if human circumstances made that advisable.

The result of this argument was that private property did not violate a precept of natural right; rather it was a legal supplement devised by human reason in accordance with postlapsarian conditions.[187] Private property thus manifested a legitimate change in the legal order by adding to natural right rather than by subtracting from it. As Soto said, recapitulating this position:

> With respect to *dominium*, the right of nature never prevented a division of things by a precept that would have made a contrary law into a derogation from it. Common possession is said to belong to the right of nature only in the negative sense that the natural law never required that division but permitted possession to be in whatever way was more convenient and advantageous to the different conditions of man. Therefore, it was not natural right that was changed but the circumstances.[188]

Instead of negating the right of nature by contradicting it – and thereby depriving itself of the legitimacy attendant on compatibility with it – the institution of private property leaves the right of nature intact but limits its operation in the particular circumstances of the fallen world.

This distinction between negating a norm and limiting it is jurisprudentially crucial. To the extent that a norm is negated, it no longer has an effective existence. According to Duns Scotus, this was the fate of the precept of common possession after it was revoked. In contrast, a norm that is limited continues in existence, its scope unaffected, but its operation justifiably restricted in certain circumstances.

Consider the stock example of not returning the sword to the owner who might use it to do harm. The influential theologian Luis de Molina invoked this example to explain what it means to say that contravening a right without legitimate cause does wrong to the right-holder.[189] A person who entrusts something to another has a right to have it returned. Suppose that the person entrusted with a sword refuses to return it because of the danger created by the owner's supervening madness. That refusal is a contravention of the owner's right, but because it is for a legitimate

---

186 For a clear statement of this, see the work of Soto's younger contemporary, Domingo Báñez, commenting on Aquinas, *De Iure et Iustitia Decisiones*, q. 1 art. 2 comment. 1 comment. para. "Ad secundum argumentum" (p. 15).
187 Aquinas, *Summa Theologiae*, II-II, q. 66, a. 2, ad 1.
188 Soto, *De Iustitia et Iure*, IV, q. 3, a. 1 (p. 299).
189 Molina, *De Iustitia et Iure/Über Gerechtigkeit und Recht, Teil I*, Tract. II, Disp. I (p. 100).

cause, it neither destroys that right considered in itself (*nec tollit facultatem illam in se spectatam esse ius illius*) nor does it do the owner wrong. Although the owner's right to the sword remains intact, he suffers no wrong, because that right is not operative in the particular circumstances of his madness. In Soto's terms, it is not the right that was changed but the circumstances. Using the distinction formulated here, one might say that the owner's right is limited but not negated.

Although it makes the owner's right to the sword inoperative in the circumstances, the permissible withholding of the sword affirms rather than repudiates that right. The owner's madness provides what Molina calls a "legitimate cause" for the contravention of his right in exceptional circumstances, on grounds narrowly tailored to the danger that it poses. One may surmise, for example, that withholding the sword must be for a proper purpose (the prevention of the sword's harmful use), and that it must be suitable and necessary for avoiding the harm (the depositee, for instance, cannot destroy the sword or retain it indefinitely after the danger has passed). In scholastic literature,[190] this limit on the owner's right is formulated as a matter of proportionality, in which the return of the sword prejudices the common good to a far greater extent than the minor and temporary inconvenience that its non-return causes the owner. Given this disparity, the owner cannot rationally wish the sword's return. Accordingly, even though generally the law insists with the utmost strictness on the return of deposits, withholding the sword is not unjust so long as the depositee intends to return it at the opportune time. The significance of this intent attests to the notion that the limit does not affect the continuing validity and effectiveness of the owner's right. Because it is circumscribed by a reason applicable to specific circumstances, the limit presupposes, normatively depends on, and operates within the context of the owner's continuing entitlement to the sword. In this way the danger of returning the sword to the owner limits but does not negate the owner's right to the sword.

The distinction between a limit and a negation is relevant not only to the occasional contravention of specific legal rules, as with the withheld sword, but also more systemically. A striking example is a suggestive passage from the work of the fourteenth-century Franciscan, William of Ockham, that deals with the very issue at hand, the ongoing significance of Eden's communality of goods:

> [T]o use temporal things pertains to a right of nature that no one can licitly renounce. However, it does not pertain to natural right in such a way that it cannot in many cases be limited (*limitari*) and in some way restricted (*coartari*) and impeded (*impediri*) so that it does not licitly issue in an act. In this way, according to Isidore, as we read in dist. I, c. *Ius naturale*, "The common possession of all things and the one liberty of all" pertain to natural right, and yet that right is in a way restricted

---

190 Duns Scotus, *Ordinatio*, IV, d. 15, q. 2, nn. 188–92.

(*coartatur*), because, also, temporal things are appropriated … However, this natural right cannot be emptied totally (*totaliter evacuari*), because temporal things can never be appropriated in such a way that it is not true that they ought to be common in time of necessity. Thus the power to use temporal things can in a way be restricted (*coartari*) by human law and by a free man's own will and can sometimes be impeded (*impediri*) so as not to issue in any act of using (for thus one can by vow resolve that one will abstain from flesh, thus also men are prohibited from using the things of others), but the power to use temporal things cannot be eradicated totally (*totaliter evelli*). And therefore, anyone can use by right of heaven any temporal thing whatever that he is not prohibited from using either by natural law or by divine law or by his own act. And therefore, in time of extreme necessity, anyone can use by the law of heaven any temporal thing whatever without which he cannot preserve his own life; for in this case he is not obliged not to use a temporal thing by any law whatever or by his own act.[191]

This passage fully deploys the contrast between negating and limiting. Starting with the natural right to use anything ("the power to use temporal things"), Ockham emphasizes that when human law creates private property, this original right to use is not negated ("totally emptied" or "totally eradicated"), even though under a regime of private property "men are prohibited from using the things of others." Private property "limits" and "restricts" the natural right of all to use everything, but it does not completely do away with it. Ockham's conception of private property as a limit on (rather than as a negation of) the natural right to use anything signifies that this right continues in existence, generally quiescent in the face of private property but reasserting itself when necessity is extreme. Whatever a person owns can always legitimately be taken by those who cannot otherwise save their lives. Because the original communality of goods residually survives in the permissibility of using others' things for one's self-preservation, the right to private property which limits that communality can be ignored under circumstances of extreme necessity. Then an indigent person is allowed to invoke the natural right to use temporal things, because "no one can licitly renounce" that right when continuation of one's own existence is at stake.

Although Ockham recognized the importance of distinguishing between "limiting" and "totally eradicating" the right of nature, he understandably did not work out the jurisprudential framework implicit in the very idea of allowing a right to be limited. Presumably he regarded the distinction as so obvious that stating it was sufficient. However, quite apart from medieval intellectual history, the elaboration of that jurisprudential framework has been a central theme of global

---

191 Ockham, *Opus Nonaginta Dierum*, Chapter 65, in *Opera Politica* II, 577–8, trans. in William of Ockham, *A Letter to the Friars Minor*, 55–6.

constitutional theory in the modern world. The modern treatment specifies the conditions under which, despite their high normative status, constitutional rights can justifiably be limited. Perhaps paradoxically, modern constitutionalism provides a conceptual apparatus that illuminates the relationship between the three ideas (common possession, private property, and extreme necessity) that preoccupied the medieval scholastics.

To grossly oversimplify a matter of great complexity: modern constitutions entrench the protection of rights from legislative and governmental measures that would infringe them. These rights are not absolute; they are subject to limits appropriate to the vindication of human dignity within free and democratic societies. The point of setting out a normative framework for these limits is highly practical. The framework provides a legal methodology for dealing with situations in which two rights have conflicting effects, or where the exercise of one right may conflict with the values inherent in the system of rights. For example, the exercise of the right to free expression may, if taken alone, give access to information that would be protected from publication by a countervailing right to privacy, if taken alone. Or the dissemination of hate speech under the cover of the right of free expression may undermine the idea of human dignity that undergirds the entire rights-protecting system.

When the constitutionality of legislation that engages rights in this way is impugned, courts embark on a "proportionality" analysis,[192] which is a distant descendant of the scholastic proportionality mentioned above in connection with the withheld sword. The object of the modern proportionality analysis is to evaluate the constitutionality of a legislative measure that limits a right. This it does by employing criteria that, in the light of the rationale underlying a system of rights, serve to limit the very endeavour of legislatively limiting a right. This proportionality analysis proceeds through a sequence of steps, all of which are viewed from the standpoint of the values of a free and democratic society.[193] The first step is to identify and assess the public purpose that the impugned legislation serves. If that public purpose is constitutionally acceptable, one then enquires into the connection between that purpose and the right that the legislation contravened. Throughout, the purpose constitutes the fixed point of reference around which the ensuing analysis revolves. One then asks three questions that determine whether limiting the right is justified. The first question deals with the suitability of the limit: Is the impugned legislation rationally connected to the achievement of that purpose? If it is not, the limiting legislation is struck down as arbitrary, and indeed pointless. The second question deals with the necessity of the limit: is the purpose being pursued in a manner that minimally

---

192 Barak, *Proportionality*.

193 On proportionality analysis as a sequence, see Weinrib, *Impasse of Constitutional Rights*, 59–66 (the analysis moves from the ends for which a constitutional right may be limited, to the means for achieving these ends, to the extent of the limit's effect on the right).

impairs the right? If the purpose could have been achieved in a manner less injurious to the right, the legislation is struck down as needless or is declared inoperative to the extent of its overbreadth. The third question deals with the proportionality of the limit: from the standpoint of the system of rights, are the effects of impairing the right proportional to the benefits that will be attained by forwarding the purpose? If the deleterious effects are disproportionate to the benefit, the limiting legislation is struck down because of its failure to achieve the optimal mutual accommodation of the constitutionally acceptable legislative purpose and the entrenched constitutional right. These criteria are assessed with close attention to the particular social and factual circumstances to which they are applied. In this sense, the scholastic formula is apt: the change to the right is not in the law but in the circumstances.

Proportionality is thus a sequenced form of argument that, under an overarching public purpose, reconciles considerations that, if taken independently, are in tension with one another. Although developed to deal with limits on rights in the modern constitutional context, it provides a disciplined and systematic framework for understanding limits on rights (and other norms) more generally. Of course, in the medieval context the touchstone for these limits is not the concept of a free and democratic society, but consistency with the rationale of the natural right to common possession. Moreover, the point of applying proportionality analysis to the medieval material is not to test the constitutional validity of a specific legal arrangement but to understand the relationship among the components of the scholastic approach to property. Structurally, however, the medieval problem of reconciling common possession, private property, and the right of necessity is similar to the issue raised by limits on rights in modern constitutional law. Taken on their own, common possession and private property are in tension with each other. So are private property and the right to take another's things in a situation of extreme necessity. So is the availability of everything to everyone and the more limited availability of something owned to someone in extreme necessity. And yet the three may achieve a measure of concordance when situated in a sequence of thought that moves from common possession to private property and then to the right of necessity.

This endeavour to achieve concordance works sequentially in the following way. The rationale for a natural right to common possession is to make external things available for the use, and especially for the physical sustenance, of human beings. As Aquinas says, "Man has a natural dominion over external things because, by his reason and will, he can use external things for his own utility, as if they were made for his sake, because the more imperfect is always made for the sake of the more perfect ... God directed certain things to the bodily sustenance of man, and because of this man has a natural dominion over things, as regards the power to use them."[194]

---

194 Aquinas, *Summa Theologiae*, II-II, q. 66, a. 1, ad 1.

The notion that external things are for human use and bodily sustenance – that is, for the sustenance of every individual person – is central both to the original natural right and to the way in which that right can properly be limited. In the terminology of modern constitutional law, this rationale for mankind's dominion over external things both provides the conceptual genesis for considering common possession to be a natural right and constitutes the ultimate standard for justifying the limiting of that natural right.[195]

The right of nature by which everyone can access and use everything is the perfect and most comprehensive realization of the notion that external things are for human use and bodily sustenance, as it treats every person as equally capable of and entitled to making use of what the world contains and produces. Every single person thereby both enjoys an abundance sufficient for their needs and participates in peaceful and frictionless social relations. However, this right of nature presupposes a corresponding perfection of the natural world and of humankind, which is present only in the ideal circumstances of the Garden of Eden. After the Fall, the right to partake of the communality of goods remains valid, but it must be limited to fit the changed circumstances. Only through arduous human effort can the natural world now produce what human beings need. Moreover, human beings are now driven by avarice to be disputatious and to free-ride on the labour of others. The combination of these changes in the world and in mankind frustrate the production of what is needed for human sustenance and social peace. Private property is introduced to adjust the original and still valid right of common possession to the exigencies of mankind's new circumstances. The purpose for limiting the natural right by instituting private property is to forward the natural right's underlying rationale by creating the legal mechanism that yields the social stability and material productivity conducive to the sustenance of everyone under postlapsarian conditions. This purpose plays the same role in the scholastic analysis of the function of external things as the constitutionally acceptable public purpose does in limiting a modern constitutional right.

In the postlapsarian world, limiting the right of nature in this way is both suitable and necessary for realizing the underlying rationale for mankind's dominion over things. It is *suitable* because, by creating the incentives required for producing what will satisfy human needs, private property is rationally connected to the process of using external things to keep human beings alive. It is *necessary* because private property is a systemic arrangement that impairs the natural right to the minimal extent possible, given that in a world of labour and avarice the

---

195 Compare the description *in R. v Oakes,* [1986] 1 Supreme Court Reports, para. 54, of the
  relation between right and limit in the Canadian constitutional context: "The underlying values
  and principles of a free and democratic society are the genesis of the rights and freedoms guaranteed
  by the Charter, and the ultimate standard against which a limit on a right and freedom
  must be shown, despite its effect, to be reasonable and demonstrably justified."

sustainability of human life cannot otherwise be achieved across the entire gamut of social relations. Soto observes that in the cloisters of monasteries, monks still live peacefully in common – a mode of life that is possible for small numbers of devout persons but not "for vast republics of mortals who avidly long for secular things."[196] Soto also adverts to the argument that instituting private property has not completely eliminated the laziness that allows fields to remain uncultivated and the avarice that leads to encroachments on others' rights. His response is that "it is not necessary for a law's equity that it achieve its end perfectly; it is sufficient that in accordance with its capability it establishes those things that are suitable to its end, for man's unbridled freedom cannot be totally restrained by any reins."[197]

So far, the limiting of the right of nature has been examined without considering the permissibility of taking something that belongs to someone else in a situation of extreme necessity. The significance of this permissibility, the third of our triad of medieval ideas, requires reference to the role of what is termed "proportionality." As noted, the point of insisting on proportionality in this mode of analysis is to bring about the optimal mutual accommodation of the purpose of the limit (in this case, the promotion of productivity and social stability through the instituting of private property) on the one hand, and the underlying rationale for the original right of common possession (in this case, sustaining the lives of all) on the other.

The element of proportionality has a different focus than do the elements of suitability and necessity. The latter two elements deal with the relationship between the limit as a means for accomplishing an acceptable purpose and the purpose itself: Is the limit rationally connected to that purpose, and can that purpose be achieved by a more modest limit? In contrast, proportionality deals with the relationship between the pursuit of that purpose and the underlying rationale for that right. Even if the purpose for the limit is acceptable, and the means are suitable because they are rationally connected to the purpose, and the means are also necessary because the purpose cannot be achieved by a lesser impairment of the right, the limit may still not be justified in particular circumstances. This is because, from the standpoint of the underlying rationale for the right, the degree to which the right is limited may, in particular circumstances, exceed the advantages derived from the limit's pursuit of the acceptable purpose. When this happens, the mutual accommodation of right and limit is not optimal.

In the context at hand, the suitability and necessity of private property influence the realization of the rationale only indirectly through the incentives for productivity that private property provides. However, private property also has the countervailing shortcoming that in specific situations, persons may face the

---

196 Soto, *De Iustitia et Iure*, IV, q. 3, a. 1 (p. 299); Soto, *De Dominio*, para. 22.
197 Soto, *De Iustitia et Iure*, IV, q. 3, a. 1 (p. 297).

prospect of probable death or serious injury without having anything that they can use to fend off the disaster. This shortcoming – which is not adventitious but is an inevitable concomitant of the operation of private property in a fallen world of selfishness and hard work – renders the underlying rationale that external things should be deployed to sustain each and every person unrealizable for those who are extremely poor. Although in comparison with common possession, private property increases the pool of goods that humans produce and use, it dooms those for whom nothing is legally available for use when their continued existence is at stake. It thereby sacrifices the lives of some for the increased prosperity of others. Private property thus mitigates life-threatening scarcity systemically but recreates it for individuals. In Ockham's terms, the introduction of private property allows an endangered person to be deprived of what, under the right of nature, "no one can licitly renounce."[198] From the standpoint of the purpose that legal arrangements about external things are supposed to achieve, private property increases the quantity of goods but makes those goods unavailable to everyone who needs them. Taken on its own, private property disproportionately limits the original natural right because in extreme circumstances it completely deprives certain persons of the benefit of arrangements that fulfil the right's rationale.

The solution to this difficulty is to supplement private property by permitting the desperately poor to take what belongs to another when they are in extreme necessity. Then persons with nothing have an entitlement to preserve themselves by using things owned by others. The result is that the rationale underlying mankind's dominion over things is fulfilled for everyone. The purpose of the limit and the rationale of the original right are brought into optimal alignment with each other. On the one hand, the existence of private property facilitates social peace and provides the incentives for maximizing the resources generally available for human use. On the other hand, the survival of common possession under conditions of extreme necessity affords everyone the right to use what others own to preserve oneself in an emergency. In accordance with the notion of proportionality, the purpose of the limit and the rationale underlying the right are, when a situation of extreme necessity arises, brought into mutual concordance. Put another way, unless the introduction of private property was accompanied by the proviso of permissible use in extreme necessity, it would not constitute a justifiable limit on the natural right of common possession. In this way, the underlying rationale for mankind's dominion over things is both the genesis of the natural right of common possession and the ultimate standard against which the institution of private property that limits that right must be justified.

The quoted passage from Ockham conforms to this pattern of thinking. By instituting private property human law limits the natural right to use things.

---

198 Ockham, *Letter to the Friars Minor*, 55.

However, that limit does not extend to situations of extreme necessity, where the original right to use things continues to be valid. Within its now limited sphere the commonality of goods still prevails, unabsorbed by the operation of private property. Private property is regarded as a limit on the right of nature; the right of necessity, which is a residue of that original right, marks a limit on that limit that enables the achievement of the underlying rationale for legal arrangements regarding external things. In this alignment of the three ideas of common possession, private property, and the right to take things when in extreme necessity, private property functions as a justified limit on – rather than in contradiction of – the natural right to common possession.

Of course, this picture does not reflect the full complexity of the situation. The common possession that survives in a situation of extreme necessity is importantly different from the common possession of the Edenic world of natural right of which it is an enduring vestige. The common possession in extreme necessity is for the benefit of a single person only rather than of humankind at large, and it must coexist with the private property that occupies the rest of the normative space in which things are used – including the very thing owned by another that the indigent person takes. What does it mean to say that the proprietary status of something owned by one person is so transformed when extreme necessity supervenes upon another person that the thing becomes an object of common possession for the sole benefit of the latter? As the next sections show, the tension generated by this intermingling of private property and common possession gave rise to further controversy about the implications of the limited form of common possession pertinent to extreme necessity.

Half a century after Soto's account of the effects of the Fall, Leonardus Lessius summed up the three components of the theory of property in a way that emphasized their sequential interdependence. Explaining the right to take what belongs to another in conditions of extreme necessity, Lessius referred to the "received principle" that in extreme necessity everything is in common, and then wrote,

> The purpose of inferior things is to assist mankind in its necessity, so that through these things they should be able to preserve and protect their lives. This right accordingly belongs to everyone by nature. Nor could the division of things introduced by the right of nations remove this right, because the right of nations supposes rather than overturns natural right, especially because it is so necessary for the preservation of life. One should therefore think that the division was made with a reservation of natural right to the extent necessary to protect life. Otherwise, it would not have been made in a rational way.[199]

---

199 Lessius, *De Iustitia et Iure Ceterisque Virtutibus Cardinalibus*, Lib. 2, Cap. 12, dub. 12.

Lessius in this passage confirms that, starting with mankind's natural right to the communality of goods, the underlying rationale for the availability of things is the preservation of each person's life. This natural right and the rationale it reflects are presupposed in and then complemented by the subsequent stages. Far from removing this natural right, the introduction of private property contributes to the achievement of its rationale by providing the incentives for the productive management of the world's things. However, in circumstances of extreme necessity, where the very survival of the indigent is at risk, the rationale would be frustrated unless private property were qualified by a reservation that enabled the original communality of goods to resurface. Thus, to realize individual preservation, the introduction of private property limits but does not do away with the original natural right; and because private property would, if unrestricted, doom the desperately situated, it is in its turn limited through the availability of what is owned to those who suffer extreme necessity. Lessius's formulation of the scholastic conception of property provides a concise but clear exhibition of the sequential structure that characterizes modern proportionality analysis.

The point of adducing modern proportionality in a discussion of the scholastic tradition is not to claim that medieval thinkers formulated it or consciously adverted to it. Rather, it provides a conceptual framework for thinking about the combination, which they explicitly postulated, of (i) a categorial difference between "limiting" and "totally eradicating" a right of nature; (ii) three ideas, each of which if taken on its own is not consistent with the other two; and (iii) a sequential ordering that moves from the Garden of Eden to postlapsarian society. Under proportionality analysis, these elements of the scholastic account of early human history are modulated into a conceptually ordered sequence of normative moments consequent on the distinction between a limit and a negation. That distinction is central to the scholastic treatment of the fundaments of law. It expresses itself in the distinction between a norm that was contrary to the right of nature and one that merely limited the right of nature, or (to put the distinction in another way) between impermissibly subtracting from natural law and legitimately supplementing it, or (to put it in still another way) between the immutable part of the legal order and the part that responds to the contingencies of human circumstances.

IX   Extreme Necessity

One can now turn to a closer examination of the relationship between the first two of these ideas and the third. In Soto's time and in the following century different versions of the significance of extreme necessity were current. These attached differing meanings to the reappearance of common possession within a world normally characterized by the existence of private property. The principal axis of dispute among the proponents of these versions was whether extreme necessity gave rise to an issue of charity or an issue of justice.

An especially influential account of extreme necessity was that of Grotius seven decades after Soto, who while muting its theological aspect drew on the scholastic notion that extreme necessity occasioned the re-emergence of the original communality of goods. In presenting this as an idea held by theologians, Grotius expressly acknowledged Soto for the point that one who takes another's property to save his own life does not commit theft.[200] However, he then immediately added, without specifically referencing anyone but nonetheless repudiating the reason that Soto himself had offered, that this rule is not founded on an owner's obligation to give anything to the indigent person as a matter of charity. In Grotius's opinion, the reason for the rule was that those who introduced private property must be supposed to have intended to recede as little as possible from the natural equity of common possession and, therefore, to have benignly retained common possession in life-threatening situations.

Grotius's view is oriented toward justice in a sense that is, one may say, narrowly juridical. It is *juridical* in that it accounted for the rule about extreme necessity in terms not of charity but of the just evolution of the legal institution of private property in accordance with a sequence of arguments that can be traced back to the primeval natural equity of common possession. It is *narrowly* juridical in that it applied to the desperate person's right to take what was needed from a person of means, without however imposing on the person of means a legal obligation benevolently to offer what the desperate person needed to preserve his life. Although the rule bars him from interfering with the indigent person's right to save himself, the owner cannot be held liable for the damage that would ensue from his failure to assist in the provision of aid.

In presenting this view, Grotius drew on material that was present and continued to be developed in the scholastic literature. For example, Lessius (to whom Grotius referred on another point) had crisply outlined the same position.[201] Lessius observed, drawing on the work of Soto's Salamanca colleague Martin de Azpilcueta,[202] that the fundamental idea that in extreme necessity everything was in common concerned itself solely with the right to use something. The common possession that was brought about by extreme necessity did not effect an immediate transfer of *dominium*. Lessius's unspoken reason for insisting on this was that a transfer of *dominium* would have given the indigent person a right to the thing, and so would have placed the owner under an obligation to give it to him. Instead, the thing became common only in the sense that the indigent person had a right to use it. As a result, persons pressed by extreme necessity had a right to seize for their use whatever they needed to save themselves. Because they were exercising

---

200 Grotius, *De Iure Belli*, II, 2, 7, 4.
201 Lessius, *De Iustitia et Iure*, Lib. 2. Cap. 12, dub. 12.
202 Azpilcueta, *Manuel de Confessoribus*, cap. 17, n. 61.

their right to preserve themselves, the owners were prohibited from impeding the seizure. Owners who attempted to interfere, Lessius asserted, would be subject to the indigent person's legitimate exercise of self-defence.

This narrowly juridical position focused on the indigent person's right to take something on his own initiative. However, the owner's obligation to provide assistance to someone suffering extreme necessity was a matter of charity, not justice. Consequently, an indigent person facing death had the right to take something from an owner, but the owner was under no corresponding legal obligation to give that thing before it was taken. This might seem odd. If an indigent person had a right to the thing, why was that right exercisable only through self-help? A century after Soto, Juan de Lugo noted the view that without a legal obligation to give, the pauper's right to take would make no sense. He put the argument this way: "Unless the pauper had a right as a matter of justice with respect to what belongs to another, he would not be able to take it against the will of the owner, even though the rich person was obligated to give it in accordance with another virtue."[203] Lugo's rebuttal of this view was that the pauper's right was not to the seized object, but to the act of seizing and using the object, which the owner could not resist or impede. "Extreme necessity gives the pauper the right to take what is another's, and by the very taking of it he acquires a right in the thing itself or in its use as necessity demands."[204] This statement sealed off the pauper's right to take from the suggestion that because the pauper had a right to the thing taken, this right obligated the owner to give it antecedently. Nothing in the conclusion that the indigent person was entitled to take the thing implied that the thing itself was the object of the indigent person's right. The right was to an action, not to a thing. To put the issue in Hohfeldian terms, the indigent person's right was a liberty to use the thing, not a claim-right with respect to the thing itself.

A second version of extreme necessity was oriented toward justice in a broader sense: not only did the indigent person have a legal right to take the thing, but the owner was legally obligated to give it to him. The leading proponent of this position was Cajetan, the great commentator on Aquinas. Expounding the assertion of Aquinas that a person is obligated to give one's goods to the poor in accordance with a *debitum legale*,[205] Cajetan remarked that this was easy to understand in the case of extreme necessity: "For in a time of extreme necessity everything is in common, and because of this another's goods become mine if I suffer from extreme necessity." For Cajetan the meaning of possession in common in the context of extreme necessity is that the thing in question becomes the pauper's, so that the owner should give it to him on his own initiative. Only because the owner fails

---

203 Lugo, *De Iustitia et Iure*, Disp. XVI, Sec. VII, para 142.
204 Lugo, *De Iustitia et Iure*, Disp. XVI, Sec. VII, para. 143.
205 Aquinas, *Summa Theologiae*, II-II, q. 118, a. 4 ad 2, and Cajetan ad loc.

to comply with this legal obligation does the pauper become authorized to take what is due to him. In so doing, the pauper takes "not what belongs to another, but what is common yet denied to him" (*non accipio aliena sed communia negata*), because "extreme necessity makes another's things common to me, because they are owed to me in accordance with a legal debt" (*quia extrema necessitas facit res alienas mihi communes, quod ex debito legali mihi debentur*). Presumably, the notion that things can be "common to me" (which seems problematically to combine something's being both common to a plurality of persons yet reserved to a single person) reflects the idea that in this context possession in common is for the benefit of the pauper and no one else because the proprietary status of the goods is tied to the presence of a specific pauper's extreme necessity. Thus, the pauper's right to take is merely the sequela of the transfer of ownership that ensues from the situation of extreme necessity.

Cajetan's position was criticized on several grounds. First, it treated almsgiving – usually considered to be an expression of the donor's compassion – as the discharge of a legal obligation. Alms were the response of mercy to indigence. The greater the indigence (as in the case of extreme necessity) the more urgent the reason for exercising mercy.[206] By transforming almsgiving into the payment of a debt, Cajetan's position was alleged to contradict the essential nature of almsgiving as an act of mercy.

Moreover, Cajetan's interpretation of common possession was said to have misconstrued the effect of extreme necessity. As Lessius, Azpilcueta, and others pointed out, extreme necessity did not by its own juridical force make anything the property of the person suffering it.[207] Rather, it created the normative space for paupers to save themselves by using the thing in question. This criticism reflects the function that the communality of goods served before private property was instituted. The original communality of goods gave everyone a right to use everything, but it posited no duty of beneficence. On this model, once private property is established subject to the resumption of common possession when necessity is extreme, those facing extreme necessity have the right to use what belongs to another, just as everyone had the right to use everything when things were in common. However, just as in the original communality of goods, no one is under a legal obligation to give anyone anything.

Furthermore, the consequence of postulating a legal duty to assist the person facing extreme necessity is that one would be held liable for the damages resulting from a failure to fulfil that duty. On this basis the person of means who did not rescue a pauper from extreme necessity would, as a matter of justice, be required

---

206 Sanchez, *Consilia seu Opuscula Moralia* I, V, dub. V, 61; Lugo, *De Iustitia et Jure*, Disp. XVI, Sec. VII, para. 141.

207 Azpilcueta, *Libri de Reditibus Ecclesiasticis*, 215n25: *necessitatem extremam patientis non fiunt ipso iure ei necessaria.*

to compensate the pauper's family for his death. Later critics pointed out that this was implausible: as a general matter no one was liable to compensate another for failing to prevent a loss. Otherwise, a person who failed to defend someone who was under attack would be liable for his death – which, the critics said, was a position that no one held.[208]

In Soto's time, his colleague Francisco de Vitoria had been willing to entertain the possibility (one can put it no higher than that) that the failure to assist someone in extreme necessity did indeed entail legal consequences.[209] Vitoria canvassed two kinds of liability if that failure resulted in the death of the indigent person. First, the non-giver might be liable to the indigent person's family to make restitution for the damage they suffered. Just as a person who owes money because of a loan or purchase would be liable for the total damage (including the consequential losses, such as a resulting death) caused by defaulting on the payment, so the indigent person had a similar right to the alms that should have been received. Although no debt was owed, the obligation to give made the alms notionally the pauper's, so that the indigent person should be treated as if he was deprived of money in hand. Alternatively, Vitoria argued that even if the failure to give alms is distinguishable from the non-payment of a debt because the requisite but ungiven alms cannot be included in the indigent's patrimony, nonetheless the withholding of the alms caused the indigent's death. The non-giver should therefore be held liable for homicide but not for restitution.

These arguments were in line with Cajetan's position, in that they assumed the juridical significance of the non-giver's obligation. Especially striking was Vitoria's argument about restitution for loss, which compared the non-giving of alms with the non-payment of a debt. Through this analogy Vitoria sought to bring extreme necessity within the framework of commutative justice, of which the reimbursement of a loan was the paradigmatic case. The difference between them, however, was that the case of the loan belonged to commutative justice because of the transactional equality between what the lender had given and what the borrower was repaying, whereas the case of extreme necessity demands a unilateral giving by or taking from the person of means to satisfy the pauper's need, with no similar equality being apparent. Implicitly responding to Vitoria, Soto asserted in his commentary on almsgiving that compensating the family of the pauper who had been allowed to die would not be completely absurd. He noted, however, that the common opinion rejected this on the ground that one was "not obligated to give alms by a precept of distributive justice but by a precept of mercy."[210] This actually

---

208 Gabriel Vásquez, *Tractatus de Eleemosyna*, Caput Primum, dub. V; Juan de Lugo, *De Iustitia et Iure*, Disp. XVI, Sec. VII, para. 141.

209 Vitoria, Commentary on Aquinas *Summa Theologiae*, II-II, q. 32, a. 5, in Deuringer, *Probleme der Caritas*, 181–2.

210 Soto, Commentary, s. 32.

misstated and weakened Vitoria's argument, because even if giving were considered an obligation of distributive justice, the restitution of loss is a remedy for the contravention of justice that is commutative rather than distributive. At any rate, by the time of the *De Iustitia et Iure* more than a decade and a half later, Soto had more definitively come around to the view that the implausibility of holding the non-giver liable for damages for the death of the pauper indicated that giving alms to a person facing extreme necessity was not a matter of justice.[211]

A third version of extreme necessity was the converse of Cajetan's. Whereas Cajetan had postulated that both the obligation to give and the right to take were matters of justice, the third version treated them both as matters of charity.

The chief impediment to this version was the ubiquitous – and apparently justice-oriented – idea that under conditions of extreme necessity, private property gave way to the re-emergence of the primeval communality of goods, so that the pauper's taking of something did not count as theft. The justice-oriented versions of the right of necessity treated common possession as the basis for the pauper's right to take what belonged to another. In contrast, the charity-oriented version reversed the polarity of this argument by treating common possession as a construct expressive of the underlying obligation to provide aid. Common possession was understood as the meaning and not the basis of the right to take. In other words, common possession does not authorize the taking of the thing; rather the permissibility of taking it (which flows from charity not justice) enables the thing to be regarded as being in common possession: "Everything is in common in this sense, that an extremely indigent person can take the thing that he needs that belongs to another."[212]

Especially revealing to proponents of this view was the narrow artificiality of common possession in this context. Instead of making what was owned available to everyone (as true common possession would), it operated only for the benefit of the person facing extreme necessity. This indicated that the point of the right of necessity was not to dissolve private property into common possession, but to prevent the existence of private property from dooming a specific indigent person. What motivated this conclusion was not justice but the inviolateness of the principle of charity, which applied despite the existence of private property. In the context of the right of necessity, common possession was not a distinctive regime of justice in holdings, but an affirmation that the issue of who owned what was irrelevant to charity: "Although the right of nations appropriated what belonged to each person, nonetheless in the necessities that make almsgiving obligatory, charity does not enquire into what each person owns but makes everything be in common; this is not a matter of justice, and the person who needs something

---

211 Soto, *De Iustitia et Iure*, V, q. 3, a. 4 (p. 428).
212 Sanchez, *Consilia seu Opuscula Moralia*, I, V, dub. 5, 61.

can use it without injustice."[213] Because the owner is obligated to give the thing to the indigent person as a matter of charity, the taking of the thing is not rationally against the owner's will.[214] This charitable obligation to assist when necessity is extreme is a precept of natural right that is normatively prior to the justice-oriented arrangements about private property introduced by the law of nations. Those arrangements must yield to this precept; they cannot supplant it.[215]

Soto favoured this third version. This is apparent in his treatment in the *De Iustitia et Iure* of the permissibility of stealing in a situation of extreme necessity. There Soto invokes the third version to bridge two seemingly inconsistent principles. The first principle is that almsgiving is an obligation not of justice but of charity, to which no one can be unwillingly compelled. If the obligation were one of justice, a person who failed to assist would be bound to compensate for the loss resulting from his omission – which Soto asserts is not the case. This principle, Soto asserts, excludes compulsion not only by public power but also by private takings. Yet the second principle is that in a situation of extreme necessity, an indigent person can take what belongs to another. (Indeed, in the *Deliberatio* Soto even countenanced state action to penalize the failure to give alms when necessity was extreme.)[216] Addressing this inconsistency, Soto remarked that "it makes little difference whether you say in such necessity that some reason of justice intervenes; indeed, properly speaking it is nothing but compassion that nonetheless strictly obliges. Compulsion then plays a role because of the singular right accruing to everyone of saving one's own life."[217]

In this passage Soto treats with relative indifference what he considers to be loose talk about extreme necessity as occasioning an intervention of justice. However, he explicitly confirms that properly understood, the right to take another's property when necessity is extreme is not a démarche of justice. Despite its coerciveness, the taking falls within the range of the charitable obligation of compassion because of the unique status of saving a life. Precept obligates the sacrifice of one person's superfluities to save the life of another. For Soto, it does not matter whether that sacrifice involves an act of assistance by a person of means or an act of self-help by a person in danger. Compassion "strictly obliges" because what counts is the resultant saving of life, not the identity of the actor who accomplished that result.

---

213 Vásquez, *Tractatus de Eleemosyna*, Caput Primum, dub. V, paras. 41–2: *Et licet ius gentium unicuique suum appropriaverit, tamen in necessitatibus quae ad eleemosynam obligant, charitas quae non quaerit quae sua sunt omnia facit communia, non iustitia, et quod ille sic egens re sine iniustitia possit ea uti.* My description of the third version draws principally on this text.

214 Vásquez, *Tractatus de Eleemosyna*, Caput Primum, dub. V, paras. 41–2

215 Vásquez, *Tractatus de Eleemosyna*, Caput Primum, dub. V, paras. 41–2: *et ita ius gentium non potuit ius charitatis auferre per appropriationem.*

216 Soto, *Deliberatio*, Chapter IV.

217 Soto, *De Iustitia et Iure,* V, q. 3, a. 4 (p. 428).

Such taking cannot be considered theft of one's private property because, when extreme necessity (in distinction from lesser forms of necessity) identifies the specific target of one's charitable obligation, one's right to private property starts only at the point at which the obligation of charity ends. To be sure, theft is a prohibited wrong that does not admit of exceptions. Taking something when in extreme necessity, however, is not an exception to the prohibition but rather an act that does not fall within the prohibition's scope, as the prohibition cannot preclude a taking "that nature itself allows."[218] Thus, the relief of extreme necessity is not a part of the justice of property arrangements, but is a charitable obligation prior to justice.

As against the second version, the first and third versions share the view that the right of necessity does not flow from the indigent person's temporary ownership of the thing being used. Where they differ as between themselves is in their assumptions about the significance of the owner's proprietary right. These assumptions can be formulated as follows.

The first version treats private property as the point of departure for the right of necessity. The purpose of that right is to loosen the control exercised by the property owner over the thing needed by the indigent person. What the right of necessity limits is integral to the conception of the purpose of the limit. As Grotius put it, the point of allowing a taking when necessity is extreme is "to preserve natural equity against the rigour of ownership."[219] In this Grotius explicitly referenced his scholastic predecessor Covarrubias, who wrote that "when necessity is extreme everything is in common in conformity with the reason for moderating what is right (*iuxta recti moderaminis rationem*), that is, to relieve the necessity."[220] To forward the underlying rationale of sustaining every person through the use of external things – a rationale that private property helps effectuate by providing incentives for productive use – the right of necessity tempers private property's harsh effect when a person's life is in danger.

In contrast to its justice-oriented alternative, Soto's charity-oriented version treats the existence of private property as incidental. To be sure, on this version the permissibility of taking what belongs to another has the effect of moderating private property, but that is not its point. Its point is to fulfil a precept of charity that is conceptually anterior to and independent of private property and that directly corresponds to the notion that in extreme necessity everything is in common. The property right is regarded not as merely attenuated or qualified by the taker's right to satisfy his need, but as immaterial to it. The pauper's taking is to be understood as the use not of what belongs to another but of what is available

---

218 Soto, *De Iustitia et Iure*, V, q. 3, a. 4 ad 2 (p. 429).
219 Grotius, *De Iure Belli*, II, 2, 9.
220 Covarrubias, *Regulae, Peccatum*, II, 1, 4

as a matter of charity regardless of private property. Far from being the point of departure for the right of necessity, the existence of private property is normatively irrelevant to the pauper's necessitous use.

X Restitution

Does this contrast between the versions of extreme necessity have any practical bearing? Considered as a matter of justice, what paupers take is conceived as affecting another's rights. It would not be surprising that this approach has more stringent implications for desperate paupers than does understanding such takings as instances of obligatory compassion.

A circumstance in which the contrast between justice and charity seems to matter is this: suppose that a pauper who in extreme necessity takes and uses something belonging to someone else, subsequently experiences an improvement in fortune that makes it feasible to compensate the owner for the object used. Is such compensation obligatory? This arcane issue has had a perhaps surprisingly long afterlife. In a famous case from the early twentieth century a court in the United States observed that "theologians hold that a starving man may, without moral guilt, take what is necessary to sustain life, but it could hardly be said that the obligation would not be upon such person to pay the value of the property so taken when he becomes able to do so."[221] In fact, among the theologians of the sixteenth and seventeenth centuries this issue was a matter of considerable dispute. Writing in the mid-seventeenth century Juan de Lugo asserted that "the common opinion of scholars and non-scholars" was that there was no such obligation.[222] The contrary view, however, was popularized by Grotius, who on this point followed a line of thought favoured by some eminent scholastic writers, such as Adrian of Utrecht (later Pope Adrian VI), Covarrubias, Azpilcueta, and Lessius.[223]

In his treatment of this issue Soto outlines the arguments on both sides while in the end minimizing the obligation to make restitution.[224] Soto first presents the position he opposes, offering two general reasons for the existence of this obligation.[225] The principal reason is that in extreme necessity everything is in

---

221 *Vincent v Lake Erie Transportation Co.,* 124 N.W. 221 (Minnesota Supreme Court, 1910).

222 Lugo, *De Iustitia et Iure,* Disp. XVI, Sec. VII, para. 170.

223 Grotius, *De Iure Belli,* II, 2, 9; Covarrubias, *Regulae, Peccatum* II, 2, 9; Azpilcueta, *Manuel de Confessoribus,* cap. 17, nn. 59–61; Lessius, *De Iustitia et Iure,* Lib. 2. Cap. 16, dub. 1. Adrian's treatment of the issue, in his *Quaestiones de sacramentis in quartum Sententiarum librum,* 4 *de restitutione,* question beginning *Quia dictum est de lucro* (1516), was the basis of Soto's presentation of this side of the controversy and was the common point of reference for other writers about it.

224 Soto, IV, q. 7, a. 1 (p. 366).

225 A third, more specific reason dealing with the provision of emergency medical assistance is here ignored.

common with respect to use but not with respect to ownership. If it were other-wise, a person of means who failed to provide assistance would be withholding what belonged to the pauper and, therefore, should be held liable to compensate the pauper for the consequences of that wrong – a conclusion that Soto regards as implausible because in his view (and in the view also of those, unlike Soto, who adhered to the first and narrowly juridical version of extreme necessity) the obligation to assist is one of charity only, not justice. Correspondingly, what paupers take on their own initiative is not something that already belonged to them when necessity was extreme. Common possession allows the pauper no more than the right to relieve the necessity by using the thing, "so that once the use is completed one is obligated to make restitution of the thing (*ut transacto usu tenearis ad restitutionem rei*)."

The full scope of this statement about making "restitution of the thing" should be appreciated. Soto is here presenting the position he opposes, which he says posits an "absolute" (that is, an exceptionless) obligation on the pauper, when fortune smiles more favourably, to make restitution of what he took when his need was extreme.[226] The position that he opposes comprehends the taking of items that are both non-consumable and consumable. Suppose – an example that Soto himself adduces – that a person facing mortal danger escapes by commandeering and riding off on another's horse. Once the danger has passed, the horse must be returned to its owner, because the danger gave the imperilled person the right to use the horse but did not change its ownership. Soto accepts this conclusion, treating it as a paradigmatic example of the notion that in extreme necessity everything is in common with respect to use and not ownership. Soto's disagreement with the opposite view does not concern this example. Rather, the dispute is about items that were consumed, such as food. Even if the thing was no longer in existence or was ruined, the pauper upon whom fortune subsequently smiled had, on the view that Soto rejected, to make restitution of its equivalent to the person of means, who owned it while the pauper was legitimately using it and who continued to have a right to it. At issue was whether the person who saved himself by using a consumable thing was obligated to make restitution for consuming it.

A second reason for restitution – later underlined by Grotius – was that the assistance had merely to be sufficient for the purpose of relieving the pauper's extreme necessity. Anything more, such as the pauper's permanent retention of the

---

226 Soto mentions that "everyone acknowledges that no obligation to make restitution remains when the thing is of small value." This should not be considered an exception to the existence of a general obligation to make restitution, but rather a presumed gift, as Adrian thought, or a presumed waiver on the part of the owner, as in Azpilcueta, *Manuel de Confessoribus*, cap. 17, n. 61: "When a person in such need takes a small thing, such as a piece of bread, some clothes, a torn dress, or something like that, he can think that its owner would be content that he take it entirely for himself and that he would be forever excused from making restitution of it."

benefit under more prosperous circumstances, would derogate from the owner's property right while being superfluous to the elimination of the emergency. To achieve sufficiency for its purpose without needlessly impairing the owner's property right, the pauper's taking should be interpreted – so the proponents of this view held – not as a gift but as a loan. In the terminology of Roman law, the thing taken was the object of a *mutuum*, a loan for consumption to be reimbursed through the return of an equivalent.[227] Repayment of this notional loan, accordingly, was due when the borrower's fortunes improved. This interpretation of the taking ran parallel to the suggestion, also controversial, that the charitable obligation to assist a person in extreme necessity could be satisfied by making a loan rather than giving a gift.[228]

Construing the taking as a loan repayable on the improvement of the pauper's situation treated the basis for the taking as its limit. Not only was the taking justified by the pauper's extreme necessity, but the taking also could be no more extensive than was needed to relieve that necessity. A marginal note to Azpilcueta's exposition of this view articulated the underlying principle, that "a limited cause produces a limited effect."[229] In a similar vein Lugo later noted the "speculative rigour" of this position: "The indigent person cannot take what belongs to someone else except with that burden, because he has the right to take only to the extent required for his need, and so with the least possible loss to the owner."[230]

Lugo's formulation brings out the conformity of this position with the proportionality aspect of the conceptual framework elaborated above. Recall that one of the elements of that framework is that the natural right of common possession and the limiting of that right through the institution of private property should be proportionally aligned to each other from the standpoint of the rationale underlying the production and use of things. The point of this proportionality is to produce the optimal mutual accommodation of the natural right and its limit. However, unless the obligation to make restitution is included within the limit on private property, then the permissibility of the taking will operate more extensively than is needed to achieve its purpose. The postulating of an obligation to make restitution when feasible achieves the desired accommodation by impairing

---

227 Birks, *The Roman Law of Obligations*, 131–5.

228 Sanchez, *Consilia Seu Opuscula Moralia* I, V, dub V, 45–57; Lugo, *De Iustitia et Iure*, Disp. XVI, Sec. VII, paras. 141–72.

229 Azpilcueta, *Manuel de Confessoribus*, cap. 17, n. 61: *limitata causa limitatum producit effectum.* Similarly, Adrian, *Quaestiones de sacramentis,* 4 had invoked the principle *cessante causa cessare debet effectus.*

230 Lugo, *De Iustitia et Iure*, Disp. XVI, Sec. VII, para. 172: *in rigore quidem speculativo indigentem, per se loquendo, non posse nisi cum illo onere alienum sibi accipere, quia non habet jus accipiendi nisi quatenus ad suam necessitatem requiritur, atque ideo cum minori domini damno si fieri possit.* Lugo contrasted this speculative rigour with the practical reality that such repayment would be rare.

the owner's right to the minimal extent consistent with facilitating the pauper's survival. Then common possession and private property are each modulated in the light of the other: common possession reasserts itself within a regime of private property, while not derogating from private property more than is necessary for effectuating the rationale that underlies both common possession and private property.

After presenting these reasons for requiring restitution of what was taken, Soto moves to his preferred position. Because he opposes a general requirement of restitution but allows for restitution in particular circumstances, his conclusions are factually more nuanced than the opposing view. Soto affirms that in three situations the person in need is obligated to make restitution. These three situations are as follows.

One situation – this is a distinction that Soto says was "elegantly" drawn by Duns Scotus – is when the person in need is already, before the extreme necessity arose, obligated to give back to the owner the thing taken. The example that Duns Scotus had posited was that of a person who wrongly had taken food belonging to another and then subsequently, when he fell into extreme necessity, saved himself by eating that food.[231] Scotus analysed this situation as one in which the obligation to return the food or its value was dormant but not extinguished (*non est extincta sed sopita*) during the period of extreme necessity. The obligation had already arisen through the wrongful acquisition of the food, but the subsequent extreme necessity had a practical effect: although the obligation subsisted, the extreme necessity rendered pointless any attempt by the owner to sue for the recovery of what had been taken. When the poor person became more prosperous, the obligation revived, in the sense that suing for restitution was no longer pointless. Soto drew from this the conclusion that extreme necessity allows something to be taken without creating a new obligation, but it does not dissolve an already existing debt. That debt is a continuing obligation that aims not at making restitution for the food consumed under extreme necessity, but at satisfying what was already owing regardless of the extreme necessity. The converse of this was that, because the consumption of food taken once necessity became extreme was not wrongful, no new obligation to repay the value of the food arose.

A second restitutionary situation arises when the person who took the thing was not "needy without qualification" (*simpliciter indigens*). This designation refers to a person who has resources or the possibility of resources that are not available in the present emergency, such as a Spanish merchant shipwrecked on the French coast. Only a person who is (in the later formulation) a *pauper re et spe*[232] – a pauper

---

231 Duns Scotus, *Ordinatio*, IV, d. 15, q. 2, n. 104 and n. 203.

232 Lugo, *De Iustitia et Iure,* Disp. XVI, Sec. VII, para. 162; compare Vitoria, *Commentary on Aquinas Summa Theologiae*, II-II, q. 66, a. 7: *Ille dicitur esse in extrema necessitate qui nihil habet nec aliunde sperat.*

who has nothing anywhere and who has no hope of having anything by virtue of a special skill or occupation – properly falls within the category of persons in extreme necessity who do not have to make restitution for what they took or were given. In contrast, assistance to those who lack resources here and now but have or can secure the means to repay is to be regarded as a loan.

Finally, a third restitutionary situation occurs when the means of salvation survive the emergency for which its use was required. As already noted, the paradigmatic example is the horse that was used to escape danger. In such cases use of the thing can readily be distinguished from ownership. The person endangered is entitled to use it when in extreme necessity, but subsequently it must be returned to its owner.

The crucial disagreement between Soto and the opposing view concerns the use of consumables. Basing itself on the idea that common possession went to use and not ownership, the opposing view claimed that this ongoing ownership implied an obligation to restore the value of the thing consumed if the user's fortunes improved. Soto rejected this. In a difficult argument, Soto postulated that the person who took and used the thing exercised some kind of ownership over it as an aspect of the consumption of consumable things. In this way, Soto avoided a general obligation to make restitution by remaining faithful to the notion that in extreme necessity everything is in common with respect to use, while at the same time specifically distinguishing the case of consumables. As Soto put it:

> If he is needy without qualification, it should be beyond controversy that he does not remain liable to make restitution for taking what he needs. For although it is the case that then everything is held in common only with respect to use, nonetheless for things that are consumed by use, ownership follows use by natural law [*ad usum lege naturae sequitur dominium*]; for example, the person who takes food or drink or money becomes its owner. In this matter, if we are not mistaken, the contrary opinion deceives its adherents. For the fact that everything is in common with respect to use means that to that extent the needy person could take another's goods as if they were his own. Therefore, he is not obligated to take them as something to be repaid, but the other is obligated to give them for nothing. But if the thing is something that is not consumed by use, then when the necessity passed, he would be obligated to return them, for example, if someone uses another's horse to escape the danger of death, or if he needed a bed while ill.[233]

Taken at face value, the argument that no compensation is due because ownership for consumables follows use by natural law is problematic on several counts, as Soto's sometime colleague at Salamanca, the canon lawyer Martin

---

233 Soto, *De Iustitia et Iure*, IV, q. 7, a. 1 (p. 366).

de Azpilcueta, pointed out.[234] First, a tension exists between this argument and Soto's defence earlier in the *De Iustita et Iure* and elsewhere of the Franciscan position that the right to use consumables does not involve ownership.[235] More importantly, the argument proves too much. If the argument about restitution hinges on the mechanics of ownership through consumption, it would apply also to the consumption of what was taken by a person who was not "needy without qualification," that is, a person of means who did not have resources immediately available, and who was, as everyone agreed, under an obligation to make restitution. Finally, it is not the case that one to whom ownership has passed never has an obligation to restore an equivalent. Those who favoured restitution argued that the taking should be thought of as a loan of consumables, a *mutuum*. In Roman law this form of loan always involved a passing of ownership (*ex meo tuum* in the fanciful Roman etymology), and yet the loan had to be repaid.

Soto's reference to ownership in this context must be interpreted to spare him these difficulties. He cannot plausibly be regarded as repudiating in one sentence the position on the Franciscan controversy that he had methodically elaborated in this very work and had consistently maintained in earlier writing. Whatever he means by the statement that "*dominium* follows use by natural law," *dominium* here cannot have the significance that it had in his treatment of the Franciscan claim.

If one keeps in mind the precise point that Soto was making about the Franciscan right to use, the difficulty is abated. Soto's position regarding the Franciscans was that the right to use was not a form of ownership. Because under Soto's definition, ownership gave the owner the right to use a thing for any purpose whatsoever permitted by law, it subjected the thing to the full range of legal operations, including the owner's right to alienate.[236] This the Franciscans did not have; they enjoyed a right merely to a bare use that did not allow for alienation.

Soto's observations on extreme necessity are consistent with this. Paupers who took something under extreme necessity could use that thing solely for the purpose for which it was legitimately taken, that is, for the relief of their necessity. If the thing or any part of it remained unused for that purpose, it could be reclaimed by the original owner; that would merely be a variant on the horse example. Within that purpose, however, the fate of the thing was entirely in the pauper's hands. So long as the pauper acts in execution of the permitted purpose, no one else (including the original owner) has a legally cognizable interest in the thing taken. Moreover, just as the pauper's use is permitted, so is his consumption of it, because consumption is simply the way that consumable things are used. Thus, given the

---

234 *Azpilcueta, Manuel de Confessoribus*, cap. 17, n. 61.
235 Soto, *De Iustitia et Iure*, IV, q. 1, a. 1 (pp. 281–3); Soto, *De Dominio*, ss. 5–8.
236 Money was in a category of its own, because money could be used only through alienation. Soto was of the view that money given to the Franciscans always remained within the *dominium* of the donor (*De Dominio*, s. 8).

nature of use for a consumable thing, persons who have nothing but the right to use it can, by consuming the thing, exert a control so complete that it resembles ownership, even though they lack the owner's full range of powers. Such control of the thing for the permitted purpose is what Soto here calls *dominium*. This *dominium* follows use by natural law because the right to use is permitted by natural law, and the consumption – the exercise of *dominium* in this narrow sense – is the fulfilment (and the only practical fulfilment) of the purpose for which the use is permitted. Far from referring to legal operations, such as alienation, that are distinct from the permitted bare use, the *dominium* to which Soto is here referring is continuous with that use. This is why Soto thinks that no claim for restitution arises. The consumption of the thing in accordance with the permitted purpose has the same permissibility as the taking itself. By acting within the scope of an entitlement to use and consume what was needed for survival, the pauper incurred no obligation to the owner, because one should not be held liable for doing what one was entitled to do in the only way that one could practically do it.

Accordingly, when Soto says that "ownership follows use by natural law" he is referring to a special kind of ownership that is not the basis of the user's legal position but is a representation of the control he exercises when acting pursuant to the purpose that renders the taking legitimate. That purpose is not limited in duration; at the time of the taking, the pauper has no reason to assume that his fortunes will sufficiently change to the point of being able to repay. He therefore does not take the benefit subject to an obligation to repay. In contrast, the person who is not "needy without qualification" knows that the purpose of the taking is to satisfy a temporary need, so that the entitlement to retain the benefit expires when the emergency that occasioned it comes to its anticipated end. Similarly, in the case of *mutuum*, the obligation to repay is built into the loan. Regardless of how *dominium* is characterized in these situations, they differ from the position of the desperate pauper whose prospects are more or less fixed.

Defending Soto's formulation from Azpilcueta's critique several decades later, Gabriel Vásquez noted the special meaning that *dominium* has in the situation Soto is discussing:

> It well follows that if in that necessity goods are common with respect to use, they are also common with respect to *dominium*. For it matters little that *dominium* remains with the former owner, if the thing is to be consumed justly by the pauper. Nor are they obligated to make restitution if their fortunes improve, just as the Franciscans to whom a bare use is granted are also not obligated. It must, therefore, be said that goods are common even with respect to *dominium*, not absolutely, but sufficiently to relieve the necessity.[237]

---

237 Vásquez, *Tractatus de Eleemosyna*, Caput I, dub. VI, para. 49.

The objective of Soto's s argument is to counteract the first reason offered by his opponents on the issue of restitution. Recall that they had argued that restitution was due because common possession was with respect to use and not with respect to ownership, so that the owner continued to have a claim to the value of the thing consumed. Soto's response was that in a certain sense common possession was indeed with respect to ownership, that is, to the special kind of ownership relevant to what was consumed under extreme necessity. Soto argued that this undercut the basis for the original owner's ongoing entitlement to be reimbursed.

Thus, Soto concluded that by acting within the scope of an entitlement to use and consume something that was needed for survival in a situation of extreme necessity, the pauper incurred no obligation to the thing's original owner. Implicit in Soto's handling of the issue was the view that the situation provided no ground for imposing a legal obligation to make restitution: the pauper neither committed a wrong in consuming the thing, nor was the pauper unjustly enriched by consuming something that was within his entitlement when extreme necessity reactivated common possession, nor was the original owner's right effective given the pauper's legitimate control of the owned thing, nor (in contrast to the case of the horse) did anything survive the consumption that the original owner could demand be returned.[238]

Colouring Soto's exposition was his fundamental assumption that the pauper's taking and use of the thing was oriented to the precept of charity. Requiring that the imperilled pauper make restitution to the person of means for using what was needed to save his life would have been a cold-blooded expression of compassion. Alluding to Soto subsequently, the well-known Jesuit casuist Thomas Sanchez, in his explanation of why giving a loan cannot satisfy the precept of almsgiving, expanded on what he thought must have been Soto's thinking:

The reason is that relieving a necessity is not sufficient, but a person is obligated to relieve it by giving alms. But although almsgiving is not an act of liberality, it nevertheless supposes a gratuitous donation, as a genus to which indigence is added as a species. Otherwise giving a loan to a rich person would be considered

---

238 Half a century after Soto, the respected moral theologian Juan Azor, in *Institutionum Moralium, in quibus universae quaestiones ad conscientiam recte aut prave factorum pertinentes breviter tractantur,* para. 3, lib. 4, c 39, summed up the position of Scotus and Soto on this issue by reference to the inapplicability of the standard grounds for restitution formulated by Aquinas. In *Summa Theologiae,* II-II, q. 66, a. 6, Aquinas had said that restitution could be claimed either by reason of the retention of a thing taken or by reason of the act of taking the thing. Azor wrote that taking and consuming something in extreme necessity falls neither under the first of these grounds, because the thing no longer exists, nor under the second, because the act of taking was not unjust. One may suppose that proponents of the opposite view would have pointed to the example of *mutuum,* where the loaned thing might no longer exist and had not been unjustly acquired by the borrower. Aquinas thought *mutuum* fell under both grounds of restitution.

almsgiving – which is absurd. And so common linguistic usage understands the word "almsgiving" as a gratuitous donation.[239]

That Soto may well have thought along these lines is evident from his assertion in the *Deliberatio* that the point of being merciful lies not in the concrete assistance provided to the poor but in the soul's inward compassion at the pauper's plight.[240]

This orientation of extreme necessity toward charity was matched by the assumption that by taking and consuming what they needed, paupers violated no right of the owners. As already noted, Soto held that such taking, far from being an exception to the prohibition on theft, did not fall within its scope at all.[241] In Soto's view the effect of the Fall was not that private property completely replaced common possession, but that common possession continued to exist in a shrunken form that consisted in the charitable obligation to be beneficent to the poor.[242] The existence of private property did not even for a moment oust or extinguish this obligation. The consequence of this was, as Soto had already asserted in the *Deliberatio*, that the wealthy do not give alms out of the goods they own.[243] This in turn implied that by taking what was necessary for survival, paupers were not depriving owners of what they owned; rather, they were exercising a specific entitlement – the entitlement to use what would save their lives – that simply was not within the scope of the owner's proprietary right. Soto construed private property as having been incomprehensively instituted, so that common possession continued to be available to those facing extreme necessity. It followed that the owners' right to the exclusive use of what they owned did not include the exclusive use of it in circumstances of extreme necessity. Whereas Soto's opponents treated the pauper's use as a compensable derogation from the rights of ownership, Soto assumed that the relevant right had never belonged to the owner to begin with. Thus, for Soto no restitution was due, because the owner had lost nothing.

When the dispute between Soto and his opponents is seen in this light, the underlying issue is one of considerable jurisprudential interest: Does the pauper's entitlement go to the scope of ownership or to its operation?[244] If the non-owner's entitlement to use what is necessary for survival falls outside the scope of ownership, then the owner has no grounds for claiming restitution for the effects of that use. Although the pauper's consumption of the thing left the owner worse off,

---

239 Sanchez, *Consilia seu Opuscula Moralia* I, V, dub. V, 56.
240 Soto, *Deliberatio*, Chapter XI.
241 Soto, *De Iustitia et Iure*, V, q. 3, a. 4 (p. 429).
242 Soto, *De Iustitia et Iure*, V, q. 3, a. 4 (p. 428).
243 Soto, *Deliberatio*, Chapter VIII.
244 On the significance of the distinction between the scope and the operation of a right, see Weinrib, "Defending the Juridical."

in that what the pauper had consumed no longer existed, it did not injure the owner's right to his property, because that right did not include an entitlement to control what was needed for another's survival. On this view, as Soto concluded, the pauper could not be obligated to restore the value of an entitlement that was not within the scope of what the owner owned.

In contrast, Soto's opponents – mostly lawyers like Covarrubias, Azpilcueta, and (later) Grotius – assumed that ownership gave the owner the right to complete control of the owned thing. To be sure, this right could not operate under circumstances of another's extreme necessity, because that would be inconsistent with the idea that the purpose of the world's things was to sustain each and every member of mankind. However, that the pauper was permitted to consume the thing did not change the fact that what had been consumed was something that belonged to the owner. Hence, the owner could insist on the restitution of its value if a change in the pauper's condition made restitution feasible. In this respect the consumed thing was parallel to the withheld sword: the thing in question continued to belong to the owner, even though special circumstances justified the contravention of the owner's right of ownership.

Finally, although Soto responded expressly to the first of the two general reasons for restitution that he listed – that common possession is with respect to use not ownership – he did not respond to the second reason, which based the obligation to make restitution on the sufficiency of the use itself for an end that had already been achieved when restitution became feasible. In historical retrospect this has a certain irony, because it was the second reason that made its way into subsequent legal notice through the writing of Grotius, who ignored the first one. Soto's motivation for not responding to the second reason is obvious. In preserving property rights to the extent possible by envisaging the possibility of restitution, this second reason belonged to a justice-oriented account of extreme necessity in which compensation was due for the adverse effects of one's actions on another's property. In contrast, in Soto's view, once the opposing argument about ownership was countered, justice had no stake in the controversy regarding the taking of consumables by a sufferer from extreme necessity. Soto gave no response the second reason because, so far as he was concerned, there was nothing to respond to. The issue to which such extreme necessity gave rise was fundamentally one of charity, not justice.

XI   Conclusion

The present treatment of Soto's views on poverty has primarily focused on his opposition to restrictions on the movements and activities of beggars, and on his conception of the relationship between the right of necessity and the notion of private property. The leitmotif running through his handling of both these issues was the precept of charity as an expression of Christian compassion. That precept anchored the idea that, when necessity was extreme, common possession re-emerged, and paupers were permitted to seize and use what, regardless of ownership, they needed to survive. The precept also gave rise to an obligation to give alms. Soto interpreted this obligation very broadly as requiring the donation of one's superfluous resources to paupers even if their need was grave but not extreme. Even more expansive was Soto's delineation of the permissible scope of begging, which was available even to persons whose needs were less than grave, provided only that their presentation of need was not an exercise in fraud. Although Soto doubted that government had the legitimate authority to enforce almsgiving except in cases of extreme necessity, he thought that considerations of legality barred restrictions on the travel of beggars or on their direct solicitations.

"To those of us who know the end of the story – state taxation and implementation of welfare – Domingo de Soto seems to be arguing for an outdated system."[245] In this observation by the historian Linda Martz, the word "seems" is important, as she goes on to affirm the enduring significance of Soto's views about the treatment of poverty. Soto wrote at a fateful juncture in the evolution of the theory and practice of the treatment of pauperism, and he occupies a distinctive place in the intellectual history of the relations between the law and the poor. His position incorporates a view of the state of nature, of private property, of extreme necessity, and of rights that include a right to beg.

The centrality of the issues that Soto raises is confirmed, if any confirmation were necessary, by their reappearance in Immanuel Kant's arguments in the opposite direction. Adapting and transforming the elements that figured in scholastic philosophy, Kant explicitly affirmed the state's duty to support the poor.[246] He postulated a state of nature that, unlike Soto's, was not an ideal but rather a presentation of the axiom that right consists in the totality of conditions in which one person's action can coexist with the freedom of others.[247] From this emerged both a conception of property under which free beings relate to one another through external things, and a conception of the state as the institutional framework for protecting and realizing the freedom of everyone with respect to everyone else. For Kant the state's duty to the poor was an essential aspect of the reciprocal freedom that animated the state's existence. Correspondingly, he dismissed begging as closely akin to robbery,[248] perhaps because he regarded it as an open appeal to the emotions of others designed to deprive them of what was theirs. Kant also reduced a privately exercised right of necessity to an injustice that violated another's rights

---

245 Martz, *Poverty and Welfare in Hapsburg Spain*, 28.

246 Kant, *Metaphysics of Morals*, 109 [6:236]. On the interpretation of this passage, see Weinrib, *Corrective Justice*, 283–96.

247 The transformation of the state of nature from an ideal to an axiom is first evident in Grotius; see Schermaier, *"Res Communes Omnium,"* 20.

248 Kant, *Metaphysics of Morals*, 110 [6:236].

but was excused by virtue of the limitations of state coercion in the face of threats to one's life.[249]

Be that as it may, Soto's themes have a continuing resonance. Among current issues of public interest are such questions as: What is the connection between a system of rights and a system of welfare? Is poverty a concern of charity or also of justice, and if the latter, how should justice be deployed? Should the poor have freedom of movement within and across political borders? Should public solicitation by the poor be regulated? Should access of the poor (especially the homeless) to public spaces be controlled? What should be the eligibility requirements for receiving assistance? How can the administration of assistance be made consistent with the dignity and privacy of the poor? Should the public provision of assistance be tied to creating incentives for certain kinds of social behaviour? Soto's treatment of poverty refers to versions of all these questions, while emphasizing that being poor is not itself a wrong. In the effort to understand these contemporary issues it is still worth attending to the compassionate words of Domingo de Soto, and to the tradition of thinking that they represent.

---

249 Kant, *Metaphysics of Morals,* 31 [6:235].

TRANSLATED TEXTS

Deliberation in the Matter of the Poor (1545)

TO THE SUPREME AND MOST ILLUSTRIOUS PRINCE OF THE SPANIARDS LORD PHILIP, OLDEST SON OF THE INVINCIBLE EMPEROR CHARLES V

From FRIAR DOMINGO SOTO of SEGOVIA, OF THE ORDER OF PREACHERS, PROFESSOR OF THEOLOGY IN SALAMANCA AND PRIOR OF THE MONASTERY OF SAN ESTABAN

No reason, great Prince, could ever have induced me to submit this document to Your Majesty, unless I had often read how much humanity a prince should have, and with how much gentleness those of you who hold exalted rank among mortals ought to listen to persons of every condition, and equally unless I had heard from many how much gentleness you exhibit with the signal humanity characteristic of your family and your ancestry. And yet now especially I surmise that you will not only listen with humanity to the opinions of many but will also ask for them. When Your Highness, as the person sitting on throne of the Emperor, will make his judgment about this matter, nothing else will be incumbent on all than to hear your decision and obey your commands.

It does not escape me that I am not among those whose authority has any weight to alter in one direction or another a matter discussed by so many and confirmed by such long consultation. Nor do I take up the task of speaking to contend that what is being done should be changed. I would consider it sufficient if a decision is made after all of the inconveniences one way or the other are explored more diligently, more carefully, with more foresight, and with greater divine approval, that is, in a manner more attentive to the unfortunate poor. In this matter nothing could be either a greater service to Your Imperial Majesty and your consequent greatness or a larger good to the state. Christ our Saviour not only wished, preached, and admonished us to care for the poor, but he ordered us to do so with both the greatest promises and the greatest threats.

There are some cities – and not the least – in this imperial patrimony of the Spanish that in the last four years have begun to separate the poor from the vagabonds, to bring the poor into line, to collect and distribute the alms on a certain basis and in a certain manner. That is: beggars should be prevented from going around door to door, so that the poor should be relieved of this labour and the rich of their improbity, and so that the alms should not be squandered recklessly, but the poor should be a culled, so that those whom the law terms "able-bodied" should be removed and the others – the truly indigent – should be better provided for. There can be no one who does not think that this undertaking is deservedly noble in its origin or does not see it proceed from a Christian heart, and therefore does not consider it worthy of praising with all one's strength, of cherishing, and of enthusiastically embracing.

But because the matter is so important, it is necessarily subject to the law governing other important matters, that unanimity about it is not readily attained. Although a particular work may deal with the most honourable matters, its subject matter does not necessarily entitle it to be called excellent, as it does not straightway attain to the standard of excellence. Rather, the requirement that something first be wrapped around by many considerations that are explored and surveyed as a whole cannot happen without the judgment of many people. And yet it often happens that from the unschooled doubts of those of us who are inexperienced, prudent and even extremely astute men may foresee many reasons to be cautious. For as Solomon's proverb says [Proverbs 1:5], "The wise person who listens will become wiser."

Therefore, Your Majesty, neither you nor anyone else should attribute the words I am setting out here to a desire to be critical or contentious. For I neither presume to have such ability in any matter, nor in this particular matter could proceeding with such an intention be without fault. Therefore, no one has reason to oppose me for the sake of strife or argument. As I just said, I direct the strength of my remarks – if they have any – only so that the laws providing for the poor should be enacted as carefully as possible. On this basis let it be the case that, while in this matter there are those who daily contribute very generously, I with my limited means should, along with the poor woman mentioned in the gospel [Mark 12:42] make two small offerings.

For the alms that we owe the poor do not consist in bread alone. To the contrary, to quote the words of Gregory [*Homiliae XL in Evangelia* 9, 7], "A person of intelligence should take care not to be silent, a person of wealth should be alert not to become listless about being mercifully generous, a person whose conduct is guided by a skill should zealously strive to share its use and utility with his neighbour, a person who has the opportunity to speak to someone of wealth should fear damnation for holding his talent back when, if he is able, he does not intercede with him on behalf of the poor." These are the words of Gregory. Therefore, the service of the tongue can sometimes significantly assist the suffering poor. For as it says in Ecclesiasticus [13:3], "The rich man acts unjustly and roars, but the poor man when injured keeps silent." And as Isidore says, as it is stated in *Decreta* [*Decretum Gratiani*], Cause 11, q. 3, "When the poor person has nothing to present in court, not only is he heard with contempt, but he is even oppressed against the truth." For this reason whoever protects the poor imitates God, who, as Job the patron of the poor attests [Job 5:15], "snatches the poor from the hand of the violent", and as David also attests [Psalms 108:31], "He stands at the right hand of the poor person, to save his life from his pursuers."

Therefore, in determining something that the Christian religion treats as so important to the life of the poor and also not without great danger to the rich, no one could omit his duty without immediately incurring blame, just as in the gospel parable [Luke 12:23], the master would not so harshly have rebuked his faithless servant who preferred to bury his talent in the earth, if by lending it at interest he could have increased it and returned it to his master multiplied.

Let no one think that I say this because I want to condemn anyone. Whoever has taken up this care and business of the poor, whatever side they favour, are led by the zeal of piety and religion, and therefore an abundant reward is laid up for them with God. But the deep point of what I am saying is that each person, to the extent of his talent and judgment, ought to bring his reasoning in this matter into the open, so that on each side it can be discussed and examined more precisely.

With respect to my intention to address Your Majesty, in the absence of the Emperor there is no other legitimate judge before whom I could either choose or certainly be obliged to speak about the matter of the poor. God himself, through whom kings reign and legislators enact just laws [Proverbs 8:15], as a mark of respect often and repeatedly calls himself the judge, patron, and father of the poor. Hence the fifth Synod of Carthage wanted prelates to be admonished that they should request protection of the poor from the glorious emperors. Moreover, this matter has already long been referred to the Emperor and to the Royal Council.

I have written this not only in Latin, the language in which I have explained the matter more broadly and precisely, but also in Spanish. First, as I remember saying to Your Highness on another occasion, when you honoured our school with the wish to be present at our lectures, that although you fully understand both languages, one is permitted to address princes only in their native tongue. Moreover, because the matter about which I am to speak concerns the populace, in that knowledge of it also pertains to the masses, it was worthwhile to present it in the language that even the people might understand.

Chapter II
Containing the Narration

The first stone on which this edifice rests was Petition 46 in the Cortes that assembled in Valladolid in 1523 AD. This petition complained to the Emperor that beggars had traversed their native borders and were ranging over the kingdom, and because of the wanderings of such people the state, as they alleged, had suffered much damage. Because of that, they implored the Emperor for a law by which beggars would be confined each to his own territory and would not be permitted to wander around. However, although the answer was given that this would be provided for, no public edict was issued at that time. Therefore, in the Cortes assembled in Madrid in 1528 complaint was again made about the wanderings of the destitute, and just as on the previous occasion the delegates did not bring back a response.

Then, in the Cortes convened in 1534, in Petition 117 another request was made in different terms, i.e., that in each city in the kingdom a prudent and circumspect man be assigned to deal with the poor, and that without his attestation and signature no one should be permitted to beg door to door, so that in this way one could discover which paupers were legitimate. Considering this a just request, the Emperor replied that that vagabonds whom the law calls "able-bodied" should be expelled from the towns, and that foreigners who under the cover of poverty are begging under false pretences should be removed from the Court. To these he added that the legitimate poor should be provided for and fed in their respective dioceses. No penalty was decreed for the legitimate poor no matter where in the kingdom they had travelled to beg.

Subsequently – and this is more relevant to the matter – in 1540, the Emperor's Council made a decree ordering that the contents of the aforementioned petitions be observed. And after the signatures of the councillors, an instruction was appended signed solely by the hand of the Chamber notary, in which the form for executing the law was specifically prescribed.

In summary, what pertains to this matter consists of six articles. First of all, it is provided that no one is permitted to beg before his poverty undergoes an examination for its legitimacy. Second, that it be permissible even for a legitimate beggar to beg only within the fixed limits of his own homeland, except in time of extreme famine or some other great calamity. Third, that no one may beg without a certificate of the priest or the person to whom this responsibility has been delegated. Fourth, that such certificates for begging be granted only to those who have first made confession in church. Fifth, pilgrims to Santiago are forbidden to tarry long on the road or to deviate from the direct route more than twelve miles, which we Spaniards call four leagues. The rest of the provisions are most justly enacted and are uncontroversial.

Finally, a last article was added that the diocesan and city authorities, according to their respective abilities, should occupy themselves in refurbishing the hospitals and should exact endowments for them from their debtors and patrons; in this way they would take care, if possible, that the poor would be sustained in their own territory, so that no necessity would compel them to wander about. These instructions were sent for printing in Medina last year, in 1544.

On these foundations the cities began to make regulations. Among these were: first, that vagabonds should be expelled from the city; next, that foreign beggars, after being provided for and refreshed by a certain amount of assistance, should be forced to move on immediately; and finally, that the native poor should not be allowed to run around begging from door to door, but should stay home while others selected for this service would collect and procure alms for them. Certain officials, especially the praetors, were designated to perform these services.

All this was full of holy zeal and piety; on this basis, legitimate poor who because of their extreme sense of shame preferred to put up with being confined to their homes rather than to go out and beg could receive greater assistance. For how otherwise than by holy intention could these regulations have been made, especially at Zamora – the foremost of these cities – where the prior of the world-famous religious order of Saint John was stationed? This person (whose other titles of honour it is not permissible to mention in the presence of Your Highness), who both generally is a true Christian and is most Christianly high-minded toward the poor, and (if the words go together) most sacredly prodigal in alms, would never have allowed anything to be decided about the poor unless he had known by the judgment of the religious and the wise that it was to their benefit.

Afterwards, when murmurs about these kinds of regulations began to arise in this University, some of us were consulted by Zamora, and we did not approve of the articles in their entirety. However, we promised that if some of them were excised in accordance with our judgment, we would sign the rest. Then after several days, the same city wrote certain sections of the articles for us to sign. I freely acknowledge my ignorance and rashness. I believed that there was nothing in the document except what I had promised to sign. And so I signed a document I had not read. Among so numerous and so distinguished a group of wise men there was nothing that the authority of my signature could add or subtract. Nonetheless, I hear that the document contained some things which, if I had read it, I would not have been able to so ignorantly approve.

I have said this because after the most reverend cardinal of Toledo recently in Valladolid asked me my opinion about this treatment of alms and I responded that I did not fully understand everything, these Zamoran articles were exhibited signed with my name. Subsequently, as I hear, the supporters of these articles produced them in your presence.

However, I do not have the authority that the Pythagoreans attributed to their Pythagoras – who sought no other testimony for the truth than what Pythagoras had said – but rather what I want prescribed both to all who speak about this matter and especially to myself is the rule of Saint Augustine to Jerome included in the *Decretum* [*Decretum Gratiani*, dist. 9, c. 5], where he says that aside from the canonical books no one, no matter how weighty he is religiously or doctrinally, should be given greater credit than the persuasiveness of his reasons. What I have signed elsewhere is almost of no importance, but I call this pamphlet as the witness to the truth of the matter.

Therefore, to return to the matter at hand, this city then accepted from Zamora the same regulations, although there was opposition. From here they have migrated to Valladolid, where – this is the rumour I have heard from there – Your Majesty has deservedly received them with uncertainty. That is why I had the idea of writing this *Deliberatio* to Your Majesty.

I fear that I have prolonged this narration to the point of weariness. But I thought it necessary to set before your eyes the entire summary of the matter about which I am going to speak.

Chapter III
On Vagabonds

As generally with everything that comes up for discussion, it is worthwhile immediately to divide this deliberation into two. One should first decide what is permissible and impermissible, and then discuss what seems to be beneficial from among the things that are permissible. The Apostle outlines this distinction in his first epistle to the Corinthians [6:12; 10:23] in these words: "All things are permissible to me, but not all things are beneficial. All things are permissible to me, but not all things edify." Nor are both to be examined in the same way; rather, they should be weighed in different scales. Whatever is permissible is done by law. For as the jurists note in the passage *Prospeximus* in *Qui et a Quibus* [Justinian, *Digest* 40, 9, 12], concerning something about which there is written law, no opportunity for dispute is allowed. But when we deliberate which of two legally permissible alternatives is beneficial, then the matter is to be interpreted according to what is fair and good and by arguments based on prudence.

And because distinguishing among things often casts light on matters of knowledge and counsel, it is very important that one understand the difference between vagabonds and the genuine paupers who travel around the world begging. For with respect to the former class of persons not only does the particular law of the kingdom provide, but also the more ancient common law and even the most ancient divine and natural law, that they are not to be permitted to do this with impunity in the state. With respect to the latter class, even if they are newcomers and foreigners, I see no law – with all respect to those who excel in jurisprudence – that prevents them from travelling wherever in the world they want. Indeed, if we pay attention to what both the gospel and natural reason suggest, neither does there appear to be any such law as a matter of what is fair and good.

With respect to the former category, although at first sound the noun "vagabond" seems to designate only the person who without his own abode and domicile seems to wander over the world – as the jurists learnedly note in the final chapter of *De foro competenti* [*Decretales Gregorii IX*, II, 2, 20] and the passage *Haerens absens* [Justinian, *Digest* 5, 1, 19] – it must be added that this notion refers to people who wander not out of necessity but for their convenience and utility.

Otherwise, it would not be, as it plainly is, a noun of infamy by which we denote people who are idle. Accordingly, those who leave their native territory to work as artisans or to do business or for necessity or utility are not disparaged or censured with the infamous name of "vagabond."

Therefore, the class of men who do not have the means to avoid servile work or are not legitimately considered incapable of servile labours because of disability or some other impediment should not be able to wander around with impunity. The first argument for this is from the divine law. God wanted us to have this admonishment immediately at the beginning of the creation of the world, when God, on deservedly expelling man from that most pleasant paradise – in which, if he had persevered in justice and fairness, man would have enjoyed the sweetest leisure for contemplation – said that you shall eat your bread in the sweat of your brow [Genesis 3:19]. Subsequently he confirmed this figuratively, when he commanded in Deuteronomy [25:4] that an ox should not have his mouth muzzled while threshing. As Paul interpreted this in his Epistle to the Corinthians [I Corinthians 9:9], God did not so much express the care he has for cattle, as that men who work and are busy are worthy of eating bread, but those who do not work are not.

That is what Christ our Saviour himself teaches in the gospel, where he says that the labourer is worthy of his wage [Matthew 10:10] and where he criticizes those men standing idle in the forum, although they had excused their idleness because no-one was hiring them [Matthew 20]. And in his Epistle to the Thessalonians [II Thessalonians 3:6–10] Paul harshly rebuked certain brothers because, when they were idle and without work and disorderly, they were receiving alms from the people. Paul concluded that whoever does not work should not eat.

Although some people who are thoughtless and incautious in speech (not to call them by another name) have tried to interpret this passage adversely to religious mendicants, Paul there and elsewhere frequently and explicitly teaches that sowers of the spiritual can rightfully reap the temporal. But this is not the place for this digression; let us return to the proposed conclusion.

The same conclusion is approved by natural reason. Whoever does not have wealth of his own from which to live has no right to seek what belongs to someone else, unless by his skill or by some other labour or by what he does he can serve others in turn. On either grounds God and nature have looked out for human affairs by wisely arranging that there should be both rich and poor; that is, that the rich should be like the soul that governs the body, and the poor should be like the body that serves the soul by cultivating the earth and exercising the skills without which human life could not be conducted. For, as Aristotle wrote in the tenth book of *On the Nature of Animals*, God and nature have never made anything in vain. Therefore, those who waste their lives in idleness live against the law of nature. Thence, as is attested by Seneca in *Ad Lucilius* Book XIX and by Cicero in Book II of the *De Natura Deorum*, men who live idly are as if they did not exist. And the philosopher Demetrius calls idle men "the Dead Sea." Accordingly, even grandees – who exact tribute from their subordinates – can rightly accept it only because of the care, the skilfulness, and, if necessary, the great exertions that they undergo in governing their subordinates. Why, even princes – as the Emperor has found in his long experience of brilliant achievements, and as you, celebrated Prince, are just now beginning to experience – have an entirely deserved right to the revenues that are conferred upon them by the state because, as was famously said [Horace, *Epistles* 2, 1], they bear the burden of many great labours in defending the state with arms, adorning it with morals, and improving it with laws.

The following is the third reason for the aforementioned conclusion. As Solomon says [Ecclesiasticus 33:29], idleness teaches much evil. He explains the cause of this in another proverb [Proverbs 21:26]. For since an idle person is always pregnant with cravings, to what else could he give birth except evil and iniquity? The first thing immediately annexed to the habit of seeking what belongs to another is adulation. What is next broken is the sense of shame, which is the bridle that holds men back from the precipice of vice. Thirdly the flesh is softened to lust. For as the poet famously wrote [Ovid, *Remedia Amoris* 139], "Remove idleness, and Cupid's bow is broken." Fourth, the vagabond's begging is the teacher of stealing.

In short, since this class of lost men has no interaction or business with people of higher quality by whom they might be imbued with good morals, it happens that they readily forget the whole Christian religion and proceed to besmirch and contaminate others with the colouring with which they have been infected. For this reason, Plato in the *Republic* says that idleness is the pestilence of mortals; because of this he most accurately provides that there should be no one in the Republic who lives a life of idleness. And among our saintly theologians, Jerome, as is recorded in *Ad Rusticum, de consecratione, dist V, cap. Numquam*, warned that the shield that protects us against the weapons of the devil is if that adversary never finds us idle. And Augustine in the letter *Ad Vercellenses* [Ambrose, Epistle 63, 99] says "There is no fruit of idleness that is not a greater loss. Idle Esau lost the blessing of his birthright because he preferred to accept food rather than to seek it." And Chrysostom, *Super Ioannem*: "We are made perverse by idleness; not working is wont to corrupt us." And Seneca in his *De Clementia*, "Idleness softens our strength, as rust does iron. A motionless torch is inert, shaking it restores its fire" [Seneca, *Controversiae* 2, 2, 8]. And among the many other notable testimonies that can easily be accumulated to this effect, the prophet Ezekiel [16:49], after a long execration of the Jerusalemites in which he lays bare the source of all evils, says "Behold, this was the iniquity of your sister Sodom; she and her daughters had pride, excess of food, abundance and idleness; and they did not stretch forth their hand to the needy and the poor."

Instructed by these and other testimonies and arguments, everyone who instituted the state with written precepts or governed it with famous deeds wanted idle people of this sort removed from its midst. According to the statement of

Solomon [Proverbs 10:26], they were like acid for the teeth and smoke for the eyes. Thus, Aristotle in Book VII of the *Politics* divides the state into those who are idle and those who are not. He instructs those of outstanding intelligence, whom he calls "free," to be idle in that they are exempt from the mechanical skills and other bodily labours of that sort. Some of these sit at the helm of the state, others are in charge of military affairs, others apply themselves to the study of books, and still others are devoted to divine worship. But those whose capacities lie more in physical strength than intelligence – the servile multitude – should, he said, be allowed no idleness, but should always be occupied in labour and work. For this reason, as the philosopher recounts, the Spartans, who were savage warriors, trained their young men in arms and military matters perhaps more than was right. And in contrast, as Livy says, Numa Pompilius, the second king of the Romans, a man of peaceful and religious disposition, instituted so many sacrifices and ceremonies not only for the worship of the gods, but especially so that those who had become inured to war should not luxuriate in idleness of spirit.

To proceed now to the common law, this is the reason that the emperor Justinian enacted a law (Codex Book I) with the title "Concerning Able-bodied Beggars" [Justinian, *Codex* 11, 26]. This law deals with persons who, although they are not only healthy but strong enough to work, make up and simulate an infirmity with which they wander over the world begging, thereby wrongly usurping the alms of the legitimate poor. Furthermore, the law gives anyone the power and the ability to enslave persons of that sort if they are of servile condition, and to press them into the condition of a *colonus perpetuus* [a tenant farmer tied hereditarily to the land] if they are free. Approximately the same thing is prescribed in the *Authenticum (De quaesitore* 2, collation VI) [*Corpus Juris Civilis, Novellae* 80] that the quaesitor should take care to examine the identity and condition of newcomers to the city, and to have them readily explain the causes of the business or the chance that has brought them into the city. If they wish to remain and are capable and suitable for work, they should be compelled to work. If the are of servile status, they should be transferred to their owners.

From this are derived the particular laws of the kingdom. The forefathers of Your Highness confirmed that on this matter they would subscribe to the common law. First, among those laws called *Partidas* (*Partida* II, tit. 20) is an edict that approves of the law Concerning Able-bodied Beggars. Such "sobeiani" – as the law calls them – and vagabonds are to be excluded from the state as enemies. The same is prescribed, though in more words, by another law among those called the Ordinance: Book VIII, Title XV, first law, promulgated in Briviesca in 1387 AD. That law refers to a new harm (in addition to those we mentioned above) that the state suffers from vagabonds, that is, when a crowd of idle persons is allowed, the fields lie empty of farm workers and the state suffers from a shortage of craftsmen. Moderating the rigour of the penalty decreed for vagabonds under the law Concerning Able-bodied Beggars, the law gives anyone the power to force the vagabond into personal service for a whole month without pay except for food; or he can be flogged and banished from the city.

These, most righteous Prince, are what divine and natural law and subsequently positive and common law and the particular law of the kingdom have most justly established about driving out the vagabonds. In my view, these sufficiently support and confirm the first conclusion, that is, that vagabonds are not to be permitted, as the Emperor wisely ordered by public edict at the Cortes in Madrid in 1534 and frequently elsewhere.

Chapter IV
On Foreign Beggars

Next, we should consider the second member of the above-mentioned list of articles: Is it permissible for any person – provided that he is a genuine pauper and not a fake one – to leave his native borders and go to beg anywhere in the kingdom, or on the contrary can beggars be prohibited by law and restricted within those borders, as is said in the aforementioned petitions of the kingdom to the Emperor? I would be apprehensive speaking about this if a law of the Emperor had already been promulgated and had long been in use, although even then, if it was advantageous, the just Emperor and the wise Council could change the law. For no injury is done to the laws if they change with the temper of the times. But not only has that law not been put into practice, but – if one examines the Council's resolution of 1540 – it was not enacted with the status of a law. I therefore consider it an act of deference to present these considerations, such as they are, to Your Highness.

First of all, these petitions are something new about which no law was ever anywhere proposed or enacted. Nor do I fear that I am rash to affirm this, but all laws divine and human will attest to it. That is certainly a great and very valid argument against this novelty. For you may certainly believe, most illustrious Prince, that if this matter was as much in accord with what was fair and good as they think, antiquity would never have been so improvident as not to have enacted a law about it. But the contrary is what the common and the particular law of the kingdom admonish, what natural reason persuades, and what Holy Scripture explicitly preaches.

The aforementioned *Authenticum de quaesitore* provides for an examination of the causes and the business that brought the foreigners, and it prescribes that when this is executed, the able-bodied and strong either be sent back to their native lands or be compelled to work. It then sets out an exception in these words: "We order that men and women who are injured in body or hoary of head be allowed to remain in our city without disturbance." No further distinction is made between natives and foreigners.

In the law that we Spanish call the Ordinance, to which I referred just now, there is an express provision. For after it provides that vagabonds are to be sent into exile, it then exempts those who are so old or crippled or sickly that it can be surmised from their appearance that they cannot sustain themselves by physical work or labour. These persons the law permits to beg with impunity, without distinguishing between citizen and foreigner. King Henry subsequently reconfirmed this law word for word in his edict in Toro.

For this reason I cannot understand how from these common laws or laws of the kingdom it can be inferred that borders and boundary lines are prescribed for beggars beyond which they are not free to beg. Up to this point no law distinguished foreign from resident paupers – provided they actually are paupers; all of them distinguished only between fake and feigned paupers and legitimate ones. For this reason, if one may conjecture, both His Imperial Majesty and his Royal Council delayed for seventeen years to give a certain response to these Supplications, which they suspected proceeded not so much from a Christian feeling toward legitimate paupers as from being fed up with beggars.

Nor against this can it be objected that Petition 117 was answered in the Cortes in Madrid in 1534, in which it was clearly declared that vagabonds should be subject to punishment by law. Concerning legitimate paupers, the Emperor added that they should be taken care of in their respective dioceses, preferring royal clemency to legal harshness. When he made this subject to the condition that those who were abundantly provided with necessaries should not be permitted to beg, that just prescription did not differentiate foreigners and residents. Nor did the Council in 1540 want to ordain anything else than that if it was clearly established that everything was abundantly available to paupers at home, they would not be permitted to beg. But never were legitimate paupers subject to a penalty, no matter where they were begging, whether in their own homeland or elsewhere.

At this point, subject to correction by more knowledgeable men, one can conclude that paupers who are truly in need cannot be expelled from any part of the kingdom, but just like natives and residents, are either to be permitted to beg or are to be maintained in some other way. In my humble opinion I can affirm this conclusion for five or six reasons.

Apart from the testimonies that I will submit from the Holy Scriptures, the first is this: no one except someone who is an enemy or subverter of the state or who has committed some crime or some shameful act can be kept from any town. The reason for this is obvious. For since by the law of nature and of nations roads and cities are open to everyone without discrimination, no one can by right be prevented from staying wherever he wishes, except because of his fault. That is why exile is among the harshest penalties of the law, to the extent that in the passage *Capitalium, De Poenis* [*Digest* 48, 19, 28], it is considered if not completely capital, at least the closest thing to it. And although sending a foreigner back to his native soil is not a harsh exile, it is nonetheless a violation of the right whereby anyone can stay wherever he wishes. Therefore, since for legitimate paupers begging is not directly a crime or shameful act, there is certainly no right by which they can be ejected from any town as long as they themselves wish to stay there.

The second reason is perhaps more evident. Princes or the state cannot enact laws about alms that restrict citizens by a greater fetter than the laws of nature and the gospel. To explain this point: there is a dispute among theologians. Some teach that the precept, whether natural or divine, that one commits a mortal sin by not giving alms does not apply except to *extreme* necessity. Others add that people are bound to give alms on pain of mortal sin out of what is superfluous for each person's status and condition not only then but in *grave* necessity. Saint Thomas, among others, holds this view. But even in this case [i.e., when the necessity is grave but not extreme] no one is necessarily bound to give to a particular person or at a particular time, but it is enough if someone contributes from his superfluity to some needy persons at some time.

To these laws the prince can add no other, except to compel alms by threat of penalty when the necessity is extreme. However, beyond that case he cannot compel alms under a penalty, because the gospel's precept does not extend more widely than what obliges under mortal sin.

Nonetheless, even those who are not under extreme or grave necessity have the right to beg for the relief of some other necessity. To assist these is the virtue and function of mercy. Nor did the Emperor or the Council, when it enacted that paupers be supported in their own respective territories, intend to compel citizens to support their paupers generously so that they would not need to beg, but ordered only that endowments for hospitals should be exacted from their debtors. But it added within its order that the diocesan and city authorities should do their best to somehow keep the paupers sustained within their own homelands.

From this the following second reason can be inferred. No one of any authority or power can restrict paupers from departing from where they live in order to go begging, unless he compels citizens by law to feed and clothe paupers and to minister to their other necessaries not only out of mercy but as their due. For if he restrained the poor with a tighter fetter than could open the purses of the wealthy, he would compel these unfortunates to suffer extreme deprivation. But the prince cannot so harshly force citizens to support the beggars; at least, he has not done it so far. Therefore, he cannot shut them up in their own territories. For even if the harshest law was enacted – that all bishoprics should, on pain of severe penalty, support their own impoverished citizens – they still would not provide for all of them; the paupers would then be free of the edict and would be able to go wherever they wanted to beg. For how, I ask, can the law prohibit the paupers from leaving their homelands if doing that is neither a crime nor a wrong? And how can it be a wrong, if necessaries are not copiously provided for themselves and their families?

The third reason, which casts more light on the preceding one, is this: just as within the walls of a single city some are rich and others are poor, and within the borders of the same bishopric some towns overflow with riches and goods and others struggle with want and need, so in the whole kingdom some bishoprics are very prosperous, for instance, where the soil is more fertile and the earth is more unstintingly productive or the population is more wealthy through commerce, and others are infertile and impoverished. Therefore, just as rich citizens are obligated to sustain the paupers of that city with alms, and the richer towns the paupers of other places in that bishopric – as the authors of those petitions acknowledge – so the rich bishoprics cannot exclude foreign paupers of infertile regions. Now the inference is clear. For just as a city and a bishopric, so also is the whole kingdom one body and one state of which all the cities are members. For why, if this ever occurred to you, most wise Prince, did God place fertile and fat fields, supplemented by the kingdom of Toledo, adjacent to the borders of Asturias and of the mountainous regions that he had inserted into that stony, thin, and infertile soil, unless to relieve the want of some with the fertility of others? Nor is it sufficient to say that this applies when famine or some other grave calamity happens. Not only the extremely indigent, but others also suffer from needs for the relief of which they have a right to beg. In the Royal Council of Your Highness, where so many thousands of ducats are paid out, how are not many more beggars to be admitted than in another entire province where the house of any prelate or grandee suffices to feed more beggars than any hundred other citizens? When unfortunate people of this sort are regarded as worms in the state and are trampled underfoot, they should at least be permitted to ascend with the ants to the treetops looking for food.

When I just now seemed to regard only one kingdom as a single body, I was speaking "by way of indulgence," as Paul says [I Corinthians 7:6]. I would add that under Christ's law, entry from one kingdom to another is available to paupers. For when the Apostle taught the Corinthians [I Corinthians 12:13] that we are all members of a single body, he did not reduce the metaphor to the confines of a single kingdom, but, he said, "we have all been baptized by a single spirit into a single body." It is not the case that only one kingdom is also one body. Rather, by a single baptism we Christians are all reborn into a single body, so that we are each reciprocally the various limbs, differentiated by diverse functions and duties, of a single entity.

Just as in the Greek tales where the blind man carried the lame one on his shoulders so that the lame man would in turn direct the steps of the blind one, so among Christians the intelligent ought to be the eyes of the ignorant, and the physically strong should be the arms and legs of the crippled, but the rich who have the wealth of this world are obligated to act as stomach to the poor, so that Christ should then be the head of all. Nor for Paul is there according to the gospel [Romans 10:12] any distinction in Christ between Jews and Greeks, for everyone has the same lord. Indeed, if the matter is referred up to the law of nature, humankind is by its own nature joined in so tight a bond that, unless they are our enemies or we fear from them some harm to our faith, even mendicant infidels may not be expelled from our state.

The fourth reason is this. Beside the fact that some provinces of the kingdom have greater wealth than others, some peoples are more merciful towards paupers than are others; indeed, out of avarice or even cruelty some are extremely stingy about giving alms. And since men cannot be constrained to give alms otherwise than as I have explained above, paupers would be treated cruelly if these unfortunates were not allowed to betake themselves from one province to another. Add that because of an inclement climate infirm and sickly paupers very often find it necessary to seek a region where they can more healthfully refresh themselves. And continuous and frequent solicitations by the same pauper may engender weariness in the inhabitants of a particular city, whatever the reason for being an annoyance, so that he is compelled to move to another area. Add that perhaps he has enemies there or some other opportunity for wrongdoing or he has done something for which he fears punishment. Nor can he rightfully be compelled to explain why he left his homeland any more than if he were wealthy.

The fifth reason is taken from the right of hospitality. In antiquity there never was a nation or a state in which this was not greatly valued and religiously cultivated. Plato made hospitality the third part of friendship. Theophrastus, as referred to in Cicero, *De Officiis,* Book One [II, 18, 64], extolled it with the highest praise. The pagans even honoured their own Jupiter, whom they worshipped as the best and greatest of the gods, with the name Hospitalis. Under that name they erected temples and altars to Jupiter, because he was the judge and fiercest avenger of the violation of the right of guests.

And so as not to seek testimonies only from pagans, Paul in his Epistle to the Hebrews [13:2] says, "Do not forget hospitality, for through this some have unknowingly welcomed angels." He alludes to the hospitality with which both Abraham and Lot received the angels, on the merit of which Lot and his family escaped the destruction of Sodom. Of such honour did God think hospitality worthy that he dispatched angels to earth to receive the benefit of hospitality. And because of the duty of hospitality Rahab the harlot in Jericho was saved from the destruction and sacking of her city. Because of this there are many rules by which guests are committed to the trust of Christians. So, if the duty of hospitality was always so celebrated, with what greater praise and merit, I ask, can Christians show themselves to be hospitable than to the needy and the mendicant? Hospitality is practised not so much to our own inhabitants and citizens as to newcomers and foreigners. For although one has a duty to accept any needy person under one's roof, the word hospitality properly applies to newcomers.

And finally, to confirm this conclusion with scriptural testimonies, never in Holy Scripture do we read of any distinction between native persons and foreigners, provided that they are paupers. Rather, everywhere does the Sacred Communication commend to us with equal right and importance paupers who are foreign and native. First, in Exodus 24 [23:9], God says, "You shall not oppress the stranger, for you know the heart of the stranger because you too were strangers in the land of Egypt." And Leviticus 23 [23:22], "When you harvest the produce of your land, you shall not cut it down to the right the ground, nor shall you collect the gleanings that remain, but you will leave them to the poor and the strangers." And Deuteronomy 10 [10:18–19], "God loves the stranger and gives him food and clothing; therefore, you are to love the stranger." And a little later, in Chapter 14 [14:21], "Give it to the stranger who is within your gates to eat, or sell it to him," the former if he is a pauper, the latter if he has the means to buy it. And most importantly of all, among those things about which Christ our Saviour warns us that he will exact an account, one (and not the least) is whether we hospitably received a stranger in need of lodging [Matthew 25:35].

Therefore, I ask, let those who drive away foreign paupers respond to me. If we both eliminate the vagabonds and are inhospitable to foreign paupers, who is left toward whom we can exercise this mercy, unless they perhaps say rich and illustrious men who are the guests of their peers. But although this may be a duty, I do not think that these are the people to whom Christ alluded when, among other acts of mercy to the poor, he also listed hospitality. Therefore, unless I am mistaken, I think that the poor have a right to go and beg anywhere in the kingdom. Nor is it enough that they be maintained for two or three days, if they wish to stay there longer.

Chapter V
Response to Objections

I have never seen any law that contradicts this, unless what I hear has recently been instituted in Ypres in Flanders is considered a law. There, among other ordinances instituted in a wise and Christian manner, it was decreed that the city should not be open to foreign paupers. However, not every example is to be regarded as a law. They say that the professors in Paris have subscribed to the decree, which I could certainly never believe. For what they could approve is only this, that they are not bound to provide for all of them. But that they are not to be admitted into the city – there is no way that the Parisians or anyone else learned in the Holy Scriptures or in law could have affirmed that.

The greatest testimony that could be adduced by those who assert that paupers can legitimately be restricted to their native borders is from the Second Council of Tours, celebrated under Pelagius I almost one thousand years ago. To quote from Chapter V of that document: "That each city should feed its poor and needy inhabitants with suitable food according to its ability, that the neighbourhood presbyters as well as all citizens should support the poor so that they will not be wearied by going to other cities." However, this most fair and holy decree manifestly supports us rather than the opposite opinion, for paupers are not here prohibited from freely going out anywhere to beg. In favour of the poor, each city is admonished to maintain its local poor, to prevent them (as it says) from being wearied by going to other cities. Nor is this a new posited precept, that each city should appropriately maintain its native inhabitants; they are merely admonished according to gospel truth to so conduct themselves in relation to the poor that they do not force these unfortunates to seek food elsewhere. In those days the poor were treated by the prelates with such care, by their subordinates with such charity, and by everyone with such kindness that not only did they not have to go elsewhere to beg but they did not have to beg even in their homeland, unless the city was so impoverished that it did not have enough to support its poor.

This is what we read especially in Cyprian. To quote Book 1, Epistle 10: "If a church there" (he was speaking about an impoverished city) "does not have enough to provide food to those who are suffering, they can transfer themselves to us, so that they can receive food and clothing here." And in Book 3, Epistle 10: "Meanwhile have as much care as possible for the poor, so that through your diligence expenditures can be made for them to tolerate their poverty." And Epistle 23: "I ask you to diligently have care for the infirm and all the poor. And make expenditures also for indigent foreigners from my own money … In case that money has already all been spent, I have sent another portion so that the beneficence to those who are suffering might be larger and quicker." About this, more below.

I have adduced these passages only to show how the primitive church, still moist and inflamed with the blood of Christ, took care that the poor should not wander to foreign places. It did not fence them in from leaving by any boundaries or prohibitions, but it so took thought for their needs that they were not forced to leave.

Accordingly, I cannot sufficiently marvel that the Emperor was requested to ask for a papal bull that would prevent paupers from begging outside their native soil. For how would the Pope have granted a document of this sort, unless both the Pope and the Emperor had by a most stringent precept so obligated every city to support its poor that that they could be compelled through the praetors – just as with other taxes – to contribute the appropriate food, clothing, and other necessaries to the paupers, as I said above? This law, as I was implying there, could neither be justly enacted nor conveniently put into practice. But about this, still more later.

The reasons that might have led the authors of those petitions to believe that they were seeking only fairness could have been something like this: First, they could have pleaded that a province is obligated not to the paupers of another province but only each to its own; otherwise, the burden of the poor would unfairly weigh more on one province than on another. But this reasoning has a twofold weakness. First, as can be inferred from what we have already said, we grant that no binding rule places a province under an obligation to the paupers of another province; this is because one is compelled to bestow a benefit only when the person seeking it is under extreme necessity. But it does not immediately follow from this that the beggar can be confined to his home to prevent him from having the right – without detriment to anyone's freedom – to entreat and move anyone anywhere to mercy through his plea. Moreover, the more persons of wealth there are in a province by reason of God's having distributed the goods of fortune to them more fruitfully and plentifully, the more bountiful are the alms they owe to the poor of Christ regardless of origin. Otherwise, God as the lord of all would not prudently have provided for human life.

But perhaps someone will reply that by the manner and order of charity we have a greater and prior obligation to those to whom we are connected by blood or some other relationship, and so to our fellow citizens, than we have to strangers. That is what Paul taught the Galatians when he said [Galatians 6:10]: "While we have time, let us do good to all, especially to those in the household of believers." The response to this is, first, that Paul admonished us to be beneficent not only to our family, but to all those of any nation or condition. The verse teaches us only that if the opportunity to do more is not present, we should start with those who are closer to us.

A further response is to pay more careful attention to what the verse says. It is one thing to be more fully obligated to one's own than to others, as Paul teaches. It is quite another to deprive foreigners and outsiders of their right to ask for alms from anyone, especially among Christians; this is never permitted.

Perhaps while a city is so beset with extreme need and famine that it cannot provide for itself, it has the right to keep foreigners away because it suffers from extreme want, although even in such a time I could scarcely advise it. Rather, when a calamitous famine is ravaging the entire kingdom, everyone has the right to seek food wherever it can be found. But it would be sufficient to admonish the populace at that time that whoever could not help everyone should first help his own.

The other reason that is offered to make this petition plausible is that there are people who, although they can live from what they have, move somewhere else, pretend they are poor, and fraudulently usurp alms that could better be allocated to the legitimate paupers who live there. And moreover, they spread contagious diseases and pestilences from one region to another. And other similar inconveniences are referred to in these petitions.

I acknowledge what is perfectly obvious: there is no status or order of persons among whom there are not good and bad, honest and dishonest, as I will elaborate shortly and in its proper place. Nonetheless, because it is permissible to be of every status and condition, the bad should be punished in a way that does not inflict injustice on any status. Since the condition of being a pauper is permissible among us – even paupers who are outsiders and foreigners – it should be sufficient that whenever fake paupers are apprehended they should suffer punishment, just as happens by law and custom for all other orders of people. This is not a reason for completely uprooting foreign paupers. This is especially true because persons of means in their hometowns so rarely move elsewhere in order to fraudulently beg, that no law is needed for such a small number. Nor is there any reason to fear that any province or city may ever be impoverished by a multitude of poor people.

As for the allegation about contagion, foreigners do not often transmit these diseases. But a throng of poor people at any place, even of native poor, not infrequently is the cause of disease and pestilence.

Beyond this no argument comes to mind that anyone could plausibly make against outsiders and foreigners who are legitimate paupers.

Chapter VI
On Pilgrims to Santiago

Immediately attached to this article is the one about pilgrims who go to Santiago: they are not to tarry long on the road or deviate from the direct route more than twelve miles. So that my speaking may not seem to contaminate everything, I do not want to waste many words on this. The following brief remarks will suffice.

First, because this pilgrimage is an honourable and religious work, and certainly not the least of all those that pertain to the worship of God, it is not fitting to make any decision that appears to be offensive toward the pilgrimage just because one or two people play the vagabond while dressed as a pilgrim. This is especially because it is foreign pilgrims more than others who come to us out of religious feeling. Because of this we could scandalize other kingdoms by constraining the pilgrims to proceed like cattle along roads that are marked out and enclosed.

Add the barrenness of the route, on which so large a throng of pilgrims can scarcely be fed, even though by the right of both hospitality and religion they ought to be refreshed more lavishly and generously. Moreover, in the innermost parts of the kingdom are other stations, to which one should turn off out of religious respect.

Moreover, if any should happen to desire to visit the Court of Your Highness or other principal cities of the kingdom, would it not show a lack of courtesy and even of humanity to bar them from roads or alms? I believe without doubt that they could accuse us of having violated the law of nations, even if they could then determine in advance the time of their return to their own lands. I think that the Council decided only that those who carelessly or otherwise were long tarrying in the kingdom dressed as pilgrims should be sent back to where they lived, pursuant to the *Authentiticum de quaesitore*, for then they are to be adjudged to be vagabonds. Only these people were the ones whom His Imperial Majesty in 1534 ordered removed from the Court.

These, most virtuous Prince, are the matters that seemed worth bringing forward in the first part of this disputation, where I proposed discussing what according to the laws can permissibly or impermissibly be decided concerning the poor. My intention was to convince you (I do not know if I succeeded) that exactly what had to be decided about paupers was whether they were legitimate or whether they were fake and feigned. In neither case is it permitted by law to further distinguish whether they are native and resident or whether they are foreign and outsiders. For if they are legitimate the outsiders and foreigners have a right to beg without discrimination. All that the order of charity demands is that if they cannot give alms to everyone, they should (all other things being equal) give first to the resident poor, provided that the others do not have their right to beg erased. In contrast, the pseudo-paupers, whether native or foreign, are to be driven out as idlers.

Chapter VII
On the End Applicable to Arrangements about the Poor

The theme of the second part of this *Deliberatio* is: for the measures that are legally permissible to institute and carry out regarding the poor, by what reasoning and method might they be improved and brought closer to the Christian religion? Above we included the six reported articles about what is to be decided with respect to the poor: First, that no one should beg without the legitimacy of his poverty being examined. Second, that one can beg only on one's native soil. Third, that this is permitted to no one without a certificate. Fourth, that certificates are granted only to those who have confessed in church. The fifth is about the pilgrims to Santiago. The sixth and most notable of all is that paupers should not be allowed to beg in the streets from door to door. The second and fifth of these have been dealt with so fully, I think, that they need not be brought back into the discussion. The first, about the examination, has the authority of right, as was evident in the third chapter. The only thing that is called into doubt is exactly how this examination is to take place. Accordingly, our treatment should include the third and fourth articles. Finally, the last place is left to the sixth article.

First of all, we must determine the end to which the entire account and duty with respect to the poor ought to be referred. This is what Aristotle frequently tells us. For he says in *Ethics* VII [1151a16] that in every act and likewise in every deliberation, the end is first of all. As he had said in Book I [1094a23], in every exercise of wisdom and foresight it is like the target towards which the archer directs the arrow. From this he infers in Book V [VI, 1142b35] that the means should be assessed according to the end, that is, that one should consider the suitability of means to end. Because of this Cicero [*De Inventione* 1, 5] says that one must first posit, as more significant than the content of oratory, the end toward which oratory's entire function refers.

In the issue at hand, it first should not be the case that those petitions, regulations, and considerations proceed from the weariness and nausea that the appearance and improper behaviour of beggars are wont to inspire in certain fastidious people of the present age. Aside from this wise and equitable Royal Council – in whom there could be only a sacred intention and evangelical zeal to give a wise response to so improper a demand – those whom I know who have the responsibility of dealing with this matter have a heart full of mercy and piety in order better to consult the interests of the legitimate poor and of those who are perishing of hunger.

Nonetheless, the words of these laws cannot fail to cause unease in the suspicious. Among the leading authors there were perhaps some – so that we do not cast blame and suspicion on all – who devised these holy laws not so much to better allocate alms, as to free themselves of the throng and the trouble of beggars. If Ambrose or certainly if Chrysostom had heard that this unfortunate condition and rank of the poor had been hedged around with so many laws – that only those who had been diligently examined and had first confessed and had a certificate and were within their native borders and were shut up at home would be able to receive the paltry stipend with which they could barely carry on their lives – they would think only that these laws had been devised out of hatred for this unfortunate group. And so that we do not say hatred, at least they do not exhibit the heart and inner feelings that Christ, the father of the poor, wished us to have toward his poor children.

To the extent you deem fit, distinguished and celebrated Prince, one must take care that the term "mendicant poor" not become hateful to Christians or be considered a term of denigration or mockery. Clearly on that awful day those very persons who hold it in disrespect will be – as is written in the Wisdom of Solomon [5:2–5] – "terrified with horrible fear and amazed at the suddenness of unexpected salvation" – when they see the fortunes and vicissitudes of rich and poor so completely changed. Then he says, "Groaning in anguish and repenting within themselves" they will confess in these words: "These were those whom we once held in derision and like a reproach. We foolishly accounted their lives a madness and their end without honour. Behold, now they are numbered among the children of God, and their lot is among the saints."

Indeed, inasmuch as the rank of the poor had been commended to Christians under no other name, and this name was considered honoured and most beloved precisely because Christ our Saviour (who must be believed to have chosen only the best rank of mortals) selected the rank and condition of a poor man, this term was amply glorious. Add that in the Holy Scriptures he never speaks well of the wealthy, whereas the whole gospel is replete with verses that favour, privilege, and commend the poor. Not that the status of princes and the order of other persons who are invested with office and power are not given the greatest approval in the Gospel. For as Paul teaches [Romans 13:1], because every power is from the Lord God, it is most right that they be regarded with the greatest honour and worth.

And yet Christ nowhere considered an abundance of riches and of goods of fortune as worthy of honour as he did poverty. We may pass over the royal psalmist who in this verse [Psalms 72:4] where he prophesies the coming of Christ says

that "He will judge the poor of the people and will save the sons of the needy."
And so that the patience of the poor may not pass away but he may hearken to
their desire, Christ our Saviour takes as the exordium of his prophecy the crushing
of the error of those who located happiness in great wealth and fortune. He says
[Matthew 5:3], "Happy are the poor in spirit, because theirs is the kingdom of
heaven." He calls the poor in spirit not only those who freely profess poverty in
a religious vow, but also those who bear indigence and begging with equanimity.
From the multitude of the poor he elevated those whom he established as princes
of the world and givers of laws. To avoid making a nuisance of myself by mentioning all the verses, I will say only that Christ never compared the poor to the rich
except to honour the poor.

In the nascent Church the apostles who had been instructed by Christ attached
such worth to the poor that James [2:2] wrote that if a man comes into our meeting wearing a gold ring and dressed in white, and a poor person comes in with
filthy clothing, we should not stand up more for the rich man than for the poor
man; otherwise, he says, we would make unjust distinctions among persons. The
apostles instructed the Christians that – except for those who hold office – we
should value and assess persons solely according to the merit of their virtue. For
regard for this is to be had only when, after the completion of the comedy of this
world and the laying down of the masks that make an appearance, the truth of
their merits will be revealed. Can we more sublimely praise the fate of the poor?

Since according to David's testimony [Psalms 15:2], God does not stand in
need of our goods, he thought up a marvellous device for needing the assistance of
the wealthy. He did not think it sufficient to say that "what you have done to one
of the least of my brethren you have done *for* me," and I will recompense you, although putting it this way would have been an excellent commendation for giving
alms; but what he said [Matthew 25:40] was "What you have done to one of the
least of my brethren you have done *to* me." For I am that famished person whom
you fed and clothed, and that naked person whom you took in as a guest. And
that not only in this world, where divine majesty deigned to assume the role of a
pauper, but on that day on which he will manifestly demonstrate his boundless
majesty to all the orders in the heavens, on earth, and below the earth, then, I say,
he will not disdain to confess that he lived among us as an indigent and a beggar.

Take it in good part, Prince laden with all the adornments of the virtues, if I
have digressed slightly to celebrate the name of the poor; in my judgment this
contributes greatly to the present purpose.

To return to the point from which we digressed, it will not be sufficient if the
prescribed end for this enterprise was that by driving out the vagabonds the state
should be relieved of the burden of alms.

For it is not necessary just for the sake of this that so much attention be given
and that so many officials be appointed who are learned in so many laws. For in
the state there are people who, through illicit contracts and even through fraud

and trickery, filch what belongs to others in much greater quantities, without having contrivances of this sort arrayed against them.

I would add that unless the alms that on this basis are taken away from the vagabonds accrue in their entirety to the legitimate paupers, so that the order of paupers, purged of the vagabonds, is held in greater worth and is loaded up with larger alms, the rich would suffer a loss from the removal of the vagabonds rather than a gain. For whatever alms they now give, they do not fulfil the just measure of their obligation. If, therefore, all that the state would achieve from these laws is that alms would decrease, it would be very clear that those whom mercy does not suffice to make more receptive to the poor are not only overcome by the improbity of legitimate beggars but also deceived by the cleverness of fake ones.

Nor is it a sufficiently just end of these institutions to improve the morals of the poor. For if the poor had the opportunity, they would surely find more to correct in us. Moreover, it is enough, as I will say at greater length a bit farther on, if the secular and ecclesiastical eminences who attend to the rich also undertake this care toward the poor. Yet I would not disapprove if those who have charge of the poor in temporal matters also incidentally paid attention to their morals.

Therefore, the principal end and target of the institutions that deal with the poor is that alms should better provide for genuine paupers, that is, that they should receive greater temporal assistance and that alms should on this basis increase rather than decrease. This is the end toward which all the regulations should precisely be referred. And whatever is more conducive to securing this should be chosen and carried out.

Chapter VIII
On the Obligation to Give Alms Incumbent on Christians

With this placed before our eyes like a target, it is next worthwhile to forewarn that the wealthy do not contribute the alms that help the poor from the goods they own so much as is commonly thought. The alms are owed to the poor under a far greater obligation than people realize. God, the most provident of all, who takes care not only to bring forth hay for beasts of burden, but he puts the hay itself which lives today and tomorrow into a vessel, and he clothes the lilies of the field so beautifully that even Solomon in all his splendour was not so attired [Matthew 6:29]. He would never have been so neglectful of the human race that he would have left paupers among the very wealthy as destitute of assistance as we now find happens among Christians. Accordingly, unless he ever permits it to be a calamity to its possessors, he provided that the wealthy abound in goods not so that the goods would overflow, but so that the excess would flow out to the poor and needy.

Nor did he arrange this without the most profound deliberation. His goal was to tie the human race in a tighter relationship and, as it were, in a knot of charity, that is, that they would be like members of a body who by their own nature so dearly love one another that they reciprocally sustain one another's activity; and even that they would recognize that rich and poor have the same lord and father, since he had appointed the rich as stewards of the poor. Similarly, in the composition of the natural world, God wanted the earth to be naturally subject to the heavenly motions, so that they might dispense their goodness to it. From this the theologians adduce the most powerful argument in favour of a single God, because the parts of the universe hold themselves so amiably in a reciprocal embrace of friendship that they would never love each other so dearly without having shared the same beginning. Therefore, the apostle John [I John 3:17] (according to Christ, the greatest teacher of love) is absolutely certain that he who has the wealth of this world and sees his brother in need, can by no means be in God's love.

From this Saint Thomas wisely inferred not only that almsgiving is a matter of precept for those in extreme need, as Ambrose, cited in *Decretum* dist. 86, admonishes with the words: "Feed the person dying of hunger; if you did not feed him, you killed him." The Saintly Doctor even adds that people are obligated to give alms out of what is surplus for their present respective conditions.

The inference is manifest. If according to the gospel we are obligated to love our neighbours as ourselves, and if (as the apostle attests) a person having the wealth of this world and seeing his brother in need, does not love his brother, because he is not in [God's] love, a person of this sort transgresses the law and commits a mortal sin, because [God's] love is lost by this sin alone. Nor can anyone find an excuse under the colour of John's mention of the brother being in extreme necessity. For if he was speaking only of that kind of necessity, he would not have added "Whoever has the wealth of this world." For a person is obligated in the case of extreme necessity even if he does not have wealth, that is, an abundance of goods by which he can help. Accordingly, wealthy persons are sometimes obligated by precept to give alms even when there is no extreme necessity.

Moreover, this is corroborated by divine testimony. In Luke [3:9–11, where the story is told about John the Baptist rather than Jesus] Christ rebuked certain people because they bore no fruit of virtue, and just like a sterile tree should be cut down and thrown into the fire. When several of them asked how best they could guard against this danger, he responded that whoever had two tunics should give one to someone who did not have any, and whoever had food should do the same. Extreme necessity is not mentioned here. But in order to remove himself from the fire of Hell – into which one will be thrown only because of a mortal sin – he is ordered to share his goods with the poor. Nor is any great wealth required. But whoever has two tunics should give one to a person who has no tunic. This is because one tunic is ample for life; whoever has more is ordered to share with the needy.

To avoid seeming to thoroughly terrify the wealthy, the scholastic theologians mixed in many factors before they obligated people to give alms on pain of mortal sin, namely, that the rich should have a superfluity, that the poor should be in grave need, and other things of this sort. This is something that I do not intend to define succinctly and carefully, because I am not engaged in a scholastic dispute. But when I read the Holy Fathers attentively, I think that they wished to require alms on pain of mortal sin neither when the need of the paupers was so grave nor the superfluity over what fitted the status of the wealthy was so great. Rather, they perhaps believed that there was scarcely anyone, unless himself a pauper, who did not have something that he was obligated to give. If he did not have a thousand to spare, perhaps he had a hundred; if not a hundred, then at least ten. In short, who was there who could not give some assistance to the poor without prejudice to his own household?

Thence Ambrose says in his *On Luke*, in the canon *In singulis*, dist. 86: "The use and obligation of mercy are common to all. There is no exception for the soldier, nor for the farmer or city dweller; the rich and the poor, all are admonished in common that they should give to those who do not have. Mercy is the fullness of the virtues, and therefore presented to everyone as the form of perfect virtue." These are the words of Ambrose. As for the poverties of the unfortunate and the calamities with which they are afflicted that we consider light, I cannot but grievously fear that on the Day of Judgment it will be established that they had been the ones that we were obligated to relieve.

From this flows that peculiar expression in which the Holy Fathers call the avarice and stinginess of the rich toward the poor nothing less than theft and robbery. These are the words of Jerome in the canon *Hospitalem*, dist. 42 [*Decretum Gratiani*, dist. 86, c. 19]: "The person shown to retain for himself what is beyond his needs is guilty of stealing another's goods." And Ambrose, *On Luke*, in telling the parable of rich man who suddenly died while thinking that he would not give away his fruit but would pile it up. Ambrose added the even harsher words found in [*Decretum Gratiani*] *Sicut hi*, dist. 47. Expostulating with the rich man as to why he was holding on to what he should have given to paupers, he has the avaricious rich man make this answer: "What is the injustice in assiduously keeping your own property, provided that you do not encroach on another's?" To which Ambrose makes this riposte: "What a shameless thing to say! What do you call your own property? Of the things that you stored up, what did you bring into this world? ... Let no one call his own what is common, what would be more than enough for his own expenditure and has even been gained by violence. Is God unfair, that he unequally distributed the things that support life, so that you would be overflowing in wealth, but others would be lacking and in need? Or was it rather that he wanted to confer on you the experience of his generosity and to crown another for the virtue of patience?"

They wisely and (as they were) most piously thought that God gave these goods to the human race in common. These were subsequently distributed by the law of nations on the basis that in case of necessity everyone would have common use of everything. Is it at all surprising that the saints would have spoken this way, when (if Chrysostom, *Contione de Lazaro secunda* is to be believed) the very saying of Isaiah 3 [3:14] issued by the divine mouth, "What was robbed from the poor is in your houses" was to be interpreted as referring to the alms of the poor that the rich retained. The adornments of the rich that Isaiah mentions there with reproach, namely, the moon ornaments, the necklaces, the collars, the bracelets, the head-dresses, and all the other things of that sort are just the things that are stolen from the poor by being superfluous to the rich.

But beyond all this, two things about this matter strongly move me – and not only me but Augustine. The first is the famous statement of the Lord [Matthew 6:24; Luke 16:13] that "You cannot serve both God and money." Is this anything else but that you cannot at the same time give yourself over to the desire for wealth and have the great concern for mercy toward paupers that the Lord instructed you to have? The second is about what that most saintly and wise father greatly admires in the interpretation of the same passage. Although there are so many sins, crimes, and disgraceful acts for which people are to be condemned for all eternity, the only mention that the gospel makes of what is put forward as a cause of eternal damnation on the day of the Lord is that I was hungry and you did not feed me, I was thirsty and you gave me nothing to drink, I was naked and you did not cover me, I was a stranger and you did not receive me. This is what Augustine says [*Sermones de Scripturis*, LX, cap. 10].

If avarice did not keep us blind and if we were not snakes deaf to divine utter-ances, it is patently obvious that the injunction to give alms has much wider scope and includes many other occasions than people falsely persuade themselves. Oth-erwise, how on that day would the statement about the neglect of mercy envelop everyone generally?

Because this is not the place and I do not now intend to examine the matter in detail, it will be enough if I just add this final word. Let us represent God as the father of everyone both rich and poor, who like a paterfamilias is solicitous to do what is best for everyone and to provide for them. It necessarily follows either that God was improvident to leave the needy and the mendicant bereft of protec-tion or that the wealthy are to be held guilty of perfidy and inhumanity, because although God committed the poor to their trust and placed them within their power, they appropriate for themselves the goods entrusted to them, they repudi-ate what has been deposited with them, and they break their faith.

Chapter IX
On Examining the Poverty of Beggars

Instructed and informed by these fundamentals, we can now at last proceed to the first article, which is about the examination of the paupers. Although examination is in accordance with the law, the issue for deliberation is how rigorously it should be conducted.

The articles delineate two matters about which the paupers are to be examined. One is an examination of their poverty and need – whether they are genuine paupers or fake ones; the other is an examination of their morals and life.

The first is introduced in the third article, the other in the fourth article. So far as the first is concerned, it is equitable and worthwhile to remove fake and feigned beggars from among the poor. That was abundantly demonstrated in the first conclusion. But first of all, it is worth considering that being merciful to the paupers is one thing, and being just to the evil and iniquitous is another. God enjoins mercy on all men, but he delegates the punishment of malefactors to a small number of persons who administer justice. For this reason, as the Apostle attests [Romans 13:4], these bear a sword, to execute wrath on evildoers.

Because of this, we must attend to the question of whether it is sufficient that those who are set over the other orders of mankind, who administer justice, who emend morals, and who punish sins should also investigate, punish, and take charge of eliminating vagabonds. Or perhaps the cities' councillors and governors would every week or month gather together the beggars, and the ones they adjudged to be able-bodied they would subject to punishment or assign to work or expel from the city. For to set more officials as administrators against the poor than against the rich with their only task being to examine their poverty, to summon them to trial, to investigate them and drive them out – one could perhaps easily judge that this was done not so much out of mercy to the genuine paupers as out of hatred against the whole order of paupers, and this especially because the officials do not subject the crimes of the rich to such meticulous scrutiny, but discharge their duties sufficiently by chastising according to law those who are accused before them. Therefore, there is no need for a more searching enquiry against the poor.

Secondly, one should consider that persons of this unfortunate, abject, and weak class cannot defend themselves. Earlier we quoted Ecclesiasticus [13:3], "The rich man acts unjustly and roars, but the poor man when injured keeps silent"; and Ecclesiastes [9:16] says "The wisdom of the poor is held in contempt and his words are unheard." When a rich person is accused of some crime or debt, he defends himself in court or by arms or in some other way; a beggar, in contrast, even if falsely accused has no shield with which to defend himself but must put up with suffering a wrong. Add that if you wrongfully deprive a rich person of some of his property, he retains and lives off the rest; but if you were to prevent a calamitously suffering beggar from begging, you kill the unfortunate man.

For this reason, God in so many places professes to be the father of orphans, widows, and the poor. Because of this the Fathers of the Church (to cite the passages would be an immense labour) attached such great responsibility for the poor to the prelates, because a pauper can have no defence against someone powerful.

Because this class of unfortunates is full of jealousy and envy, you would scarcely find true testimony from them when enquiry is made into the poverty of anyone else. They would falsely accuse one another, each busying himself with the fraud by which what is taken from others will accrue to himself. For these reasons, these investigations and examinations should be delegated not to just anyone but to persons of standing and reputation, with a propensity more to the mildness of mercy than to the rigour of justice, who would support rather than oppose the poor. For if the administrators of this office are chosen from the common people who perhaps themselves conceal beneath their cloak the poverty that they enquire after in others, they can readily sell justice for a price, so that they may accuse of being able-bodied those who can give them nothing.

Third, in this matter one should note that a legitimate pauper is not necessarily an infirm one. It is sufficient that he be of advanced age or crippled or have some other impediment that prevents him from undergoing the labours sufficient to adequately sustain himself and his family. This has wisely been enacted in the law about able-bodied beggars, whose title is not "Concerning Healthy Beggars" but "Concerning Able-bodied Beggars." Nor did the law called the Ordinance pass this over in silence. For it says that if there are people who from their appearance can manifestly be judged to be able-bodied, they should be assigned to work and labour. Therefore, when their appearance and countenance do not betray them, the law requires no other investigation or scrutiny.

From that it follows that this lesson should be kept deeply in one's mind, that when the matter is doubtful, one should pronounce in favour of the paupers and their poverty rather than against them. It is much less evil and inconvenient to admit twenty bad vagabonds lest four legitimate paupers be excluded among them, than to exclude four persons who have the right to beg so that twenty able-bodied persons are also excluded. For this reason, as found in Matthew [13:24–30], the paterfamilias restrained the excessive zeal of the servants who were rushing to tear out darnel, so that in collecting the darnel they would not at the same time uproot the wheat as well.

Also relevant to this is that there are many who can tolerate work at some time or other, but not continuously or frequently. A person might be able to last in the job a few days in the month or in the week, but not an entire month or week. Some can work a half day but cannot complete a full day. It would be very bothersome if an unfortunate had to apply to the deputies whenever his strength failed.

Moreover, even able-bodied persons might nonetheless have the right to beg. There are those who do not find work or employers to hire them. When they do not find them no matter where they look in their own country, they can leave. Therefore, every city in the kingdom is obligated to support both natives and foreigners or allow them to beg, as long as it has not found them work or employers to whom they could hire out their services. This is what the governance of the kingdom is about, that people who cannot live in one city are humanely received in another. For this reason those wage labourers in the Gospel [Matthew 20:6–7] who were rebuked for their idleness, rightly excused themselves by saying that no one had hired them.

In addition, some persons born of good blood have neither learned a mechanical skill nor are suited for business; they are not obligated to offer themselves for cheap labour. They have the right to receive a donation, and even a larger one than others of a lower class.

These points we have conceded according to the rigour of the law. But if in this matter we consulted the ancient Fathers whom God laid down as the foundation of the Church, we would have to speak much differently about this examination of the paupers. For the strongest argument that supports this investigation into the poor derives from this: that there are more than a few who devise arts to defraud and destroy the state by faking and feigning that they are sick, injured, maimed, and crippled. No greater trickery against the state exists than this.

I will never dare to answer those who use this important argument. I refer them to that great patron of the poor, Chrysostom. I cite his words in *Homily XXXVII, Ad populum*, leaving aside several others that he repeatedly says to the same effect. I beg and beseech that hearing them should cause annoyance to no one; they are prolix, but golden. After he had strenuously demanded from the wealthy that they clothe the naked poor whose garments the moth eats and the worm consumes, he introduces their response, in which they say that paupers feign their tremors and infirmity.

Great Prince, attend to how even then in the days of Chrysostom, the wealthy put forward these excuses for not giving alms, and showered these abuses on the poor. But hear the words with which Chrysostom inveighs against those who offered them. He said:

"Do you not fear that provoked by this word a lightning bolt might strike you from heaven? I burst with indignation, spare me. You swelling with your fat belly, and prolonging your drinking well into the evening, and getting warm on your soft bedspreads, do you not think that you deserve to be punished? For when you so wickedly use the gifts of God, (for wine was not made so we could get drunk, nor was food made so that we could drink to excess, nor nourishment so we could burst our bellies) do you demand a detailed accounting from a poor man whose condition is no better than dead? Nor do you fear that awful and terrible tribunal of Christ.

"For even if he pretends, he pretends out of necessity and need because of your cruelty and inhumanity, which is not turned toward mercy by the supplications of such persons. Who is so unfortunate and troubled that without the press of necessity he would for a single loaf of bread be willing to be disfigured and to wail and to suffer such pain? His pretence is endured as the herald of your inhumanity. Because by imploring and pleading and pouring forth his words of misery, groaning and weeping, and walking after you all day, he still did not find the food he needs, he contrived this deceit that brings less disgrace and accusation on him than on you. For he is worthy of finding mercy, having come to such necessity; but we are worthy of torture without limit because this is what we force paupers to endure. For if we were more readily moved, he would never have preferred such suffering. And why am I mentioning only nudity and tremors?

"For let me say mention something even more horrible, that some are forced to blind their young children, so that they can penetrate our insensate hardness. For after they have seen that neither their nakedness nor their age nor their distress can move men from their cruelty, they add a more grievous tragedy to all these troubles in order to be free from hunger, thinking it less important to be deprived of this common light and to miss the splendour given to everyone than to do battle with continuous hunger and to die a miserable death. For because you did not learn to pity their poverty, but you rejoice in their calamities, they fill up your evil lust by kindling a fiercer flame of Hell both for themselves and for you."

With these and many other words of the same rhetorical power Chrysostom fulminates elegantly and in a Christian spirit against those who, while blaming the paupers for the cruelty of having sinned against nature by mutilating their own bodies, do not look at themselves and notice their own barbarity and savagery in not bending to the pleadings of the unfortunate, thus causing them to exercise these tragic deceits against themselves. For truly, if the wealthy had suitably assisted the poor, they never would have endured that nakedness and those scars in order to get money. But they cannot wrest away that miserable contribution without mixing in those tragedies.

Most Splendid Lord, with these words I do not contend that vagabonds and sycophants should not be chastised, but that they should be chastised in the same way as are persons of other orders and conditions. In every order and class – among artisans, among advocates and scribes, among clerics and friars, among grandees even and prelates – there are people who are weak, criminal, and shameful, and who are not worthy of the bread they eat. Yet they do not have so many inquisitors and officials arrayed against them. Their crimes are to be purged with a sieve, not a mesh of bristles. [*Decretum Gratiani*] canon 6, q. 1 says that "if all sins were punished in this world, divine judgments would have no place."

Far be it from me to wish to brand any order of mortals with shame or to traduce anyone. But I can bring forth in general what is patently obvious without injuring anyone. How many artisans or public officials in the state fraudulently pilfer much more than the entire multitude of able-bodied beggars, and then spend it with magnificence and splendour, and yet people can tolerate their frauds and robberies with equanimity! But when the fake pauper filches one or two measly and miserable coins – with no other sycophancy than making a display of nakedness, tremors, hunger, and sickness – on no account can people be persuaded to put up with it, but they proclaim that they should be deprived of the light.

Was there ever anyone who experienced the loss of anything of substance because of the phoney crowd of pseudo-paupers? I put to the side those who through illicit contracts and dealings convert the property of others into their own. However, there is perhaps no small number of persons any one of whom consumed much greater wealth through ill-gotten gains than all the able-bodied beggars in the entire kingdom. Because these are the able-bodied rich, they are endured, but because others are able-bodied beggars, we can in no way put up with them. Yet among Christians the misery and need of the poor should count for just as much as the wealth and power of the rich, so that at least along with the rich we could also spare the poor.

Add that, although there are idle and wretched men who through their inertia and folly have fallen into poverty and others who pretend to be paupers, there are also very many whom the rich have made into genuine paupers. As we read in Ecclesiasticus [13:19], "As the wild ass is the lion's prey in the wilderness, so paupers are the food of the rich." Accordingly, it would not be so incongruous if we compensated for the wrongs of the rich by tolerating the poor.

Perhaps my pity for the poor has caused me to inveigh against the rich at greater length than I had planned. But I think that I said nothing that is not either in Holy Scripture or found on everyone's lips.

Nor can I conceal in silence that whenever some public office or – even worse – benefice is being conferred, no account is taken of what Christ, the founder of benefices, thought was most important about a person's worthiness and merits; and yet for a beggar to be permitted to ask for bread, so much investigation and approval is needed.

Last of all, I fear that this diligence and care in examining and expelling able-bodied paupers will not achieve its intended purpose of keeping the state clear of robbers and wrongdoers. Those who leave the city do not do return directly to their native lands; instead, they wander about through the villages and countryside, so that the very persons whose stealing while they were pretending to be beggars was small-scale and non-violent, may practise more serious acts of theft and stealing. Nor can they all be punished with the gibbet. Just as in other kinds of crimes, lesser evils allow the avoidance of greater ones – as Augustine said, if you eliminate prostitutes, adultery will be everywhere [*De Ordine* II, IV, 12]. Similarly, although out of able-bodied beggars are born a few robbers who should be punished on a certain basis and in a certain way, it is useful and for the public good to temper rigour somewhat, so that able-bodied beggars do not become the most able-bodied robbers.

Chapter X
On Examining the Life of the Poor

The second examination of the poor before they are allowed to beg pertains to their life and morals. Do they have concubines, or are they infected with some other contagion? Do they regularly go to confession and observe other such matters required of Christians? No one disapproves of zeal respecting this practice, for there is no class of mortals to whom we do not owe fraternal reproof. And yet whenever the saintly Fathers wrote about alms, they never wanted so much justice to be connected to the mercy owed to the poor.

"Alms" is a Greek word that means the same as mercy. Underlying this corporal work of mercy as its matter and object is nothing other than the misery and need of the poor, from which immediately flows the duty to feed the hungry, clothe the naked, and provide the stranger with shelter. And so that we might exhibit this mercy to the poor, the saints investigate nothing else about the poor than that they be in need and begging. But the spiritual work of mercy, which consists in the reproof of one's brother, is distinct from this. And so the justice of restraining malefactors, as we said earlier, looks to others, to administrators of justice. Being merciful is one thing, punishing malefactors is another.

I entreat you, most Christian Prince, to listen to what Chrysostom said about this, especially in his *Second Sermon on Lazarus the Beggar* [sections 5–6]. For even in his day, the rich devised these examinations and reproofs against the poor to excuse their own avarice. Against them he issued these words, which are better the longer they go on:

"Abraham in his wisdom did not examine what kind of persons the passers-by were nor whence they came, as we now do, but he received all of them without distinction. For a person of outstanding humanity should not demand an accounting of their lives, but should remedy their need and provide for their necessity.

"The pauper has but a single defence: his need and his necessity, and you should not demand more of him. Even if he was the most wicked person of all but lacked food to live, we quiet his hunger. This is what Christ instructed [Matthew 5:45], 'Be like your Father in heaven, who makes his sun rise over the good and the bad, and makes the rain fall on the just and the unjust.' A merciful man is the port for those who are in necessity. A port receives and saves everyone who has been shipwrecked, whether they are good or bad. Whoever is in danger the port receives into its bosom.

"Similarly, when you see a person shipwrecked by need, do not judge and do not examine what he has done, but remedy his misfortune. Why do you impose this task on yourself? God freed you from all such care and solicitude. How many things would people have said and how harsh would they have been if we were to give alms only after we had accurately enquired into each person's life and deeds? Now he has freed us from all this solicitude. Why are we imposing these superfluous concerns on ourselves? It is one thing to be a judge and another to be a dispenser of alms. They are called alms because they are given even to the unworthy. That is why Paul said [Galatians 6:10], 'Let us do good to all, especially to those in the family of believers.'

"If we make a close examination and enquiry into the unworthy, not even the worthy will come to us. But if we provide assistance to those who are also unworthy, then surely the worthy too, whose virtue outweighs all the evil of those others, will come into our hands. This is what happened to the blessed Abraham [Genesis 18] who did not care what sort of people were passing by, but finally happened to provide hospitality to angels. We should imitate him, as well as his grandson Job [Job 31: 32], who also diligently imitated the generosity of his forebear, saying, 'My door is continuously open to whoever arrives.' It was not open to one person and closed to another, but without distinction it was open to all.

"Let us also imitate this example by making no improper enquiry. Need is sufficient for a pauper to be considered worthy of alms. If someone approaches us with this commendation, let us not engage in additional scrutiny. We are not giving to good morals, but to a person. We pity him not because of his virtue, but because of his calamity. By this we would gain abundant mercy for ourselves from the Lord, and we would be the most worthy objects of his kindness. For if we begin to examine the worthiness and investigate the morals of our fellow servants, God will do the same to us. And while we eagerly demand an account of their lives from our fellow servants, we will lose the kindness of God in heaven. For you will be judged in the very judgment in which you judge [Matthew 7:2]." These are the words of Chrysostom.

But if this saint is suspect because he was aflame with mercy and excessively indulgent to the poor (as befits a person of his great holiness), and his writings are like a bejewelled garment that shines with designations of honour for the poor, we will call Ambrose as guarantor. In his *Liber de Nabuthi*, chapter 8, speaking of the way to give alms, he says: "Do not enquire into what any pauper deserves. Mercy is not wont to judge about what is deserved, but to assist with necessities, to aid the poor, not to investigate justice. It is written [Psalms 41:71], Blessed is he who considers the needy and the poor." No distinction is made there between the good person and the bad one.

About this I think that one needs the testimony of Augustine, whose genius is to examine matters with precise argument. I therefore submit from this most respected Father the testimony in his *Interpretation of Psalm 102* about this verse [103:6]: "God is the maker of mercies." There he teaches that God makes mercy only for those who are themselves merciful, according to the word of the Lord [Matthew 5:7], "Blessed are the merciful for they will receive mercy." He adds that "The measure of mercy is not that it is exercised for your friend or that it fails to be exercised for your enemy," because it is written "Love your enemies and do good to those who hate you" [Luke 6:27], and Proverbs 25 [25:12], "If you see your enemy starving, feed him." Enemies, however, especially of persons who are good, cannot be good. Accordingly, if mercy is to be exercised toward enemies, then it is not the office of mercy to distinguish between good and bad. Just as merciful God makes his sun rise over the good and the bad, so Christ the father of mercies, places no limit on mercy but says [Luke 6:30] "Give it to anyone who asks you."

Augustine, however, presents the following teaching of Ecclesiasticus [12:1–5], which at first glance sems inconsistent with this view, where we read: "If you do good, know to whom you do it … Do good to the just and you will find your recompense, because the Most High hates sinners and has mercy on those who repent. Give to the merciful and do not support the sinner. Give to the good and do not assist the sinner. Do good to the lowly, and do not give to the impious." Notice how that sage doubles and piles up the words, that we should be beneficent only to the just. However, Augustine readily tempers this, because the gospel cannot be contradicted. "You fulfil both," he says. "Both do not help the sinner and give to everyone who asks; when it is a sinner who asks you, you do not give to the person who asks as a sinner but as a poor person. If you intend to relieve the pauper's need and misery, you do not support the sinner." These are the words of Augustine.

Therefore, what the sage in Ecclesiasticus wants us to know is this: when the pauper, having obtained from the bounty of alms the opportunity and power to sin, becomes a sinner, and the benefits given to him are nothing but the seeds and nourishment of sins, then they are to be withdrawn from the pauper in reproof. That is what Augustine writes in *Ad Vicentium Donatistam* and is contained in the canon *Non omnis*, V, Q. 5: "It is more useful for bread to be taken from the hungry, if secure in his food he neglects justice, than that the breaking of bread should lead the hungry into acquiescing in injustice." You should understand that this applies when it is perfectly obvious that the alms tend to damage the poor.

Otherwise, examining the poor is not permitted. We must adhere to another teaching of Augustine's which is found in his book *On the Five Heresies* [4.5]. There after commending the hospitality of Abraham and Lot who, by receiving everyone without distinction, were worthy of having angels as guests, added: "Learn to receive guests without distinction, Christians, because the person to whom you close your house and whose humanity you deny may be God himself." For the same reason, this is also to be observed in all the other duties of piety.

Therefore, to put everything where it can be seen at a glance, this is what one can conclude from these many clear testimonies of the saints: the duty of mercy makes no distinction between good and bad persons; that should be reserved to the various parts of justice and its ministers. Rather, mercy resides in this, in being present to and providing assistance for all human misery without distinction. Accordingly, in the proem written with Christian piety and wisdom at the head of the articles of this law, the boundless love, kindness, and clemency toward us of Christ our Saviour is deservedly commended, and we are most piously reminded that he has exhibited for us an outstanding exercise of his charity; that is what we ourselves should repay toward his paupers.

It is worth noticing, I say, whether it is sufficiently consistent and appropriate to this beginning that what follows is that vagabonds and false paupers should be expelled from the city, that foreign beggars should be allowed only to pass through, that the life and morals of native beggars should be diligently examined, and that the persons who adroitly carry this out should be officials and praetors.

Surely it would be more fitting to write after that proem that those of us who have given our names and pledged our faith to Christ should be merciful and kind to all without distinction.

This is what was done by Abraham, whom Christ considered worthy to be his father. This is what is almoner Tobias taught his son when he said [Tobias 4:7] "Do not turn your face away from any of the poor, and then the face of the Lord will not be turned away from you." And his servant Job [31:16] took pride in never having denied what any of the poor wanted. The Saints compare his mercy to a port that receives and saves all the shipwrecked without distinction. This is what the Teacher himself preaches [Luke 6:30] when he says "Give to everyone who asks you." For this reason, when Christ fed that enormous multitude in the wilderness, he did not exclude the vagabonds and made no separation between good persons and bad.

The word "mercy" signifies that we offer benefits to the unworthy, for what is given to the worthy is "justice." For this reason God is merciful, in that he [Matthew 5:45] "makes his sun rise over the good and the bad, and makes the rain fall on the just and the unjust." Christ wanted our version of justice to surpass that of the Pharisees, in that unlike them we were to love not only our friends but also our enemies. In this, finally, the Apostle [Romans 5:8] commends his ineffable mercy that "He died for us while we were still sinners."

In truth, those who excogitated these laws on the poor can have a pious intention, and they can be just – except in this case they are perhaps too just since they usurp the office of the praetors to act against malefactors – but they should not believe that the mercy they are exhibiting is pure and innocent of self-service, because mercy does not distinguish between the worthy and the unworthy. To be sure, it belongs to the order of charity, that when everything else is equal, we should prefer giving alms to the good rather than the bad and to the better rather than the worse.

Nevertheless, a merciful person does not so anxiously scrutinize what people deserve. Nor can it be merciful not only to give nothing to sinners, but also to prevent them from seeking from others who would give what you deny. Perhaps they would take to heart what Jesus said in Matthew [10:13], "Whenever you enter a house, say 'Peace be upon this house'; if the house is worthy, your peace will come upon it; and if it is not worthy, your peace will return to you." The same applies to alms: although the pauper may not deserve to receive them, nonetheless a reward before God awaits the benefactor.

And with respect to the equity and justice of the fourth article, rather than completely agree, I would prefer to confess my ignorance about the rigour of forcing paupers to confession. For although paupers should be instructed and admonished about the necessity of this sacrament, it is not worthwhile to thrust them into the unfortunate straits of conditioning the permissibility of begging on having confessed.

First, to require the sacrament of confession on pain of death would not only be an intolerable law but would arouse hatred against this most sacred sacrament. To prevent beggars from begging is a capital penalty for those who have no other way of saving their lives. It is therefore not permissible to compel them to confess on pain of this penalty. When I want to urge confession on the wealthy, I meet with them at their convenience. If under law it was promulgated to the wealthy that after Easter no one was permitted to eat bread without having first confessed but must rather starve to death, they would perhaps protest. I cannot imagine why they should prescribe that law to the poor.

There are, they say, among the poor some who have not attended confession for an entire decade. But likewise, there are among the wealthy some who are not so rigorous about confession. But the wealthy might say that they do not seek what belongs to another: "I do not want to be munificent toward paupers with my property unless they have confessed." Here is concealed the point of this matter; this is the harshness to which they always stick fast. Here I want their attention. Let me for the time being pass over the question of whether the needy and the poor have the same right as you to your property. Although there are holy fathers who think so, we are diffident to affirm it. This at least is too evident and certain for anyone to deny: that every pauper in any necessity, even if it is less than grave, has a right to seek alms that is equal to the right that everyone has in their own goods, and perhaps even a greater right in view of the greater necessity.

It follows that no one of whatever authority can deprive the poor of this right except for the same wrongdoing that allows the wealthy to be punished by the loss of their own property – I would even dare to say, that allows the wealthy to be condemned to starve to death; for whoever excludes the poor from the right to seek alms drives him to extreme hunger. So that if someone is so perfectly just that he intends to give food – as if it were the holy sacrament of the Eucharist – only to a man who is upright and has confessed, let him not because of that take from the unfortunate the right and power to go around and find someone, perhaps better instructed in the laws of mercy, who would provide him with bread.

Moreover – and this is what must be most guarded against – if the poor, an uninstructed multitude, are so strenuously coerced to confession, do you doubt, excellent Prince, that it can happen that many might confess false and fictitious things, contaminating the sacrament in order not to be choked by hunger? When the holy synod decreed that the sacrament of confession – which was of divine right – should be received annually, the holy fathers foresaw that if they piled on larger penalties, perhaps fewer people would transgress. Nonetheless, they were apprehensive that out of fear of the very serious penalty someone might act sacrilegiously toward the sacrament by confessing a fiction. They thought it sufficient to interdict a transgressor from entering a church and from ecclesiastical burial. Although Christians must consider this a more severe penalty than extreme hunger, the fear of it does not deter from false confession as much as does a temporal penalty. Therefore, one of the sixteen qualities and conditions of the sacrament of confession is that it be free. I cannot understand how this is compatible with such rigour in forcing people to confess.

So far as reproof of the poor is concerned, in these articles it was instituted with great holiness, if only it be diligently executed, that, first, the young children of the poor be freed from the care of their parents and allotted to patrons or assigned to training or work; and next, that the poor should occasionally be compelled to listen to public sermons where they can be instructed in religion and virtue and can be admonished and exhorted. For this it would be best to put men of virtuous life in charge, who would have them in their care and consideration. That would clearly add spiritual to corporal mercy, in imitation of God, who providentially sustains the corporal life of those for whose spiritual life also he institutes laws, counsels, and examples, admonishing and leading them to what is good and honourable.

Moreover, I think it necessary above all to call attention to this point about the method of enquiring into and investigating especially the poor who have not publicly professed to being beggars. For these people alms come at such a high cost that they are hardly gratuitous. First, although the Spanish – who value honour more than life itself – prefer to endure extreme hunger rather than to be exposed as beggars, no account is taken of secrecy when paupers are registered. The nobles to whom the task is entrusted, accompanied by a train of servants, subject paupers to a public examination, many of whom would prefer going without alms to purchasing them at this price. Everywhere, and especially in Spain, the gospel's way of giving alms [Matthew 6:3] should be observed, that the left hand should not know what the right hand is doing. This is what Ambrose, Nicolaus, Chrysostom, and other saintly fathers did most scrupulously.

But what is much worse, not to say more wrongful, is that before allowing these miserable alms to be dispensed, they sometimes extra-legally investigate hidden crimes. In the lecture that I published, *On the Reason for Concealing and Uncovering What Is Secret*, I explained to the best of my ability that there is no right to investigate and scrutinize crimes unless they have been voiced by public opinion or exposed by some indication or other. Nor even under these circumstances are the sins of the rich always tracked down. And yet greater care and diligence go into uncovering the secret sins of the poor than into relieving their misery. Unhappy is the condition of a class of people who have to endanger their reputation to receive a coin.

In this matter one must keep in mind that although miserable men afflicted with worry and misfortune very often lift their spirits by admitting sins, the wealthy commit much greater sins out of their luxury and overflowing prosperity. But if this thought does not suffice to pardon unfortunate paupers, what more severe penalties for their errors can we impose on them in this world than the ones that they pay with their own calamities, adversities, and afflictions? Excluded from honours, taking no pleasure, naked, without a bed, without a roof, carrying on a ceaseless war with cold, with heat, and – most terrible of all – with hunger (for as the prophet says [Lamentations 4:8], it is better to be slain by the sword than killed by hunger), bereft of everything that makes men happy in this life, banished from almost everywhere, the life they lead is no more coveted than death.

Add that many paupers – and this is a most cruel aspect of the matter – are thrust into crimes of this sort by their need and their begging. Because of this, the avaricious wealthy are cruel to the paupers on both counts: that by reason of their avarice and stinginess they give the poor cause to commit wrongs, and that the commission of these wrongs gives the wealthy the opportunity to selfishly nurture their avarice. There would be a healthier prospect for improving the dissolute morals of the poor and it would better provide for them to recover their senses if by providing benefits and temporal assistance we softened their hearts and attracted and led them back to the proper road. For when we remove their food, we cause their vices to flair up again in their desperation and hopelessness.

I say this not to coddle those who have strayed. Rather, I have two apprehensions. First, before we aid the unfortunate and dispense mercy, we do not want to be so just with respect to the poor that we become unjust. Moreover, by so carefully and skilfully doing away with the vagabonds, driving away the foreigners, and enquiring into the life and morals of the natives, it may turn out that the amount of alms diminishes. I can never regret saying again and again that if through these examinations of the poor the alms become less frequent and smaller, it would have been much better for the wealthy if the examinations had never come to mind. And even if the alms became much larger, they would never reach the just amount.

For Christians, alms are necessary at every turn. If you want to beat back the encroaching flame of vices, "as water quenches fire," says the wise man [Ecclesiasticus 3:30], "so alms resist sins." And if you desire redemption for sins already committed, listen to the prophet Daniel [Daniel 4:27], "Redeem your sins with alms, and your iniquities with mercies toward the poor." If you further want to atone for the smallest remnant of your sins, heed what Christ commands [Luke 11:41]: "Give alms, and behold, everything is clean for you." If when already cleansed, you intend to prepare food and all your provisions for the journey of this life, again the wise man says in Ecclesiasticus [17:22] that "the alms of a man are as a purse with him, and he will keep the kindnesses of a man as the apple of his eye." If you want to save your treasure from moths and rust and robbers, entrust it to the poor. For Christ was speaking about alms when he said [Matthew 6:19], "Do not store your treasures in the earth, where rust and moths destroy it, and where thieves dig down and steal it, but store your treasures in heaven, where neither moth nor rust destroys it, nor thieves dig down and steal it." To the wealthy of the world, for whom he says – by way of explaining the difficulty – that it is as impossible for them to enter the kingdom of heaven as for a camel to pass through the eye of a needle [Matthew 19:24], he leaves only this remedy [Matthew 16:9], that with their money of iniquity they should befriend those who would receive them into their everlasting habitations. For this reason Paul teaches Timothy [I Timothy 6:9] that he should preach to the wealthy of this world that they should readily give alms: "Those who wish to become rich fall into temptation and the snare of the devil."

Why say more? If you strive not only to be received into the everlasting habitations but also, longing for his everlasting glory, to be there among the princes and the most perfect – as should we all – Christ showed [Matthew 19:21] that the only way is to sell everything that you have, distribute it for the use of the poor, and follow him.

With this, more than enough has been said about the enquiries, examinations, and scrutinizing mentioned in the first, third, and fourth articles. The second and fourth articles we have already considered in the earlier part of this *Deliberation*.

Chapter XI
On the Reason for Permitting Solicitation from Door to Door

We have finally reached the point in our argument at which we should deal with the article that, of all the ones published, is the most strongly insisted upon. This is: Is it right and good – or to use the terminology of Paul, expedient and edifying – to keep paupers away from Christian doors and feed them in hospitals, rather than to permit them to thrust their troubles and calamities before Christian eyes? Unless I am mistaken, this issue is not as uncontroversial as the authors of these articles think.

So that we can distinguish between strict right and considerations of equity and mercy, the first conclusion of this article would be that the prince who holds the state's power has the right and authority to prohibit beggars from soliciting door to door, so long as he suitably provides them with food and clothing and the other necessaries appropriate to their status in another way, but not otherwise. No one can plausibly object to this conclusion, which is too manifest to need much testimony.

Since, as Aristotle says in Book II of the *Ethics* [1103b3], the prince is put in charge of the state by natural and divine law to make the citizens good, any prince can by edict prescribe what is needed for virtue and can restrain vices and sins. But as long as the indigent are in need, it is no sin to seek donations from door to door; after they are supplied with necessaries, they cannot on the pretext of poverty seek what belongs to others without doing wrong. Therefore, when the prince or the state provides necessaries, they can restrain soliciting from door to door, but otherwise not.

Not only do I believe that the prince has this authority, but if it could conveniently happen that the state could abundantly provide for the paupers so that they would not be forced to circulate in towns soliciting from door to door, on this basis both gospel truth and the love of Christ – of which single body we are members – would shine forth with much more splendour in a Christian state. For I ask how their conduct conforms to the law that commands them to love their neighbours as themselves, seeing that some people overflow with the excesses and superfluity of all wealth, and others suffer the greatest need and must beg.

There is a celebrated pronouncement by one of one of the natural philosophers, who on hearing an extremely wealthy man boast that he was a very close friend of an extremely poor one, is said to have responded that it is not believable that any such friendship could exist. This is what our divine apostle, whom I just mentioned, said with these words [I John 3:17]: "Whoever has the wealth of this world" and so on. Much earlier than in the gospel God had inscribed this law of friendship on the minds of mortals. The pagans expressed it in that well-known proverb, "Friends hold everything in common, and the friend is one's other self." Some make Pythagoras the author of this saying. From this Socrates concluded that everything belongs to good men, because everything belongs to the gods, whose friends they are.

This is the very law that the apostles – the interpreters of the divine and the promulgators of the evangelical law that is the consummation of all natural laws – persuasively preached at the earliest baptisms in Jerusalem and the adjacent province of Judaea, as is recounted in their Acts [4:32–7]. All those who gave their names to Christ in baptism sold their goods and laid the money they received at the feet of the apostles, who then distributed it to individuals in accordance with their need. For this reason, according to the story, there was no needy person among them. At that time, short as it was, this was observed with such holiness and regularity that one new Christian named Ananias, who with his wife's complicity hid the money that he had received for his goods, was so sharply rebuked by Peter for this avarice that he fainted in terror and died [Acts 5:1–5]. In imitation of this practice, religious monasteries were subsequently established, where people living in common replicate that Christian love in one way or another. As is said in the Acts of the Apostles [6:17], the job of taking care of the table of the widows and orphans and other paupers of that sort was placed in the charge of seven upright men, of whom Stephen was the chief. I have said this to attest that if the poor could be so plentifully provided for that they would certainly and securely have their necessaries, it would be nothing but Christian love.

I nonetheless append a second conclusion to the previous one. Under present circumstances it is not possible so to provide for the paupers that they can be restrained from begging door to door. What I mean by "possibility" is what the theologians called a "moral" possibility and what Aristotle, *On the Heavens* [1, 11] thinks is something that could well happen.

To persuade to this conclusion requires laying down two or three fundamental points. The first is this: The manner and scope of alms is not prescribed either by precept or by law. This is to say: how big a share of one's property men are obligated to pay out in alms (for instance, a tenth or a twentieth) has not been determined; nor has the number of poor that certain men or the state are obligated to maintain been defined; nor have the necessities that we are obligated to relieve been specified. We are admonished [Matthew 26:11] only that we will always have the poor with us. Christ our Saviour most vehemently draws us by promises and terrifies us by threats, that in loving our neighbours as ourselves, we are to the extent of our ability to allow no one to be in need.

The second is the fundamental point mentioned above: aside from endowments to hospitals and other income and assets decreed for the poor – which are like their own private property – men can be obligated to give alms only by a law in the gospel; as present usage has it, everyone is completely free to contribute whatever alms he wishes. I add that there are very avaricious men even in Christendom who cannot be persuaded to give alms by any disapproval however great. And there are also the very rare persons who give alms proportionate to their ability and to the need of the unfortunates in accordance with gospel truth.

I would add the third fundamental point, which I would especially want all those who are endeavouring to shut out the beggars to consider. Whoever deprives the beggars (or causes them to be deprived) of the right to solicit thereby owes them relief from their misfortune and assistance with their needs, or at least with those that morally speaking, as they say, they likely could have provided for by soliciting. For example, assume the city has a hundred or a thousand legitimate paupers, whose needs could not be sufficiently provided for with less than two hundred ducats, which they likely could have gotten if they had been permitted to beg door to door. I then understand this fundamental point in this way: although helping those who are permitted to solicit is not an obligation of justice but only a matter of mercy, nonetheless the state or the person who prevented soliciting would as a matter of justice be obligated to pay those who were so prevented the entire two hundred ducats. This is certainly obvious. The beggars have the right to seek alms, and whoever deprives a person of his right is liable for the loss according to the well-known principle that whoever is the cause of loss is looked upon as having inflicted the loss.

From the positing of these fundamental points the second conclusion follows. Before the beggars are prohibited by law from soliciting, all their necessities must be provided for in accordance with the third fundamental point that necessities are owed to them as a matter of justice. But this provisioning is, as they say, not morally possible. It is, therefore, not permissible to forbid them from soliciting. That it is not possible for them to be provided for as justice requires when they are shut in is sufficiently shown by the first and second fundamental points. For if neither the paupers nor what they need is determined in any certain number or manner – because both natives and foreigners, as we have already said, have a right to solicit – and citizens cannot be compelled to give alms, how, I ask, can the state discharge the debt that it incurred by prohibiting begging?

This is especially the case because the needs of the poor include not only food, but clothing, a bed, and if the pauper has a family, other provisions and household furniture. When they are permitted to beg, no one is obligated to bestow mercy except for extreme or perhaps grave necessity. But when they are forbidden to beg, what was mercy becomes justice. For as I just said, a person who deprives a pauper of his right becomes his debtor for all that the pauper could have acquired by begging.

The second reason concerns the meals: I cannot understand on what basis or measure one can conveniently make the portions that are distributed to the shut-in poor. For among the poor there is one person for whom, given his complexion and the heat in his stomach, the portions of three other people do not suffice; if equal baskets are distributed to all, that person would necessarily be fighting a perpetual battle with hunger, although he had the right to solicit alms up to the point of extinguishing his hunger. Someone who did not provide at least enough bread to satisfy the hunger even of his slave would deservedly be accused of cruelty and savagery.

The third reason does not have first place in this *Deliberation* but is not the least significant. After the present mode of almsgiving became current, it was discovered by experience that the fixed portions and baskets being distributed to the poor scarcely sufficed for a person with a healthy stomach to have adequate bread, or perhaps vegetables or legumes, or perhaps allow him to buy a snippet of meat once a week. Yet surely it is unsatisfactory if the difference between the rich and the poor is that the rich have the means to be nourished and indulge themselves with fat and expensive foods, whereas the poor cannot; unless on top of their most unfair condition we add that the unfortunates from whom we take away even their liberty should never be able to refresh their souls, afflicted by adversity, with the foods that God and nature granted to the human race. Although the pauper's daily food is sparse and cheap, let him, I say, be refreshed at least with this freedom, that he can on occasion happen upon a house where a kindly man is sitting and dining who offers a little platter, fruit, wine, and that sort of delicacy with which he is often accustomed to indulge his servants. I do not mention the crowded and sordidly splendid banquets, the leftovers from which fill up the family and then are set before the servants or perhaps thrown to the dogs. Why, I ask, should houses of this sort not be opened up [*pandantur*] to the poor? For if we trust certain grammarians, the verb *pando* derives its meaning from the fact that even among the pagans, to whom Christ never preached about alms, when the banquets were finished the gates were opened so that bread [*panis*] could be given to the needy, or because the temple of Ceres was always open to the needy, to whom bread was given.

Moreover, to consign the trial into the lives of the poor to the power of a small number of persons is not safe. For just as there may be two or three persons put in charge of the business with the poor who are chosen for being upright and well regarded, it can happen that others who for some reason hate the poor or are deceived by false testimony – as we said, this abounds in poor neighbourhoods – declare that a pauper does not have a legitimate reason for begging. What will that unfortunate person do then? For this reason, provision was properly made in the ordinances in Ypres in Flanders, that beggars could present their misfortunes and calamities to one of the city's notables, so that condemnation by a few would not leave them destitute of all remedy.

There is also this further point about these articles that I cannot fully understand. They admit that an authentic pauper who is a newcomer and foreigner can come, to whom they give at least three days in a hospital. Listen, great Prince, how much trouble they put him through before he can receive his morsel of bread. Consider someone reaching the city who is sick or lame or exhausted from travelling. Nevertheless, he has to make enquiries as to where the person in charge of the paupers lives, wandering around from street to street looking for the house. When he finds it, perhaps the man is not home, or he is asleep; he has to wait. Then when the pauper has the opportunity to see him, he has to answer questions about his origin and destination. Finally, all he gets is a token, and then he has to return to the treasurer or the treasury, where the money is kept. And so the unfortunate man spends a whole day before he can quiet his hunger or relieve his lassitude. I hear that this is the arrangement in certain cities; I do not know whether foreigners are treated better elsewhere. A *xenodochium*, that is, a building for receiving travellers, should be available to foreigners. Indeed, people should be stationed at the gates who would lead the poor directly to lodgings.

It seems to follow that just as it is almost impossible (as I said in Chapter IV) to provide for the native paupers with laws that leave them with neither the necessity nor the right to depart from their homelands to beg elsewhere, so it does not seem possible to appropriately give them sufficient care and assistance with laws that would leave them with no further right to beg from door to door.

I would report nothing except what is legal if I asserted that a poor person can by begging get the little bit of money by which he could change his status from his original rank and station. The unfortunates are accused of and sharply rebuked for concealing gold sewn into their clothing. I put aside that others fill their regular purses with borrowed money. I put aside that there are people who live magnificently on borrowed money; however, the poor (as was famously said [Terence, *Phormio* 44]), by stinting on their own inclinations and skimping on their own tables, sustain themselves with bread and vegetables, so that they can put aside some money in case they become sick or suffer some greater calamity.

To this I dare to add another matter: just as anyone else can change his station and rank for the better by permissible skills and transactions, so a pauper can assemble from alms a small amount of money by which he can dress and deck himself out more honourably, so that he could serve some worthy noble, or might be able to furnish himself with tools of his trade and a workshop, or to set up some small shop or business from which he might live. Those whom the law shuts in are excluded from this.

Furthermore, hospitals do not abound everywhere to receive all the paupers, and the poor can be consumed with much greater idleness and listlessness shut in than if they were allowed to go out to beg.

Putting reasons of this sort aside for the moment, let us return to the rudder that in this matter we ought never let slip from our hands. It is worth paying attention to this above all: on this basis would the aggregate of alms increase or decrease? Since there is no argument or evidence that alms should be decreased and diminished – as the authors of this arrangement publicly admit would happen – the matter is proved beyond doubt.

They especially commend this arrangement and persuade themselves because in this way fewer alms are needed. This is certainly what experience itself teaches. I hear from other cities, and in this one I see with my own eyes and hear directly from those who manage these dealings with the poor, that the total of alms is scarcely a third or a quarter of what previously was usual.

And yet because of this very Achilles whom the proponents of the arrangement think is fighting from their ranks, those who see the matter differently are convinced to reject this basis for almsgiving. For if the legitimate paupers were not more numerous and their troubles and necessities were not greater than the money for alms that is gathered on this basis, I acknowledge that men however wealthy would not be obligated to give more. However, the authentic paupers – once the fakes and the phonies are removed – and their needs and calamities are too great for the contributions from almsgiving made on this basis to suffice. Therefore, the wealthy – especially the avaricious and stingy among them – should be compelled by gospel law to greater alms. The removal of the able-bodied beggars – who fraudulently and wickedly extorted alms – should rather be reckoned to the discredit to the wealthy, unless the legitimate paupers receive everything that is taken from the able-bodied.

The reasons that alms collected on this basis are necessarily more infrequent and sparser are obvious, quite apart from what experience shows. First, what beggars solicit for themselves and what others solicit for them are as different as can be. The wealthy, no matter how imbued with mercy they may be, solicit on behalf of the poor out of honour; because they have their dinners available to them at home, they think that they have sufficiently done their duty if they go around to two or three streets, not really caring whether their solicitations are successful. But an unfortunate beggar whose dinner depends only on his begging does not think merely seeking alms is sufficient, but he demands it with the greatest effrontery until he squeezes a coin out of the most obdurate heart. Nor does he think it sufficient to run around for an hour; he needs the entire day to get some food.

Do you not think, merciful Prince, that for this reason – aside from teaching his disciples to pray – Christ, who was most mindful of paupers, introduced into the gospel [Luke 11:5–13] the parable in which a man goes to his friend in the middle of the night to ask for three loaves of bread? The friend, who had already closed his door and was lying in bed with his children, was reluctant to get up and accommodate his friend. Nonetheless, says our Teacher, he knocked so persistently on the door that he was able to make the friend get out of bed and to do what was required, if not out of friendship, at least out of the effrontery of how he was asking for it. If someone had gone to seek bread to relieve another person's necessity, he would not have been so stubbornly insistent on securing mercy.

Next, the second reason is that just as with avoiding what is bad and disgraceful, so doing what is good and required usually happens by accident. The presence of the material and of the object whether of virtue or of vice has a huge effect in moving or drawing someone to do something. It matters immensely whether a wealthy person who is healthy, well-groomed, and splendidly attired comes to you seeking mercy, or whether you see a pauper who is pallid, injured, and wearing soiled clothing supplicating and begging you by the mother of Christ and by his wounds. Everyone has had long and frequent experience of leaving his house without any intention of giving alms but changing his mind for the better at the sight of a poor person. Because of this, one of the orator's precepts is to admonish that, if it can conveniently be done, the victim of the injury should be thrust before the eyes of the judge to move him by the display of his wounds.

I admit that some of these paupers are frauds. But aside from the fact that many more infirmities and calamities are authentic, if any frauds ever deserved to be called pious frauds, these are they. This is one reason among others why the presence of the bishop in his church is useful and necessary. For if what he hears moves the bishop to send alms to his paupers, he would be persuaded to give far more when he sees their troubles and adversities with his own eyes.

The example of the religious mendicants, who (as I previously said) conduct themselves in the image of the communal life of the nascent church, shows how effective it is for a person in need to ask for help himself. For where the monasteries live by begging, a single pious person entrusted with this task abundantly collects – and that justly and piously – the whole store of food that is suitable to the frugality and poverty of the devout, because he takes care of the matter for his own monastery. If this responsibility were delegated to ten very diligent and pious laymen, they would scarcely be able to get sufficient bread for the monastery. Because of this we religious mendicants are obligated to go to the assistance of mendicant paupers.

The condition and character of the Spaniards add force to this argument. They are notable among humans for being more easily moved by the supplicants' prayers and misfortunes than by the coercion of the law. Therefore, in a city in which a hundred beggars can beg with their prayers and entreaties, scarcely forty citizens would be listed in the register if they were enrolled for permanent almsgiving, because people are afraid to sign up for alms, just as if they were taxes. If one can conjecture what happens in other places from what happens in this city, which – without my criticizing any other – is extremely generous towards paupers, much less than half as many alms have been recorded in the register of the poor than the very great number that otherwise occurred or could be believed to have occurred in any single city. And yet within three months a good part of that registered sum has been withdrawn. How much now remains I do not know.

Accordingly, let me begin to make firm the road for my response to objections. Because in other regions people are more public- and civil-minded and are more readily bound by law to the common good, no one can present what has been instituted there about almsgiving as a model for imitation by the Spanish. As for the money collected in the copper boxes [set out in the churches], it suffices to say that it is scanty and less than expected. Those very persons who freely and liberally pour out their mercy to beggars whom they encounter not only forget to put alms into the boxes when they are not face to face with paupers, but when they enter a church they are not inclined to give to mute stone and wood what they would extend to a live soliciting pauper. Consequently, those copper boxes are so without wealth that no name is less appropriate to them than *gazophylacium* ["wealth-protector"].

Moreover, the register for alms lists only the heads of families. When beggars circulate, if the husband does not give, the wife, who is more generous to paupers, might. If the father does not contribute, the son does. If the master does not give, the servant does.

Furthermore, an exceptionally important argument in this matter is that usually alms are made up not only of money but of every household furnishing. You will find that people might be very sparing in giving money, but the good ones ask their wives to contribute bread or leftovers from the meal or old clothing or a linen undershirt or a worn shoe or a bundle of wood. If you exclude all these things from the aggregate of the alms, as you must on this method, you perhaps take away half.

Aside from the decrease and loss of alms that manifestly follows from this arrangement to restrain the poor, we can approach the matter by another route. The point of mercy consists not only in the aid and assistance that someone might give to the unfortunate, but especially and indeed principally that the soul, inwardly compassionate at the pauper's calamity, might suffer along with the unfortunate person, and when he lacks the ability to render aid, this feeling is laid up for merit before God. We can see this in the case of Christ who, as we read in Matthew [15:32] and Mark [8:2], before extinguishing the hunger and refreshing the lassitude of the crowd in the desert, took pity on the crowd that sustained him for three days; out of this divine feeling external action emerged.

Those who snatch the poor away from Christian eyes remove the cream (as people say), the best in this outstanding virtue of mercy. For just as one cannot be brave and vigorous unless one has often been aroused by the sight of armed enemies, so one cannot be merciful unless one has personally seen and dealt with the troubles, calamities, adversities, and afflictions of the poor. Just as there are those in whom the sight of paupers arouses nausea and in whose ears their clamour grates, there are others – whose behaviour in this matter should rather be followed – who on seeing the troubles of the poor soften their hearts to mercy, and who hold their heads high because of their noble blood and their honours and their good fortune, but then lower them because they see people like themselves thrust down into a dissimilar fate and fortune, to whom in this life they could have been similar and equal and to whom in that everlasting felicity they may be far inferior. In the major festivals and especially during Holy Week, who doubts that the sight and clamour of the poor strongly move Christian hearts to pity, and arouse them to perceive the feeling of Christ's Passion? Last year I seemed to see people sadly saying that a Holy Week that was silent without the clamour of the poor is just like a feast celebrated without music.

It is not unimportant to ask, great Prince, how beneficial it is that young people from their earliest education be schooled to mercy, in imitation of the saintly Job who suggested [Job 31:18 Vulgate] that the root of all his virtues was the mercy that had grown in him from childhood. How can a child be imbued with this most sacred virtue, who has not seen or heard calamities with his own senses? Those who are now administering the alms of the poor can be merciful and kind toward the poor because they have seen the misfortunes of the poor with their own eyes. But assume that these regulations remain intact for an entire century, so that those who are now being born never see beggars standing on the thresholds of their houses and never visit the shut-ins. What feelings can such people have towards the poor?

It is not only for this reason that religion requires that aid and assistance be given to paupers in their presence, but also out of honour and obedience to Christ. On the verse in Paul's Timothy 5 [I Timothy 5:10] where in instructing us in works of mercy he exhorts us to wash to feet of the saints and to minister to the tribulations of sufferers, Chrysostom in *Homily XIV* comments that we ought to display works of mercy to the poor in their own persons with outstanding zeal and with total willingness of soul, and with alacrity and devotion as if it were really to Christ himself. Nor, he says, ought we to order our servants to do what we owe the poor, but we ourselves are in person obligated to give to the poor in obedience to what Christ says [Matthew 13:14]: "If I your lord and teacher have washed your feet," as if to say that he did not entrust this humble service to anyone else, "you too ought to wash one another's feet." Chrysostom adds that no matter how great a person's dignity or how effulgent his glory, he is not as superior to the poor as Christ was to his disciples. When you minister to the poor, you minister to Christ. "For whoever welcomes a small child in my name, welcomes me [Matthew 18:5]." And "what you did to one of the least of them, you did to me [Matthew 25:40]." These are the words of Chrysostom.

For this reason we should fear that in the last day Christ will confess that he lived among us as a beggar and will reproach us that we thrust the poor away from our sight. We read about almost no saintly prelates of the Church or even saintly persons of great distinction about whom the memory is not handed down that they themselves gave food to the poor and even treated their wounds with their own hands. To pass over other children of emperors, I will refer to Augusta. Flacilla Augusta, the saintly wife of Emperor Theodosius, in Book VII of the *Historia Tripartita* [Cassiodorus, *Historia Ecclesiastica Tripartita Epitome* VII, 312] has this included among her principal honours:

> At the height of her reign while wearing the purple she took the greatest care of the lame and the crippled. She did not employ servants or other agents, but acting on her own she herself came to their homes and provided each one with what was needed. Similarly, circulating through the hostels of the churches, she ministered to the sick with her own hands, cleaning their pots, tasting the soup, offering a spoon, breaking the bread, serving the food, washing the cups, and doing all the other tasks that are regularly done by slaves and maidservants.

The Christians of antiquity always had in their ears that saying about the last day [Matthew 25:31–46], on which Christ declared that he was naked and a stranger among us, suffering hunger and thirst, so that they might assist the poor as if each one of them was Christ, attending to their service, and taking delight in seeing them.

We have reviewed these matters for the satisfaction of those who are kind-hearted toward the paupers, whose absence they cannot easily bear. But even for those cruel men who out of avarice have hearts of stone toward the poor and have stopped up their ears to their prayers, it is useful to thrust the poor into their sight. I hear that some people – Christians and pious men, to be sure – add to the reasons for instituting this shutting away of the poor, that if any infidel should see that among us people beg out of extreme necessity, he would accuse us of cruelty and savagery, and he would regard our law as a matter of reproach. But if he should notice that they are withdrawn and hidden away and forbidden to go out and yet are not maintained more liberally or treated more generously than is possible on this method of providing alms, he might have an even poorer opinion of us.

But I hasten elsewhere. It cannot but happen that even in a Christian state men are unkind and rough toward the poor; let paupers, therefore, move around in their presence who, if they cannot move them to do mercy, can at least convict them of injustice on the Day of Judgment. Does Christ not teach this in the story of that rich banqueter who wore purple and fine linen and feasted sumptuously every day [Luke 16:19]? He was tortured in Hell not so much because he did not give alms to an absent beggar, but because when Lazarus was lying at his door covered with sores and wishing to be fed with the crumbs that fell from the rich man's table, the rich man had absolutely no mercy on the pauper. Notice how many details Christ brings together and heaps up to increase the shame and ignominy of that rich man, for instance, that the dogs to which the rich man gave the crumbs were more merciful to the pauper, licking his sores, than the rich man himself. Christ needs beggars lying at the doors of cruel rich men as witnesses on the Day of Judgment, to confound and reproach them.

In contrast, how beautiful is the throng of paupers at the doors of prelates and grandees who are kind and merciful toward them. Restored and refreshed they heap benedictions on their benefactors, and they commend them before God with their prayers. Perhaps dissolute men would have been among them, but also some just men who, according to the word of the Lord [Luke 16:9], will be able to welcome us into everlasting habitations.

If the example of Christ washing the feet of the poor and serving their tables still continues once a year for kings and glorious emperors, why is it not laudable and honourable for paupers to dine daily at the gates of princes and other leading men? If those saintly fathers and monarchs of the Church like Gregory, Ambrose, and Augustine heard from Christ the beggar that the houses of princes and bishops were not open and that the poor were not being received inside for a meal, they would have reflected on it and condemned it no less than if they heard that children were forbidden from the houses of their fathers. Of Gregory we read that he never sat down to dine without paupers and foreigners, and that his house was crowded with beggars. So deserving was he about paupers, that angels dressed as paupers were often given alms by him and sat at his table among the pauper guests.

To juxtapose to a pope a king distinguished both by blood and saintliness, I refer to Louis king of the French, elevated to the sainthood by his own right and merit, son of Blanche, the queen of the Spaniards and herself of royal blood. I cannot be led to believe that that he would ever have ordered this confinement of the poor or even approved of it. He is said to have been so brought up by his saintly mother that more than two hundred paupers daily were bountifully fed in the royal house. On festival days before he himself ate he would personally serve them the dishes, and on particular Sundays he would with his own hands wash their feet, wipe them, and kiss them, and then later give these paupers increased alms.

For these reasons I cannot understand how instituting a prohibition against begging by the poor can be commended by its antiquity, as its authors claim. On the contrary, the claim is rebutted principally by this argument, that just as in the case of expelling foreigners, it is a novelty never known either to the pagans or the early Christians. If it had a place among the laws of mercy, the fathers of the Church would have given it to us in writing. However, this will be more suitably dealt with in my response to the reasons by which its authors support their opinion.

Chapter XII
In Which the Reasons and Causes for Prohibiting the Poor from Begging Are Examined

The authors of the proposal to enclose the beggars contend that the first foundation supporting their view is the divine verse from Deuteronomy 15 [15:4]: "However, there will be no indigent person and beggar among you, as the Lord will bless you in the land that he will give into your possession." Saint Thomas, in [*Summa Theologiae*] *Secunda Secundae* Q. 187, refutes this argument, saying that no one is prohibited from begging by this legal precept, but that the wealthy are prohibited from being so stingy that some are forced to beg out of need. One should keep this response in one's mind to understand other utterances, whether decisions of the Church or of the saints, that speak of this matter. Nowhere in the world were paupers restrained from begging; rather, the wealthy were instructed not to force paupers to beg through their cruelty.

Moreover, the meaning of this noun "beggar" does not include only, as some think, those who go from door to door. Anyone is properly said to be a beggar who is in such need that he lives every day from contributions and alms, even if he receives them at home. A pauper is someone who has something of his own from which he barely and miserably lives; a beggar is someone who has nothing but lives off what others have. Begging consists not only in soliciting, but in receiving what others give unasked.

Aside from what was just cited from Saint Thomas, this is also implied (although not stated explicitly) by Chrysostom or whoever was the author of the *Imperfectum* [*Opus Imperfectum in Matthaeum* 9, 5], expounding the verse in Matthew V [5:3], "Blessed are the poor in spirit." The Greek text, he says, refers not to paupers but to beggars. That verse impresses upon the people not only that there should not be beggars who solicit, but that there should not be persons confined to their homes who need daily alms and food baskets – the sorts of things set up in these articles. Therefore, the authors should not think that what they are instituting is fully compliant with this precept. Nor as the words stand does the precept obligate on pain of mortal sin. Rather, it was an exhortation to charity, which should flourish in every well-governed people. That is why after that exhortation the same chapter adds that the poor will always be among us. Just as Christ in many verses in the gospel taught mercy and moved us to almsgiving, he said nonetheless, foretelling the hardness of our hearts, that you will always have the poor with you.

Moreover, they adduce as an example of this way of almsgiving that Paul instituted similar ways of contributing in Macedonia and Galatia. He mentioned these in the Epistle to the Romans [15:26] and in I Corinthians [16:1]. These contributions, as Saint Thomas everywhere interprets them, were made on a far different basis, nor do the words of Paul need interpretation, as they are so clear in themselves. They were not collections of alms made to help and support the paupers in the very cities in which they lived. The story was (as we read in Acts of the Apostles, Chapter 11) that a very strong famine had broken out in Jerusalem and in surrounding Judaea. Paul and Barnabas were sent to Macedonia and Achaia both to preach and to seek help for the Christians in Jerusalem and Judaea, especially for those engaged in preaching and worship.

This is what Paul refers to in Galatians 2 [2:10] when he says: "James and Cephas and John gave the right hand of fellowship to Barnabas and me, that we should go to the Gentiles and they to the circumcised, asking us to remember the poor, the very thing I was eager to do." The Macedonians and the Galatians sent what was collected to Jerusalem by those very apostles. To this Paul attests in Romans 15 when he says [15:25–8]: "From here I am going to Jerusalem bringing aid to the saints. For Macedonia and Achaia have been pleased to make some contribution for the poor among the saints at Jerusalem. For they were pleased that they should owe it to them. For if the Gentiles are their partners in spiritual matters, they ought also to be of service to them in matters of the flesh." This is how the contributions were especially to aid the saints who were disciples of the gospel.

He then persuaded the Corinthians as he had the Macedonians. He wrote [I Corinthians 16:1]: "Now about the collection for the saints," namely, those in Jerusalem "do what I told the Galatian churches to do." Paul tells them how to do this: "On Sabbath," that is, on Sunday, "each one of you should set aside and save a sum as you wish, so that when I come," that is, to take it to Jerusalem, "no collections will have to be made." Accordingly, those alms were not collected to restrain paupers from begging. Although I am dealing with something else, I will not pass over in silence the comment of Chrysostom, *Homily XLIII*, in interpreting this passage: in imitation of this, every Christian should set aside a small money box for the poor in his home in the place where he is accustomed to pray; and just as a priest washes his hands before making a sacrifice, he should deposit alms into this box before prayer, and thus cleansed he should proceed to prayer, as it is written [Luke 11:41], "Give alms and behold everything is clean for you."

The third point held out in support of this is that in the primitive Church beggars did not solicit from door to door. This places us in a very wide field of discourse, where many things are worth thinking about. First of all, as I just said, we read of nothing either in the *Acts of the Church* or in the writing of any of the holy fathers from which we can surmise that paupers were deprived of the freedom of going out to beg wherever they wished. Secondly, no one can doubt that there were paupers begging in the time of Christ our Saviour. For of the crowd of the poor, the lame, the blind, and the sufferers from other illnesses and weaknesses who thronged to his care, one can guess that most of these were beggars who went from place to place. Then there is Christ's advice in Luke [14:12–14] "When you give a meal or a dinner, do not invite your friends" and so on, "nor your rich neighbours, but invite the poor, the crippled, the lame, the blind, and you will be blessed," which clearly must be understood as referring to beggars.

And that no one might object that these people then lived enclosed, see what follows in the parable of the man who made a magnificent banquet [Luke 14:16]. When the invited guests refused to come, he said to his servants, "Go out to the streets and the districts of the city," and not only that, but "into the roads and the hedges, and bring the poor and the crippled and the blind and the lame." For the beggars used to be found in these parts of the city and at the crossroads.

There were beggars not only in the time of Christ, but Augustine also provides evidence, especially in his *Sermon for the Second Sunday in Advent* [*Sermones de Tempore CXVI*]. When he preaches that Christians ought to give more ample alms, he states that "in holy festivals we should give more abundantly in accordance with our resources, and above all we should more frequently invite paupers to the feasts." He speaks about beggars who were accustomed to being admitted into the homes of the wealthy to dine. To such an extent at that time was begging a well-known practice and custom, as Saint Thomas says in [*Summa Theologiae*] *Secunda Secundae,* q. 187. Evidence of this is that many Christians out of religion and humility, after selling their possessions and distributing the proceeds to the poor, submitted themselves to that most abject condition, as is said about the Roman patrician Saint Alexius and about Arsenio in *The Lives of the Fathers*. Jerome in *Ad Oceanum* even commends Fabiola for pouring out her wealth on paupers and then herself choosing to live on what was donated to paupers. Nor is someone who today takes up that form of life as worthy of reproach as some people think. I recollect this only to show that beggars who solicited were always in the Church. But there is no need in so certain a matter to adduce unnecessary evidence. All the histories in which the deeds of the holy fathers are memorialized attest that beggars have always been in the Church. Nor did the religious orders of mendicants appropriate for themselves a name that was at odds with the thing itself.

I would add this third consideration, that in the primitive Church until the times of Gregory and beyond there were very different religious scruples, different attitudes by Christians toward the poor, different institutions, and different proceeds assigned to the relief of the poor than are present today, so that paupers could be relieved of the burden of soliciting. The authors of these articles adduce what we read in the life of Pope Clement, that he had a written list of the names of the needy in each region and that he did not allow those whom he had cleansed with the sacrament of baptism to become beggars. Fairly similar statements can be cited from the recorded acts of Silvester, Gregory, Martin, and all the other fathers of that time. They take note of how they did not allow the paupers to beg. But these popes did not deny, forbid, restrain, or obstruct them by law. How did they not allow them? They had a written list of the names of the paupers to whom they sent food baskets in abundance, so that they were left with no need to beg. In this most pious way the right to beg was taken from them. If it were not boring to summon up all the laws, I could lay them out in all their abundance. For the time being, whoever consults the title "Concerning Religious Houses" both in the *Decretals* and in the *Clementinae* will clearly understand how much the care of the poor was enjoined on the prelates, how anxiously and solicitously those priests, like true fathers, managed, administered, and supported the affairs of their children the paupers with appropriate expenses.

Beside these alms to individuals, there was a zeal to erect different kinds of hospitals everywhere, as is written in the *Codex de sacrosanctis ecclesiis, l. sancimus* and cited in the canon law, [*Decretum Gratiani*], causa 23, quaestio 8, cap. *Tributum* There were *xenodochia,* (that is, houses for foreign paupers), *orphanotrophia* (shelters for orphans), *ptochotrophia,* (where needy persons and beggars were supported), *brephotrophia* (buildings in which children were raised), and *gerontocomia* (where the elderly and the cripples were maintained). Watered by the freshness of the recent blood of Christ, the Church flourished to such an extent on its kindness and mercy toward the poor that no other factor was as effective for winning over the hearts of men and drawing them to faith in Christ. Because of this, as is written in Book VI of the *Ecclesiastical History*, Julian the apostate, who declared open war against the Church, strongly exhorted the pagans to build *xenodochia* and hospitals for the poor, and he gave them gifts and endowments so that by surpassing the Christians in mercy, they might retain for paganism the pagans who were rushing toward Christianity.

Why, then, do we strive, on the example of that Church, to help the paupers, so that they do not need to solicit? In those days a fourth of all the fruits and incomes of the Church was set aside to maintain the poor, as in the decree of Gelasius, in [*Decretum Gratiani* XII, q. 2, c. 27] canon Quattuor, XII, q. 2, and in that of Simplicius, in [*Decretum Gratiani*, XII, q. 8, c. 28] canon *De redditibus*, and by the Council of Toledo, in [*Decretum Gratiani*, XII, q. 8, c. 31] canon *Sancimus*, ibid. No matter how much excellent help the paupers received, we never read that they were forbidden to solicit. On what basis in the present time, when we long to have given to us the charity that those people had, the prelates of that age, the decrees of that Church, the annual proceeds set aside for the poor – on what basis, I say, can we be led to restrain the beggars from the capacity and freedom to solicit?

Neither the people of Cologne – to whose provincial council, which neither had the validity of papal authority nor appropriately decreed anything on this matter except the common law, I offer no response – nor the people of Ypres nor any of the Germans can be an example for the Spanish in this matter. Aside from their being much more civil-minded (as we said above), they have very full public treasuries from which they decree regular subsidies to the poor, as is contained in the statutes of Cologne and Ypres. We hear the same about the Venetians and the Genoans and many other Italians. I do not know, however, how we with only the money that is begged for, can now provide the beggars with enough assistance that we can by right restrain them from begging, no matter how many well-considered laws about alms there may be.

What I reflect upon mostly is that the legitimate proposers, promulgators, and executors of these kinds of laws and ordinances are not laypersons but prelates of the Church and priests. Where in the sacred scriptures or in the sacred canons, I ask, are laypersons designated as the patrons of this service to the poor, or where are not priests of the Church and bishops assigned to this task as if they were fathers of the poor? The reason is that Christ (as his disciple Paul said) wanted the priests to be free from concern about secular matters [I Corinthians 7:32–3]: "The unmarried man is concerned about the things of the Lord, how to please the Lord. But the married man is concerned about things of the world, how to please his wife, and he is divided." To where do these comments lead?

I certainly agree that this matter and the care of the poor cannot long endure in the hands of laypersons, however great their probity and prudence. This is not what God and the Church thought it right to set up. Rather, because of its spiritual nature, the bishops should be the architects of this edifice whereas the function of the people is to supply the material and the wood. Laypersons are married, have families, and are engaged in other responsibilities, affairs, and concerns. From these they can scarcely disentangle themselves to be freely available for these duties of mercy. Without a decision to pay the attendants out of the alms of the poor, you will rarely find anyone who will persevere in the work. We see it happen that the poor are cheated out of a good part of the alms that land up with the attendants. But you say: the prelates do not have the same care for the poor as their predecessors. I acknowledge this, but I can have no hope that laypersons exercising the functions of bishops will repair the damage. They will do a good enough job, I say, if the poor can continuously be maintained in their enclosures. Those who have now undertaken the task, being leading men with outstanding Christian values, will be able to sustain this enterprise for a time, but as others subsequently succeed to this responsibility and still others succeed to them, it will necessarily totter and collapse.

Drawing in my sails as I now approach the harbour, I call as witness what has the greatest weight in all that people try to do: experience. For almost three years this method of alms has continued in use and practice. Make sure you know, most provident Prince, what its fruit has been in reality. Because, as they say, this is a matter of fact and not of law, I want you to put no faith in me. But from what I have heard and seen here and similarly from what I surmise in other places, it faces many difficulties.

But as you are most vigilant, take care that your understanding is not based on fraud.

First, among the throngs of able-bodied beggars that have been expelled from the large cities, have any legitimate paupers indiscriminately been made to leave?

Second, since we see no beggar walking around from street to street, has the number of paupers in the old hospitals grown, or have other hospitals been created that have received persons who used to circulate?

Next, are there Christians who are spreading complaints that there are no longer beggars extorting alms by force? For in this matter it was usual that the kingdom of heaven suffered violence [Matthew 11:12].

Then, have the alms withheld from the expelled vagabonds come in their entirety to the natives and those who have been ashamed to solicit – which was considered the principal goal in this matter? Or perhaps these are not better off at all or only a little, but the former total of alms has decreased.

If you determine that the matter is going well, that is, that the alms are not at all smaller but much larger, and that that the miseries, troubles, and calamities that crush the poor are alleviated by the increased alms, take care to interpose your princely authority so that this way of dealing with alms continues. Then we will all bend in the direction in which we see the mind of the prince inclines. We will applaud it, support it, favour it; we will all protect it, preach it, and assist it. But if you think that the condition of the poor is worsening, it will be sufficient that we retain, commend, and strive with all our might for the success of those endeavours and regulations for registering alms to assist the native poor who sustain their needs at home, for those regulations are inevitably the most approved and acceptable to God. But all the other beggars should be left with the right to solicit.

May we not hear that in a Christian kingdom ruled by a most Christian prince, an authentic pauper should be suffer a public penalty for begging! Although that prodigious statue whose mystery Daniel interpreted [Daniel 2:31-45] had a head of gold and a breast of silver, its legs were most miserable, being partly of iron and partly of clay; when the legs were smashed, the body with all its precious metals collapsed. Perhaps this most miserable order of paupers through the merit of the alms given it sustains the higher orders of the state, so that its removal places the entire body in peril.

I fear that my prolix document may begin to weary you. Somehow its impetus took me farther than I intended. Although it has been merely the performance of my obedience for whatever it was worth, you will not regret reading some of it to acquire the outstanding and illustrious virtue of mercy. For as the person who to the great hope of your kingdoms has by divine will and mercy been endowed with such light as nature has never produced in anyone, except your father and perhaps other very rare persons, with what else but the duties of mercy can you repay the extraordinarily great benefits that you have received?

Just as on the throne of God, so on the throne of the prince, it is fitting that both justice and mercy should sit together. As with God, so with a king, it is mercy that shines with greater splendour. May God grant that you bring about both, so that as we rejoice in the place that you deservedly hold among mortals, so may we have the joy of seeing you in a similar place among the saints forever. Farewell.

In Salamanca,
in the workshop of Juan de Junta,
on the thirtieth day of January.
1545 AD

Commentary on Aquinas, Summa Theologiae, I-II, Q. 32 on Almsgiving (1539–1540)

1 This question is famous among theologians. They debate it in [comments on Peter Lombard's *Sentences*] 4. D. 15 on the topic of restitution. Saint Thomas, as we said, first dwells on four conclusions.

The first has been accepted by all without controversy, namely, that almsgiving is a matter of precept. Indeed, it is expressly drawn from the gospel and it would be impermissible to deny it. It is included in the precept in Matthew 22:39 "You shall love your neighbour as yourself." Love bespeaks not only interior act but exterior beneficence, because interior acts toward neighbours are not necessary except because of exterior beneficence.

2 Similarly, no one is sent to Hell except because of mortal sin. But as Matthew 25:41–5 says, the damned are sent to Hell because they did not do acts of mercy: "I was hungry and you did not feed me" etc. and John in I John 3:17: "Whoever has the wealth of this world and sees his brother in need and closed his heart, how does the love of God remain in him?" If love is lost through the failure to give alms, that omission is a mortal sin, and therefore the act of almsgiving is a matter of precept.

3 Similarly, it is evident from the order of charity, as we said above, because we are obligated to love the temporal life of our neighbour more than our own temporal goods. Therefore, almsgiving is a matter of precept.

Similarly and finally, otherwise God certainly would not have sufficiently provided for his children. Either he should have given all an equal share of temporal goods, or if he permitted some to have more, he should have laid down the precept that they should assist the needy. For God in the world is like a paterfamilias in the house, who should provide for all.

4 But if you say that in the precepts of the Decalogue there is no such precept about almsgiving, Saint Thomas responds (a. 5) in the answer to objection 4, that it is reduced to the precept to love one's father, as it is interpreted in I Timothy 4:8; for piety is the virtue with respect to parents, and to it belongs assisting all one's kin, and therefore, one's neighbours.

5 From this you could have inferred that the precept about alms belongs to the right of nature, because all the precepts of the Decalogue belong to the right of nature, though not as manifestly as those that are explicit in the Decalogue. For as we have said in 1, 2, among the rights of nature are placed only those that by their natural light no one of sound mind could deny. There are three levels in the precepts of nature. Some are first principles known though themselves, which do not need to be posited but are written in our hearts, such as "Do unto others what you want done to yourself." Others are conclusions to which, if posited, we would most readily assent, and those are the ten precepts of the Decalogue. Others are conclusions in the third level that need to be explained by the wise to be admitted; these are reduced to the precepts of the Decalogue, just as the sin of usury is reduced to theft, and in the same way almsgiving is reduced to the honouring of parents. But what is posited is a precept about parents, because that is obvious and undeniable. However, the precept about almsgiving needs explication, and is not as well known. But that it is a matter of right is evident, because by the right of nature everything is held in common in a condition of necessity, and the right of nations in dividing goods could not prejudice natural right.

6 Similarly the fourth conclusion is accepted by all and is not in controversy: namely, that when the neighbour is not in extreme or very grave necessity, and a person does not have a superfluity with respect to status and person, almsgiving is a matter not of precept but of counsel.

7 Accordingly, the only doubt is with respect to the second and third conclusions. The second conclusion is that it is a precept to give alms from one's superfluity; the third is that it is a precept to give alms to one who is in extreme necessity. There is a grave difficulty about the truth of these conclusions, and not only about the truth but about the intention of Saint Thomas. Three opinions exist about these two conclusions.

8 The first is of canonists who deny both conclusions. Panormitanus 2. *Decretalium De iureiurando* cap [8] *Si vero* holds that almsgiving is a matter of precept only when two conditions are present at the same time: first, that the neighbour is in extreme necessity, and second, the person who is to give alms has a superfluity of both nature and status, so that neither part in itself makes a precept; and so he allows that although the neighbour is in extreme necessity I am not obligated to give from what is necessary to my status. That is also the opinion of Antoninus, the archbishop of Florence [*Summa*] 2 p. tit. 1 cap. 24 s. 5 *De inhumanitate*. The same is the opinion of the *Summa Rosellae* on the word "*eleemosyna*." These doctors say that this is the opinion of Saint Thomas in this place. For they read the second and third conclusions as joined together in one unit. Because of this lord Cajetan wrote a treatise *On Almsgiving*, found among his shorter works, to clarify that passage in Saint Thomas.

9 The second is an intermediate opinion, which is that of Alexander of Hales [*Summa Theologica*] 4 p. q. 113 membrum 1, followed by Gabriel [Biel,

Inventarium seu Repertorium Generale], 4 d. 16 q. 4, and consists in three propositions:

> First, no one is bound to give alms from the necessities of nature, even if the other is in extreme necessity.
>
> Second, one is obligated to give alms from necessities of status to someone who is in extreme necessity.
>
> Third, apart from a neighbour's extreme necessity, no one is bound as a matter of precept to give alms, no matter how great his superfluity of status and nature, but this is solely a matter of counsel.

10 This is the opinion of all the moderns, and so they allow the third conclusion of Saint Thomas and deny the second.

Nonetheless, we have determined that the conclusions of Saint Thomas certainly cannot be in doubt for those who are versed in the readings of the early Fathers. Let us first see whether the opinion that the canonists attribute to Saint Thomas is really his.

11 As Cajetan says in the cited treatise, it cannot be doubted that the following was the opinion of Saint Thomas: apart from a neighbour's extreme necessity, everyone is obligated to give alms solely by reason of the superfluity; and similarly in the neighbour's extreme necessity, everyone is obligated to give alms from the superfluity of status.

12 First of all, Saint Thomas in 4 sent. D. 15 q. 2a. 1 quaestiuncula 4 (sol. 4) expressly and clearly sets out the two conclusions separately, namely, that after a person has provided for himself and his status, he is obligated to pour the superfluity back to the poor, and later he adds: "Similarly, precept obligates that one relieves the absolute necessity of strangers in priority to the non-extreme necessity of oneself or one's relatives"; and he says that this was the common opinion, and this certainly was so in the time of Saint Thomas.

13 Likewise in 2, 2, q. 62 a. 3 he says that by natural right we owe the poor what is superfluous to us. And he says explicitly in 2, 2, q. 87 a.1 (ad) 4 and q. 118 a. 4 ad 2 that each person is bound by a legal debt to give his goods to the poor either because of the danger of necessity or because the superfluity of what he has, where he expressly says that either on its own suffices for a precept, that is, either superfluity in the possessor or extreme necessity in the needy; and in the following article in this question in the final words he says that in extreme necessity a person is obligated to give from what is necessary to his status, and in *De Malo* q. 13 ad 2 (ad) 4. That this is the view of Saint Thomas is undeniable.

14 But because some think that this view is unique to Saint Thomas and therefore is unauthoritative, they should know that this was the common opinion, as Saint Thomas says here, and among the scholastics Richardus [de Mediavilla] 4 sent. d. 15 expressly posits both conclusions as distinct.

15 Likewise, Adrianus [*Quaestones de sacrementis in quartum sententiarum librum*] 4 on the topic *De Resititutione* in that question, on whether the clergyman who exhibits his own goods beyond the necessity of his status is obligated to make restitution, expressly posits that the two are distinct, and he takes that opinion of all the saints as settled. Paludanus [*In quartum sententiarum*] 4. D. 15. Q. 3 and Silvester on the word "*eleemosyna*" s. 2 and extensively in the *Rosa Aurea* and Cajetan in the place cited and Durandus [*In quartum sententiarum*] 4, d, 15, q, 6 ad 2 expressly put the argument that we are obligated to give from what is necessary for our status to someone who is in extreme necessity. Nonetheless, although apart from extreme necessity we are obligated by precept to give from our superfluity, he does not dare assert that not to give is a mortal sin so as not to condemn the crowd of rich people, but he says that that is the opinion of John (I John 3:17).

16 So that the dispute should be clear, one should first note that the necessary goods under discussion are of two kinds. Some are necessary always and absolutely; they are those without which a person would not be able to live and feed his family, and they are called necessaries of life or of nature. Others are necessary conditionally, if a person is to maintain the seemly status that he has; these are called necessaries of status.

17 In the following article we shall see whether a person is permitted to give from the first necessaries. The question now is about necessaries of status, the superfluity of which is the surplus over the seemly maintenance of one's status.

18 The third conclusion of Saint Thomas is easier and is not in doubt among the theologians, as we have already said, namely, that for those who are in extreme necessity a person is obligated to give from what is necessary to his status, and he is obligated to diminish his status even considerably, if it is necessary. Alexander, Durandus, and Gabriel and all except some isolated canonists concede this, and the authorities and reasons that we adduced above for the proof of the first conclusion prove this one as well. For if there is a precept to love our neighbour as ourselves, we are obviously obligated to love the temporal life of our neighbour more than our own status, and God would not be a good father unless he had instituted and commanded this.

19 Similarly, in such a case, as we said, everything is in common, and in distributing the common goods the right of nations could not derogate from natural right. And John (I John 3:17) expressly says: "having the wealth of this world and seeing his brother in need," etc. They say that the wealth of this world refers to what is superfluous, but this is really to pervert the words from their proper meaning. For "the wealth of this world" refers to nothing but temporal goods, and Ecclesiasticus 34:25 says that "the bread of the needy is the life of the poor; whoever cheats him is a man of blood."

20 Likewise is the explicit authority of Ambrose in his book *De Officiis*, as quoted in [*Decretum Gratiani* I] d. 86 c. 21: "Feed the person dying of hunger;

if you did not feed him, you killed him." And Augustine is quoted in [*Decretum Gratiani* II] 16 q., 1 c. 66: "Tithes: However, many paupers are in a neighbourhood where someone lives who did not pay the tithe, for that many murders will he appear as a defendant before the tribunal of the judge."

21 This is argued with reason, for a pauper in extreme necessity can by natural right take that which is necessary to sustain his life; therefore, whoever that might be is obligated to give it to him.

The consequence is proven: otherwise it would be a just war on both sides if it were permissible for me to defend my goods and for another to take them.

22 Similarly, this is supported by the argument that we often make on this topic: it would be cruelty that should be excoriated by everyone, if one could help a neighbour whom one saw dying of hunger and did not do so. As Jeremiah says in Lamentations 4:9: "It was better to be slain by the sword than to be killed by hunger," for death by hunger is crueller than death by the sword. A testimony to this is that miserable spectacle that took place in our time in the province of Baetica, where many thousands of persons died of starvation. Who would say that the witnesses to this were not obligated to assist from their necessities of status, even if their status would be greatly diminished?

23 Similarly, it is argued that with the same ease they would say that I am not obligated to assist from my necessities of status if my parents, or at least my brothers and relatives, were in extreme necessity – which would be barbarous to say.

24 Finally it is argued that if the precept of almsgiving applied only when both were present – namely, the superfluity for the giver and extreme necessity for the seeker – that precept would be vain, because such a coincidence could occur only rarely or never. Yet on the Day of Judgment an innumerable crowd of people is sent to Hell because of their lack of works of mercy. One should not listen to anyone who denies this conclusion, and if Saint Thomas had said the opposite, I would never have believed him. Rather, what we should believe are the words of the gospel, by which we are obligated to give alms to someone in extreme necessity.

However, there some uncertainties about that conclusion. The first is: what counts as extreme necessity?

25 Saint Thomas responds to this that it is when urgent necessity becomes apparent. It is called extreme necessity not only when one is already on the point of death, but when it is morally imminent and one fears that it will come in the near future, and no one else is present who is prepared to assist. A moral doctrine should be treated not metaphysically but by reference to moral certainty; for example, there is some neighbour of mine who is suffering from the most serious necessity and is growing weaker, I should not wait until the point of death.

Similarly, I see that others who are more closely related to him can help him; he has a very wealthy father and brothers, but I see that they are not coming to his assistance; I am obligated, because the sin of others does not excuse mine.

26 But perhaps you say: I will assist tomorrow. I say that we should not wait for this, and about this there is no certain science but only natural judgment. We have the light of God's face (compare Psalms 4:7) written in our hearts, which does not allow us to ignore these things.

The same is to be said about other necessities. A person is in jail who suffers unjustly; although there are many people who should help, none do so; certainly, I am obligated to help if I can; the same about the sick, if I am a physician or can be of service in some other way.

27 A second uncertainty is whether it is sufficient to give assistance in extreme necessity by a loan. It seems that it is, because if he himself does not want to accept a loan, he is not in extreme necessity, as he can help himself. If he is then given what he lacks, he can become more prosperous and repay. On the other hand, it seems that it is not sufficient to give a loan, but I am obligated. In extreme necessity everything is in common; therefore, assistance is owed to him as a matter of justice. On this issue some hold an affirmative view and others a negative one.

Nonetheless, I would provide a more nuanced response, for in moral matters one should not rush to a solution.

28 So let the first proposition be: if what someone in extreme necessity needs is something of little value, a gift worth two or three argentei or one aureus or more, certainly there is an obligation to give as a matter of precept.

This is evident, because a person is obligated to suffer some loss of one's goods to relieve anther's extreme necessity.

29 The second proposition: if it is of great worth then one must distinguish; the person in need has no goods either in that place where he is in need or in any other place, then certainly whoever is able should give it gratuitously for the same reason, that it is a case of extreme necessity.

30 The third proposition: however, if the person who is in need has goods in some other place, or goods are available for him to have, then a person is not obligated to give to him gratuitously. It is sufficient that he give it to him on loan; for example, if he is a merchant who has considerable property in Flanders but he was shipwrecked on coming to Spain and here he is in extreme need for one hundred aurei, it is sufficient that I give him a loan that he can repay me; if he does not want to accept this, I am not obligated to give it to him for nothing, because he is not in extreme necessity. Perhaps that would also be the case if my neighbour stood to inherit but now is a son who has extreme need for a hundred ducats; it is sufficient that I loan it to him until his father dies, even though this is not so certain.

31 Another uncertainty is whether a person is bound to relieve anyone in any sort of extreme necessity; for example, am I bound to give the money when someone is held captive by infidels who will kill him unless I give them two hundred ducats?

The answer is that, if we can, we are completely obligated to relieve extreme necessities that come from within, such as sicknesses, hunger etc., because they do not present themselves in so serious a form, generally speaking. But as for necessities that come from outside through another's wrong, we are not all obligated to relieve them at such expense; this is extreme necessity not *simpliciter* but in a qualified sense, that is, through someone's wrong, because even the captive himself is not obligated to redeem himself with so great a loss.

32 The last uncertainty is whether someone who does not assist another in extreme necessity is obligated to make restitution for the damage suffered. It seems that he is. For as we have said quoting Ambrose and Augustine, someone who does not feed the starving but allows him to die is a murderer.

Certainly, some say that he is obligated to make restitution, and although I would not say so definitively, it would not be completely absurd if a person of means who allowed the death of an unfortunate man with a family to support would be obligated to provide some satisfaction to the family.

Nonetheless, the common opinion is that he is not obligated to make good the damage. The reason is that he is not obligated by a precept of distributive justice but by a precept of mercy. It would be different if a person to whom I owed money died of starvation because I did not pay him. I think that then I would be obligated for the damage.

33 More people reject the second conclusion. As we have said, Alexander and Gabriel and all the moderns deny that, apart from extreme necessity, one is obligated to give from one's superfluity. And Durandus does not dare assert it directly in order not to condemn the crowd of the rich.

34 But certainly I can in no way doubt that there is a precept to give from one's superfluity aside from extreme necessity. We will argue this first on the authority of scripture, then on the authority of the saints, and lastly by reason.

The most compelling authority adduced by Saint Thomas and all the others is the verse of Luke 11:41: "Regarding what is left, give alms, and behold, everything is clean for you."

35 It is true that this verse is read differently by different authors. Some read "regarding what is left" (*quod superest*) as "give what is superfluous" (*superfluum date*); this is the way Ambrose and Augustine and Bede read it, as you can see in [Aquinas] *Catena Aurea* [on Luke 11:41]. It is true that Bede [*In Lucam* on 11:41] adds another meaning, that *quod superest* refers not to superfluity but to the remedy. For there Christ is confuting the Jews, because the inner hearts of the Jews were all full of robbery and iniquity; he immediately adds *quod superest*, that is, the remedy that is left is that you should give alms, and everything will be clean for you.

Theophylactus [*In Lucam* on 11:41], however, reads it differently, that is, what is in you and available for you give as alms, as if it says: distribute the wealth that you have to the paupers. All these senses are consonant with the text.

36 Others read *quod superest* as a conjunction, as if it said "but" or "what remains is that you should give alms," and that is the way grammatically inclined theologians read it. But certainly what they think is the better reading is less consonant with the text. For the Greek text reads *ta enonta date eleemosynam; ta enonta* is the plural participle of *insum*, that is, *inhaerentia*, and what we call *ceterum* or *reliquum* the Greeks call *lipon*. It is true that the participle *enonta* is sometimes understood as *superest,* as a conjunction between sentences. But more frequently and in accordance with its proper meaning it has the force only of "what is available," and so it can perhaps be understood, as Erasmus notes [*Paraphrases in Novum Testamentum*, on Luke 11:41], to have the meaning of "give alms as is possible for you," and thus all the meanings prove our conclusion. If it is understood according to the common meaning of the saints, it clearly says, "Give your superfluity as alms"; If it is understood according to the meaning of Theophylactus, the precept is even more extensive. For it does not command to give only from what is superfluous, but to give what is possible for each; and it does not mention extreme necessity but only that the person who has should give to the person who is in need.

37 Another passage is Luke 3:11: "Anyone who has two tunics should give one to him who has none, and anyone who has food should do the same." According to all the saintly expositors, one tunic refers to what suffices for human necessity in accordance with each person's status, and to have two tunics is to have for oneself and for others. This cannot be understood to be a matter of counsel. For as is evident from the words that precede it, that every tree that does not bear fruit will be cut down and consigned to the fire, but no one is consigned to the fire except for a mortal sin. And when the crowds asked him, "What shall we do to not be cut down?" Jesus answered, "Anyone who has two tunics should give one to him has none." He commanded them with the very words with which he was going to reproach them on the Day of Judgment. Certainly, if we accept the spirit of the gospel, these words prove our conclusion.

38 The words of I John 2:17 explicitly do the same: "Whoever has the wealth of this world and sees his brother suffering in need" (he certainly does not say "extreme") "and closed his heart, the love of God does not remain in him."

Also doing this is the passage in Luke 16:19–31 about the rich banqueter who was consigned to Hell because he had not given alms to Lazarus. It is not plausible that Lazarus endured extreme necessity after begging from door to door, and yet the banqueter was consigned to Hell because while he was feasting so splendidly, he allowed the beggar to suffer in misery.

Because scriptural passages are to be understood piously in line with the interpretation of the saints, let us see what the saints thought about this.

39 Basil [Aquinas, *Catena Aurea* on Luke 3:11] on those words of Luke 3:11: "anyone who has two tunics." Here, he says, we are taught that everything more abundant than we need for our own manner of life, we should disburse to a person who does not have, for God's sake. In a sermon against the avaricious rich on the

passage in Luke 12:16-21 about the field of the wealthy man, admirable comments are made on this theme, in which he makes the rich nothing but stewards, and he says that those who do not disburse what is superfluous commit the same sin as a household manager who does not faithfully disburse the goods of his master. There he says these words, cited here by Saint Thomas in the solution to the second objection: "the bread that you have belongs to the hungry, the tunic that you store belongs to the naked etc."

Chrysostom too in a homily about the birth of John [*Homilia de navitate Ioannis*] and elsewhere completely situates in precept the giving of alms from what is superfluous, just as the steward is under a precept to distribute the goods of the master. Indeed, that is the meaning of that parable in Luke 12:16–21. Ambrose on the same parable quoted in [*Decretum Gratiani*] d. 47, c. 8, *Sicut ii,* explicitly and extensively proves that not giving to the needy is just like usurping what is another's; he says, "Let no one call his own what is in common; what is more than sufficient for one's expenses has been obtained by violence." And Augustine says in the epistle to Macedonius, quoted in [*Decretum Gratiani*] 14 q., 4 c. 11: "What am I to say? Everything that is possessed badly belongs to another; one possesses badly what one uses badly." Isidore repeats the same words, as quoted in [*Decretales Gregorii IX, lib. 5, tit. 40, c. 12*] *De verborum significatione*c. 12 *Ius dictum*. And Jerome says, as quoted in [*Decretum Gratiani* I] d. 42 c. *Hospitalem*: "The person shown to retain for himself what is beyond his needs is guilty of stealing another's goods by force."

40 But moreover, there are arguments from reason: First, as we said above, God and nature made temporal goods for the maintenance of the needy even beyond extreme necessity. But God could not otherwise provide for the needy except by commanding the rich to supply the poor; therefore, this is what he commanded; otherwise, the needy would remain without a remedy.

The second argument is that this pertains to the precept about love. Just as a person would not be thought to love his friend if, when the friend was in extreme necessity, he did not give him from his necessities of status, so he would not be thought to love him if, when the friend lacked necessities of status, he did not give him from his superfluity. For just as we are obligated to value the life of another more than our status, so we are obligated to value the status of another more than our superfluities.

And it is confirmed: if my neighbour suffered a serious necessity of status but not of person, and I had superfluous goods but did not assist him, surely no one would consider me to be his friend.

41 The third argument is this: the sequenced order of charity is a matter of precept, as we shall see below. The sequenced order of charity is that a person should assist himself first, then his connections and family, and then strangers. The first order is a matter of precept, and therefore so is the second. For I am obligated to assist my family and connections even when the necessity is less than

extreme. Who will deny, if my brother was labouring under a grave necessity of his status and I have many thousands of superfluous ducats, that I am obligated to assist him?

This is confirmed, because if I am not obligated except in extreme necessity to give from my superfluity to a stranger, neither would I be obligated to give even to my father. For, as we said above, even if I was obligated more in the case of my father than in the case of a stranger, nonetheless any kind of necessity that, to avoid mortal sin, would obligate me in the case of my father would also obligate me in the case of a stranger. But who could doubt that I am obligated to assist from my superfluity a father suffering grave necessity? This is the reason that Saint Thomas sets out in the text. For he understands that the two orders of charity are a matter of precept: first, that from my superfluity I am obligated to assist myself and then my connections and then strangers, and second that I am obligated to give priority to another's extreme necessity of nature over my own status.

42 The fourth argument: if there was no precept except to give alms solely in extreme necessity and not from one's superfluity, it would not be so dangerous to be rich as is expressed in the gospel. Why is it that Christ says hyperbolically in Matthew 19:23 that it is impossible for the rich to enter the kingdom of heaven? Those theologians say that this refers to wealthy persons who rob others of their goods, but this is to say nothing because a pauper who robs others of their goods also will not enter. Moreover, cases of extreme necessity occur only very rarely. What then is the danger of wealth? And yet Luke 12:16–21 in that parable of the rich man says only that he was buried in Hell because he accumulated grain. Certainly, Christ could not say more clearly than in that parable that it is a sin not to give what is superfluous.

Finally, such a crowd would not be condemned to Hell in Matthew 25:41–6 for not doing works of mercy solely because of cases of extreme necessity, because these are not so frequent, especially because the condemnation was for not providing hospitality to strangers and for not clothing the naked; and yet hospitality and clothing are scarcely cases of extreme necessity. I certainly will never doubt that giving alms from what is superfluous is a matter of precept.

43 There are many uncertainties about this conclusion. The first is that no one who consumes his own property is considered to have a superfluity.

I prove the conclusion: because if something is superfluous to the status that someone has now, it is not directly superfluous to the status that he can acquire; someone who has ten pair of oxen can keep them to buy an eleventh of twelfth pair, and a soldier can aspire to become a cavalry man, and a merchant can intend to get a landed estate.

44 The response to this is that it is permissible to change status. But we say secondly that anyone can aspire to this provided it is morally possible, and otherwise not. For example, someone who has been admitted to the king's household and has ingratiated himself to the king can then keep what he has with a view to that

status. But for a man who makes a living through his skill as an artisan, and has two hundred ducats, and aspires to a landed estate, that is fatuous. Therefore, we call a superfluity that which is superfluous to his present status or to that status which he very plausibly can hope for in the near future; otherwise, to keep one's goods for a future status is contrary to the Gospel of Matthew 6:34, namely, it is to be worried about tomorrow, as Saint Thomas says here in his reply to the third objection, which is to provide for long into the future.

45 Thirdly we say that a person who has temporal goods always has something superfluous, which he is obligated to give. He is an owner who has income of one thousand or two thousand aurei, he has daughters, he can save for his daughters' dowry. But he always has one aureus or ten or a hundred that are superfluous to him, and the necessities that come up are not so large that he would have to diminish his status. Therefore, all these things have to be considered by reference to moral certainty, nor can a determinate rule be established for this, but each person will be able to judge whether he has something superfluous. Certainly, the very rich should take note that it is not sufficient to give a copper farthing as alms.

46 Another uncertainty is touched upon by Saint Thomas in his third argument: inasmuch as there is an affirmative precept to give from one's superfluity, for what time does it obligate? If the necessity is extreme, it clearly obligates at that time; but beyond extreme necessity there never seems to be a time when it is necessary to give alms.

This is confirmed: because it follows that as long as one has a superfluity, one has to give to all paupers, which would be a heavy burden.

Saint Thomas responds to this in *Quidlibet* 8 a. 12, that apart from extreme necessity, there is no certain time at which one is obligated to give, nor is there a certain person to whom one is obligated to give. But one is nonetheless obligated to give. For example, a rich man is permitted not to give to this pauper who is soliciting his aid, because he can hold back for another, nor is he obligated to give today, because he can give tomorrow. Nonetheless he must give at some point, but this is to be appraised according to the judgment of the wise, and natural light dictates when a person is obligated and when not. The necessity is serious, the neighbour's status is endangered, someone is sick, there is briefly now such an opportunity to give, that a greater one probably cannot occur; we are certainly obligated to give then. But I greatly fear that we are excessively inclined to favour the rich against the gospel and against the right of the poor.

47 Against this: you then condemn all the rich people, who do not usually act this way.

In reply, first: We do not condemn all of them, for certainly devout men give alms; indeed, they support poor servants and give other alms, and they now have very great expenses.

Second, Christ responds in the gospel (Matthew 19:23): "It is impossible for the rich to enter the kingdom of heaven."

I would like to dissuade those rich people about one thing. When they have a superfluity and decide to give alms, they do not give it to the poor, but they set up memorials and prebends. It would certainly be better to give to the poor before us. This is chiefly because they seem not to give but to retain, so that it remains as if it were theirs. Secondly, this is being worried about tomorrow. God provides what is now superfluous for the paupers before us. Give to these paupers, and the Lord will provide for future ones.

48 The last uncertainty is what if someone has a superfluity but there are no paupers. Should he seek out paupers and send his alms to a distant land if his own country has none?

Christ our Saviour solved this uncertainty in Matthew 26:11: "You will always have the poor with you." The others are metaphysical cases that are not admitted in moral topics. If there are no paupers in extreme need, there at least are paupers.

De Dominio, ss. 1–8 (1535)

The Precise Notion of *Dominium* Is Explained

1. Now first of all, to reach the substance of *dominium* by a definition that people call nominal, we must first enquire into the word. The word "*dominium*" is either never or very rarely found among the ancient Latin authors. It is understood as domination (*dominatio*) or absolute control (*dominatus*), so that having *dominium* is the same as dominating or ruling, just as the emperor has *dominium* over the Spaniards, as in I Maccabees 11: "King Ptolemy obtained *dominium* of the cities right up to Seleucia Maratima."

But the theologians and the jurists use this word in a different sense, as the power or right that someone has in something, or in particular to refer in this way to ownership (*proprietas*) over something, as one is said to have *dominium* of land, a house, a horse, and other things of that sort that are one's own. This is the sense in which Jerome used it in his translation of Tobias 8 [8:21]: "Of all the things that Ragael possessed he gave half to Tobias, and he drew up a deed that the half that remained would after their deaths devolve to the *dominium* of Tobias." This is the meaning of *dominium* that we must now discuss.

2. In order that our teaching, should, in accordance with Cicero's example, start with a definition, this is how almost all scholars define *dominium*: *Dominium* is the proximate power or faculty of taking things into one's licit use in accordance with rationally instituted laws and rights. Gerson was the first to formulate this definition, which Conrad and modern scholars follow, in his treatise *De Potestate Ecclesiastica*, consider. 13 and in his treatise *De Vita Spirituali*, lec. 3. In this connection Conrad notes in *De Contractibus*, tract. 1, that a power over some thing is the same as a right [*ius*] in that same thing. Accordingly, *ius* is understood in two ways: first, it is the same as law, as when we say canon law or civil law or natural law; and second it is the same as a permission or faculty with respect to something, such as a father has with respect to his children, and a husband with respect to his wife as Paul says in I Corinthians 7 [7:4]: "A wife does not have power over herself,

but a husband does." In the same way Gerson defines *ius* as *dominium*. However, a person who has a right does not thereby have *dominium*, for *dominium* adds a certain superiority. A son has a right with respect to his father, and even a slave with respect to his master, that he feed him, but yet does not have *dominium* to use him with superiority. But neither is it the case that whoever has a right to use with superiority also has *dominium*, unless understood broadly, as is apparent. A person renting a house has a right to use it, but does not have *dominium* except broadly, as we will say below.

Those scholars also note that *dominium* is rather a faculty with respect to some thing than a power, because a power extends more broadly even to a power to do what is permitted or forbidden just as a robber has a power over something of mine. But "faculty," they say, comes from the word *fas* [permitted], and so refers to a power in accordance with right. But I would respectfully say that faculty does not come from *fas* but has the same force as "facility." Faculty is the opposite of difficulty, and having a faculty is the same as having facility. A person is said to have facility over a horse because he can use it easily (*facile*), that is, without anyone else's permission. Actually, when understood morally, power has the same meaning; in this way the robber does not have power over something of mine. Therefore, it is the same whether we say that *dominium* is a power or a faculty. Nor need the word "proximately" be added, because a remote potency is not said to be physically a potency, just as cold water is not said to have the potency to get hot. Nor do the words "permitted according to the laws" need to be added, for power means that on its own: we have the power to do what we can rightfully do. Power is the same as *ius*, and *ius* is the same as what is just [*iustum*], as Saint Thomas says in [*Summa Theologiae*] *Secunda Secundae*, q. 57, a. 1.

Accordingly, in defining *dominium* it is sufficient to say that it is the power or faculty of taking something into our use. A definition should be brief, compendious, and so on. This definition is obviously good, because a power can be defined through an act or an end, just as vision is the potency of perceiving colours. The end of *dominium* is use. *Dominium* would be in vain if it was forever without use. *Dominium* is thus defined optimally as being ordered toward use, as our definition does.

3. However, against the definition is this argument: the usuary and the usufructuary have the faculty and right to take a thing up into one's own use – as a person renting a house has the right to live in it, and the person renting a horse has the right to ride it – and yet they do not have *dominium*; therefore, the definition is invalid. The issue here is the difference between *dominium* and use and usufruct. This is better understood than can be explained. Nonetheless it must be said that, first, one can reply by denying the minor premise: indeed, the usuary is in a way the *dominus* of the thing so long as he has the right to use it. In this connection one must note the magisterial rule adduced by Conrad in the place cited above, namely, that someone has as much *dominium* in a given object as the action that

he can exercise over it. For example, the usuary has the right only to use the thing, but not to transfer it or its use to someone else, whereas the usufructuary can use the thing and can transfer the use to someone else, but he cannot transfer the thing, but the *dominus* can transfer the thing. This is clear from *Institutes, de usu et habitione* [Justinian, *Institutes* 2, 5]. For example, the person who has use of gardens can use the flowers and fruits by eating them, but cannot sell or alienate this right to use; but the usufructuary has the right to use the fruits, and he can transfer this right to use to another, but he cannot sell the gardens or give then away; but the *dominus* can even sell the gardens. Accordingly, they say that the usuary is less of a *dominus* and the usufructuary more of a *dominus*. For this reason, usufruct is in law called "*dominium utile*," which is to say full *dominium* over use, whereas the person who has ownership is absolutely the *dominus*. On this way *dominiumn* is not distinguished from use but is common to use and usufruct.

4. But doubt always remains as to how *dominium*, understood as ownership (*pro proprietate*), is distinguished from use. Therefore, one must say, secondly, that the definition of *dominium* is understood as being a power or right of one's own that is not subdelegated and is not dependent on anyone else. This is unlike the usuary, who, although he has the right to use the thing, has a right that is nonetheless dependent on someone else, namely, the true *dominus*, and is not his own, and consequently is not *dominium*. But against this, if, for example, someone in his will bequeaths the use or usufruct to his wife, and leaves the ownership of the inheritance to his son, then on her husband's death the wife has a right to use the inheritance that is not dependent on the true *dominus*, because the son does not have the power to remove that right, but nonetheless she is not the *domina*. But if you say that what is required for true *dominium* is a right to use in any way whatsoever, for example, by selling or giving it away and so on, as modern scholars commonly think, there is this on the other side: a heir who is a minor is the true *dominus* of the inheritance, and yet he cannot alienate it. The person who holds things subject to primogeniture or *mayorazgo* is the true *dominus* but cannot sell it. Therefore, this is not required for true *dominium*.

One must, therefore, formulate a third definition, by which *dominium* is a person's power or own right to take something up for any use whatsoever that is not prohibited by law. I add the latter phrase because persons holding property as minors or under a *mayorazgo*, who are true *domini* and consequently can alienate what they own according to the nature of the power that they have, are nonetheless prevented by law from alienating. Thus, our first conclusion, regarding how *dominium*, use, and usufruct are distinguished, is evident.

5. However, a doubt arises here that does not concern what something is called, but is extremely difficult, namely, whether, for some things that are consumable through use, use can be distinguished from *dominium*. Things consumable through use are those things whose use consists in their being consumed, such as money, because the use of money is to consume it, that is, to alienate it from

oneself. The same applies to food and drink. Things not consumable through use are those whose use does not consist in being consumed, such as a house and a field. To increase the doubt, we speak of things that are consumed in a single act, as they say, such as bread, wine, and money. There are other things that are consumed through use but not by a single act, and for them it is not difficult to see how use is distinguished from *dominium*, for they are rented out like a horse and a house. But about other things, there is a doubt. This is notable because of the mendicant orders, and especially because of the Friars Minor, who say that they neither as individuals nor in common have any *dominium* not only over their possessions but also over their money or over the food they eat.

About this doubt not only is there controversy among learned theologians, but there are different opinions among the popes. There is a very broad opinion of Nicholas III, *Exiit qui seminat, De verborum significatione, In sexto*, where he says in explanation of the words of Gregory IX and other popes, that the aforementioned friars do not have *dominium* in common or as individuals of their tools or of their books or all their other movables or of their money, but that the *dominium* and property of all the movables and tools is reserved for the Roman Church, and that the aforementioned friars were granted only the usufruct, and that *dominium* over the money always remains with the donors as alms. Clement says the same thing in *Exivi, eod. tit.* John XXII puts forward the opposite opinion in *Extravag. Ad conditorem*, and *Extravag. Cum inter*, and *Extravag, Quia quorundum*, where he says that in things that are consumable through use, use is not distinguished from *dominium*, and that no one can have use without *dominium*. In truth, the matter is difficult.

The first argument goes like this: especially important is the opinion of all the doctors in the matter of usury. Saint Thomas says in [*Summa Theologiae*] *Secunda Secundae*, q. 78, a. 1, that for things whose use consists in consumption of the thing itself, the use cannot be reckoned separately from *dominium*, but whoever grants use of the thing grants the thing. Thence the doctors infer that I cannot receive a gain beyond the capital for the use of money that I lent out, and the same is true in the case of bread and all the other edible things, because the proper use of bread is its consumption. But they say, as appears in the cited chapter, that use of right is one thing and use of fact is another; the use of right is the right to use, and the use of fact is the very act that we exercise on a thing, as, for instance, eating, riding, and so on; the use that the Friars Minor have is not in the first mode but in the second, as a slave has mere use of fact when he rides his master's horse. But on the other hand, the use of fact that the Friars Minor have in edible things is not unjust, and so is just. But as we said, right (*ius*)is nothing other than what is just [*iustum*], that is, a just licence to use something; therefore, they have a use of right to eat the thing, and consequently they are true *domini*.

The second argument is this: usufruct cannot forever be separated from *dominium*, as is said in the section *De usufructo* [Justinian, *Institutes* 2, 4, 1] and *in*

Institutes, eod. tit. s. Constituitur [Justinian, *Digest* 7, 1,3, 2], because *dominium* that could never be used would be in vain, inasmuch as *dominiun*, as we have said, is only for the sake of use. But the pope is forever deprived of the use of the things that the monks can consume. Therefore, the pope is *dominus* only in name; and because the things themselves are not considered abandoned, they must belong to the Friars.

The third argument is this: if use were distinguished from *dominium* in those things, it would follow that someone could rent out the bread by transferring the use and not the *dominium*, and then receive something for the eating of the bread beyond the price of the bread, just as I can rent out a horse or a house. The consequence is manifestly usurious.

The final argument is this: with respect to the thing, it makes no difference whether the pope has *dominium* or they have it, because they use those things exactly as if they were their true *domini*, and correspondingly the pope abstains from them as if he were not their *dominus*. These distinctions are solely verbal. This is confirmed because John XXII renounced this *dominium* and did not want to be *dominus*, and so then, at any rate, the monks were indeed *domini*.

7. Perhaps the dispute is verbal, but nonetheless this is our conclusion: with respect to these things, use can be distinguished from *dominium*, and the Friars Minor have use and not *dominium* either as individuals or in common. By use I mean a just licence or right of eating and drinking, which certainly can be called a "use of right" with respect to that act. Accordingly, they have a right as a way of having something, although they are not *domini*. In this connection, one should note that it does not suffice that someone can consume the thing, but one must be able to alienate it, claim it in court, and so on – which the Friars Minor cannot do either as a whole monastery or as an individual person. Indeed, the pope could take all their goods against their will as if they were his own property, or at least if he did it, the act would be valid. But the monks have a limited licence, namely, to eat and drink and wear. At any rate, we can confirm this, first by the famous verse in Acts 2 [2:45], that "all the believers were equal, and they had everything in common," and consequently no one had anything of his own. When it absolutely says "everything," it seems that food also was in common, and that anyone used it as needed. You might say that at least they were *domini* in common. But to the contrary: I can at least have use of a consumable thing, given that it is not mine, and certainly on the same reasoning I can do so given that it is not mine in common.

Similarly, the second confirmation is in *Deuteronomy* 23 [23:24]. The law says: "When you enter your neighbour's vineyard, eat as many grapes as you want, but do not carry them out with you. If you come into your neighbour's wheat field, break off the ears and rub them in your hand, but do not cut them with a scythe" – a right that the disciples also used; *Matthew* 12 [12:1]. Therefore, the ancients had the use of grapes solely for eating, but they did not have *dominium*, because they could not take them out of the vineyard or sell them like true *domini*.

Similarly, *Inst. De usu et habitatione* [Justinian, *Institutes* 2, 5, 1]: a person who has the bare use of a farm is understood to have nothing more than the daily use of the vegetables, fruit, and so on. Observe that with respect to the vegetables and fruit he has nothing but the use.

Similarly, this argument: a person in extreme necessity can use someone else's bread without acquiring *dominium*. This is obvious, because a person in that condition who takes bread cannot sell it or alienate it, if the necessity is only for bread and not for money. If he does not eat it, the other can take it back as true *dominus*. This is confirmed, because if a person in extreme necessity acquired *dominium* over what belonged to another, it would follow that if the other did not give, he would subsequently be liable to make restitution – which is false. Saint Thomas says the same in [*Summa Theologiae*] *Secunda Secundae*, q. 66, a. 2 following Basil and Ambrose.

Similarly, this argument: because a person invited to another's table uses the food by eating it, he is nonetheless not its *dominus*, because he cannot sell that food or take it home.

8. From what has been said it follows that in the case of money use cannot be distinguished from *dominium*, for the proper use of money is to alienate it, and consequently the person who has such use can use money in any way he wishes, and is, therefore, truly its *dominus*. That is why in the aforementioned chapter *Exiit*, the pope said that money should not be given to the Friars, and that *dominium* always remains with the giver of alms, and that as long as the monk does not consume the money, it remains in the power of the donor to reclaim it, and that either a layman should pay the price of something bought by a monk or that a nominee of the Order should pay it as the agent of the person who gave the money.

Secondly, from these points follows the solution of the arguments except for the third, to which we deny the consequence. Usury does not consist only in the impossibility of transferring use without *dominium*. Rather, what suffices for usury is that someone seeks a profit beyond the price of the thing after it has been used and no longer exists. As for the other point, that the pope has renounced this *dominium*, it must be said that he could not do this without revoking the statutes of the Order, and this would be too serious for an order so important in the Christian Church.

About the Division of Things

19. However, there is a great difficulty about human or civil *dominium*: When and how began the appropriation of *dominia,* so that this was mine, and that was yours? The first proposition is this: the appropriation of external goods did not begin in the state of innocent nature in Paradise. This is evident, because this appropriation was made not by divine or natural right but by human right, as Augustine says in his *Commentary on John* and as is quoted in [*Decretum Gratiani*] Distinctio VIII, can. *Quo Iure*. But that the division was not then made by human right is evident; the condition of nature did not need this division, because the necessity for it was twofold, namely, that disputes should not arise and that fields be better cultivated, as Aristotle says in *Politics* book 2; but then there were no disputes and everyone diligently did what pertained to the common good. Nonetheless, this proposition should be limited because among one's external goods are counted one's reputation and honour, and these goods were appropriated by natural right. For everyone is the owner of his reputation and honour as of his own limbs. No one else is its owner, nor could an emperor deprive me of my reputation without fault on my part. To the contrary, the rule is that by nature a person is the owner of all his natural goods.

20. But about other goods a second conclusion is posited. Such appropriation and division were made immediately after the sin. The proof is this: immediately after the sin there was reason and cause for the division, and so it was made immediately. This is evident: as I said, Aristotle adduces two reasons for this distribution, namely, so that fields would be better cultivated and disputes avoided, and those were in place immediately after the sin. Secondly, in Genesis 4 one reads that Cain obtained his gifts to the Lord from the produce of the earth, and that Abel obtained his from the firstborn of his herd. It seems therefore that some herds that belonged to Abel did not belong to Cain, and some produce that belonged to Cain did not belong to Abel, because the gifts of Abel pleased the Lord,

and He did not have regard for the gifts of Cain. This is confirmed by the authority of Augustine, *De Civitate Dei* XV, chapter 20, where he says that Cain was the king of the city that he founded. It follows, therefore, that appropriation existed.

21. But how could appropriation take place? One argument against goes like this: all persons then were equal, and the common ownership of the world had been equally conceded to all; accordingly, no one had the power to make a division whereby anyone would have use of some part of the world or some goods in a way that excluded use by others. And if it is said that Adam had such superiority, the argument proceeds: Adam's superiority was only paternal, and it did not extend to making laws. In reply, it should be said in accordance with Conrad Summenhart, *Treatise* I, q. 11, conclus, 2, that this could happen in three ways. First, Adam had for himself the power to distribute not because paternal power is such universally, but because it was unique in Adam as the beginning of nature that he had other prerogatives over other fathers. Nonetheless because his having such a coercive force does not seem based on Holy Scripture, it is better to offer a second way, that this happened with the consent of all, in that all had consented that Adam should distribute the earth to them, or they chose someone else as their superior. Or third, to eliminate disputes it was established among them that one person accepted one part and another person another part, and so one person transferred to another the common power that he had in this field so that the other would transfer to him the power that he had in another field, as is said in Genesis 13 about Abraham and Lot: "I ask that there be no quarrel between me and you. Behold the entire earth is before you. If you go to the left, I will hold what is on the right," etc.

Others say that by natural right all unowned things first belong to their occupier, as is said in the *Institutes, De rerum divisione* [Justinian, *Institutes* 2, 1, 11]; natural reason concedes to the occupier whatever is no one's, and so a distribution could occur by natural right. But this should be properly understood. By natural right what was previously no one's is not the occupier's to the extent of ownership but only to the extent of use. For by natural right everything is common to the extent of ownership. Accordingly, a division to the extent of ownership could occur only by pact and men's unanimous agreement.

After the flood in the time of Noah, when everything was reduced to being in common, the division was made in the same way as it had been made in the beginning. Thence it is said in Genesis 10, "By these" (that is, by the sons of Noah) "the islands of the nations were divided into their regions"; and Genesis 11, "Come, let us make a city and tower for ourselves" when the reign of the Chaldeans began.

22. But against this is argued: the division of things is against the law of nature; therefore, it was illicit, for human law does not obligate unless derived from the law of nature. This is evident, because by the law of nature everything is in common, as is said in [*Decretum Gratiani*] Distinctio VIII, can. 1; therefore, that this is mine and that yours is against the law of nature. Against this, Scotus [*Ordinatio*]

In Quartum, dist. XV, q. 2, replies that that law was revoked after the sin, for whereas before it was advantageous for all things to be in common, afterwards a division was advantageous for the reasons already mentioned. Others say that neither those nor their contraries are against the right of nature; those concern the right of innocent nature, and their contraries (namely, that everything is distributed) concern the right of corrupted nature. Against these Conrad rightly argues that the right of nature is immutable, and therefore what is once the right of nature is always the right of nature.

Augustine makes a similar argument in *Confessions*, Book III, chapter 7: the law of nature does not change when under the law of nature everything is in common and now everything is distributed, but the things themselves are what are variable, just as the nature of wine does not change by being useful to the healthy and harmful to the unhealthy. For this reason one must say, as Saint Thomas says in the [*Summa Theologiae*] *Secunda Secundae*, q. 66. a. 2, ad 1, that everything being in common is not a positive natural precept but is only understood negatively, that is, that appropriation was not made by the right of nature because the law was posited for healthy persons for whom such a division was not necessary, and therefore such appropriation was not contrary to but rather a determination of the natural right. The counterargument is that members of religious orders live peacefully without a division of things. The answer to this is that whereas a few people can live this way, a whole kingdom cannot.

23. From this follow many corollaries. First, not everything has been appropriated, such as rivers, roads, fountains, and the very places that people live, because by the right of nature they aways remain in common. Similarly, wild animals such as birds and fish, as is held in *Institutes, De rerum divisione* [Justinian *Institutes* 2, 1, 12]; for this reason, notwithstanding any appropriation, anyone can hunt, fish, and so on.

Secondly, it follows that if there are now any lands that have not been distributed, anyone occupying them can use them without thereby acquiring ownership.

Third, it follows that notwithstanding any appropriation, everything is in common in extreme necessity, at least so far as use is concerned.

Finally, it follows that once an appropriation has been made anyone can by natural right transfer his ownership to another. But about transfers of ownership, see below.

De Iustitia et Iure, III, Q. 1, A. 1 (1553)

Whether ius (right) is the object of justice (iustitia)

Ius pertains to justice, the virtue concerning which we have undertaken the present work. For this reason, we have entitled it *"De Iustitia et Iure."* As we said in the introduction to the first book, *ius* is used in two ways. It first stands for the rule of reason and the dictate of prudence, through which we measure the equality of justice; the laws fit that description. Secondly, it stands for the equality itself that is the object of justice, namely, what justice establishes in things. Accordingly, because we have so far completed two books about *ius* in the former sense, that is, about the laws, it follows that we should come closer to the definition of justice by speaking about *ius* in the latter sense of the word, as that through which this definition of justice is to be established. The present book, the third, contains a treatment of justice in general, and its divisions into legal and particular justice, and into distributive and commutative justice; it deals with the former form of justice, distributive justice, in our discussion of favouritism. Saint Thomas published on this topic in [*Summa Theologiae*] 2, 2, q. 57 and following.

The first question is whether *ius* is the object of justice. The negative argument comes from what the jurist Celsus says in *Digest* I, 1, *de iustitia et iure*, that *"ius* is the art of what is good and fair." Now art is not the object of justice, which is in the will, but is by itself an intellectual virtue, as Aristotle says in *Ethics* 6 [1140a7].

Second, justice especially subjects us to God, according to that famous dictum of Augustine in his book *De Moribus Ecclesiae* [15]: "Justice is love serving God alone, and consequently governing well all things subject to man." Now *ius* does not pertain to divine things, but only to human things. Thus, Isidore in in his book [*Etymologies*] v, 2) distinguishes between *fas* and *ius*, that *fas* is the divine law, and *ius* the human law. Therefore, *ius* is not the object of justice.

However, both Isidore and the Philosopher are to the contrary. Isidore says there that *ius* is so called because it is just (*iustum*), and he is quoted in [*Decretum Gratiani*] *dist. 1 [c. 2] can. ius*. And the Philosopher at the beginning of

Ethics 5 says that "all are agreed in giving the name of justice to the habit that makes men capable of doing just actions."

Immediately at the outset of the question one must first suppose that one way of understanding justice is as the general word for all virtue.

Justice in this sense is what the Philosopher in *Ethics*, 5, 1 calls complete virtue. Thence the just person is the same as the virtuous person, whatever be the virtue with which he is distinguished. The reason for this very extended meaning is that present in every virtue is a reason for obedience owed to law. Whatever includes a reason for something being owed takes the form of justice. Christ in Matthew 5 and 6 understood the word "justice" with this meaning: "Unless your justice surpasses," etc. [Matthew 5:20], and "Take care not to practice your justice in the presence of others," etc. [Matthew 6:1], and Paul in I Timothy 1:9: "The law is not made for the just person."

But here we do not deal with justice in this sense, nor does it have a specific object of its own; rather, whatever belongs to each virtue is proper to it, namely, whatever is in accordance with law. It is understood as a particular moral virtue and one of the four cardinal virtues that has the function of doing what is just. Secondly, no one should reproach us for putting things in the wrong order on the grounds that we should discuss justice before we discuss *ius*. He should know what Aristotle taught in *De Anima* 2, text 33, that one who is going to deal with a potency or a disposition should begin with the object from which the disposition derives its form and through which it should be described, just as a person who is starting a discussion of the senses should first discuss the sensible. The eye is not properly defined by its being a sense composed in this or that way, but by being a sense for perceiving colors; similarly, hearing is a sense for perceiving sound; a saw is a tool for cutting wood, and temperance is a disposition by which we rightly use what is pleasurable to the touch. Similarly, in the cited passage in *Ethics* 5, Aristotle defines justice **(p. 192)** by what is just, namely, that it is a disposition by which we want what is just and do what is just. Ulpian in *de iustitia et iure* [Justinian, *Digest* 1, 1, 10 pr} says, "Justice is the constant and perpetual will that gives to each what is rightfully his (*ius suum*)."

Having made these preliminary remarks, one can respond to the question with a single conclusion: *Ius* is the object of justice. This conclusion is sufficiently established on the authority of Isidore, of the Philosopher, and of the jurists just cited, who call *ius* what justice establishes as just in things. By nothing else is this more amply demonstrated than by considering the differences between justice and the other virtues. These differences are three.

First, although carrying out the right action characterizes every virtue, the rightness of the other virtues is thought of as ordering the agent to himself, whereas justice is thought of as ordering the agent to someone else. The reason is that justice is the virtue that orders the person who has it to another, whereas the other virtues order the person to himself. For example, temperance concerns itself with the proper use of what is pleasurable to the touch, and it therefore posits a mid-point between two affects of the temperate person himself, namely, that in the use of food and sex he neither veers from reason, nor does he take less than what is required for sustaining life. Similarly, courage constitutes the mean between fear and audacity. However, justice constructs an equality between the person who owes something and the person to whom it is owed. Thus, suppose that each of us has five units, and you lent me one, as a result of which you have only four but I have six. Justice requires that I refund one unit to you, so that each of us would have five, which is the mean between four and six. Similarly, if you have been hired to do work for me, justice demands that my payment be equal to the service rendered. For this reason, two things are said to be "adjusted" when they are made equal, as when the architect adjusts the stone to the square, or the shoemaker adjusts the shoe to the foot.

Derived from this is the second difference, that in dealing with the other virtues nothing is considered truly and legitimately right except with respect to the agent. For example, if the miser sets a sparing table not to live temperately but to avoid spending money, that act is not considered right or commensurate with virtue. But if the debtor pays his creditor as much as he owes but with the malevolent intention of causing him to be profligate, or if someone who is holding a sword as a deposit returns it to its owner knowing that the owner wanted it back for some evil use, then that act is considered just in itself because it is equal to what is owed, although the act is not a virtuous one nor is the discharger of the debt a virtuous person.

From this in turn arises the third difference, that to the virtue of justice as such the scholars rightly ascribe an object (which they call *ius* and what is just), but not to any of the other virtues. That is, in the virtue of justice what is just is itself established from the nature of the thing, whereas in the other virtues what matters is only the right intention of the agent. This is why Saint Thomas – a point that should be attentively considered – begins his treatises on the other virtues, such as courage or temperance not from their objects, but from the virtues that achieve rightness in their activities; however, the treatise on justice starts from the object that comes into existence in the things themselves. Indeed, in the other virtues one does not so appropriately speak of their object as of the subject matter with which the virtue is concerned, as the subject matter of courage is danger in war, and the subject matter of temperance is tactile pleasure. In these, the virtue establishes a mean between two affects. But the virtue of justice properly has an object, which is the equality of things itself to which the virtue strives, just as sight strives to perceive colours. We therefore conclude that *ius* is the object of justice.

However, there are some who, taking a superficial view, impugn this distinction. Buridan in his commentary on *Ethics* 5, q. 1 objects to this doctrine as follows: either Thomas is speaking of the rightness of the action inasmuch as it is a rightness of virtue, or he is speaking of rightness absolutely even though it does not come from virtue. If the former. then as with the functioning of the other virtues, so too the action of justice is not right unless it is ordered to the agent. Aristotle in *Ethics* 2, 4 teaches that no action of virtue happens except through the choice of a legitimate end. Because of this, as we were just saying, the person who returns a sword to its owner so that the latter might murder someone is not virtuous. Or if Thomas is speaking of the rightness of the action absolutely, and not inasmuch as it derives from virtue, then in the subject matter of the other virtues also, this kind of virtue is found without being ordered to the agent, as when one hypocritically observes the rules of fasting or conducts oneself energetically in war because of vainglory.

The response is that the distinction nonetheless exists in rightness considered absolutely. This distinction applies here, in that because the rightness of justice can of its own nature be found in things themselves, the person who with a bad intent and purpose pays the equivalent of what he owes performs a just action in giving the other what is his right, even though he is not a just (that is, a virtuous) person because he does not do the action when **(p. 193)**, where, and how he should. However, in the other virtues, if you remove any single circumstance of virtue, no moral rightness remains. That is, hypocritical fasting will not be a temperate action, nor will attack in war be an act of energy, because such actions have no other rightness than being ordered to a disposition of virtue.

Accordingly, to reply to the objections stated at the beginning: Buridan and others less expert in the meaning of the word deny that the word "*ius*" is to be understood as the object of justice; they say that it is the same as "law," in accordance with the saying of Isidore quoted in [*Decretum Gratiani*] dist. 1 [c. 2]: "*Ius* is a general word; law, however, is a species of *ius*." But whoever makes this denial throws himself against a truth fortified by the authority of all. For what the Philosopher termed "just" when he said [Aristotle, *Nicomachean Ethics* V, 1129a6] that justice is the disposition productive of just things, is the same as what the jurist clearly called *ius* when he said that justice is the virtue of giving each person what is rightfully his (*ius suum*). If, therefore, justice makes *ius* and what is just (*iustum*), who could deny that *ius* is the object of justice? Indeed, I would believe that through apocope, that is, through cutting off the syllable at the end of the word, *iustum* is said as *ius*, just as instead of saying "*potestis*" ["you can"] we say "*potes*." Thence the Greek word "*dikaion*" has the shared meaning of "what is just" and "*ius*." For this reason, the very same Isidore immediately adds that "it is called *ius* because it is just." Because of this the law itself is called just, because it establishes what is just in things. But just as the words for manufactured and crafted things are transferred to signify the skills as well, and just as the word for medicine, which is a thing put together by skill, is adapted to the skill itself, so the word *ius* undergoes derivation, first to signifying the art of knowing what is just, and from this in turn to signifying the law. You should take care not to think that the art of what is good and fair is the same as law. Art is not a dictate, but is rather the kind of moral knowledge that jurists have for investigating what is fair for law to ordain. Law, however, is a rule of prudence, or a practical dictate established from it, for example "Do" or "Don't do." What this is we have set out in the beginning, in Book 1, q. 1. When Isidore says that law is a species of *ius*, he does not understand species as something directly subordinate to a genus, such as man is to animal (indeed, he adds that *ius* is that which is just), but that law is a rule and written precept of *ius*. One kind of *ius* is natural, implanted in our minds, and another kind is written; according to Isidore, law is a written enactment.

Through this is revealed the meaning of the words of Celsus, that "*Ius* is the art of what is fair and good." Accursius delusionally says that what is fair is not the same as what is good, imagining some kind of distinction between those elements. But as Budé learnedly says in his note on this point, and as we have made clear above in Book I, q. 6, final article, what is fair and just is understood as standing in place of the simple noun *epieikeia*, that is, the interpretation of the law in a case in which the legislator, if present, would obviously not have wanted the law to be observed in accordance with the rigour of its text, as can be inferred from *l. nulla ff. de legib.* [Justinian, *Digest* 1, 3, 25]. A law cannot make provision for every individual case, as is said in *l. neque leges* & *l. non possunt eod. tit.* [Justinian, *Digest* 1, 3, 10 and 1, 3. 12]. Consequently, when the Jurist says that *ius* is the art of what is good and fair, *ius* is to be understood as natural, not written. By doing this contrary to the words of the written *ius*, *epieikiea* keeps the legislator's intention intact, in which the natural *ius* is preserved. Accordingly, the art of what is fair and good is the same as the art of protecting the natural *ius* when the written *ius* appears unjust. For it says in *Instit. De success. libert. 1* [Justinian, *Institutes* 3, 7, 1], "By the praetor's edict this injustice in the law was corrected etc.;" and in *quod quisque in etc. l. si quis* [Justinian, *Digest* 2, 2, 3]: "Ulpian says, If anyone should get an unjust law applied against another, he is subject to that same law." Thence flowed that famous saying that the greatest right is the greatest wrong.

From what has been said, one can assess the sense of Ulpian's statement in the same legal text [Justinian, *Digest* 1, 1, 1], that the word "*ius*" is derived from "*iustitia*." That is false if you understand, as has been said, that *ius* is the object of justice. Rather, on the contrary, *iustitia* is derived from *ius*, because a condition is assigned its species from its object. Moreover, the grammarian's rule is that a longer word is derived from a shorter one. Accordingly, the Jurist understands *ius* as the art and knowledge of making judgments about natural *ius*. Because of this, that art is born of justice, because, as Aristotle says in *Ethics* 6 [1144a35], only someone who is just has the abundant prudence to make correct judgments about what to do.

To bring these remarks to a conclusion: *Ius* is in things, whereas the art of what is fair and good is in the intellect that teaches the doing of what is just, like the art of the craftsman. Law is a rule of practical reason established by prudence, and therefore the idea for what is just (*ratio iusti*), that is, it makes and establishes what is just. As a result, when *ius* is said to be rendered to someone, it is not to be understood otherwise than as the object of justice. Saint Thomas [*Summa Theologiae* 2, 2, q. 57, a. 1, ad 1] makes somewhat of a distinction [about the extended meanings of *ius*], namely, that to render *ius* is to pronounce a judgment in favour of someone, or according to the truth of the matter, or **(p. 194)** according to what is alleged and proved even when it is unjust according to the truth. As for his adding that *ius* is also understood as the location of the tribunal, as when a defendant is said to appear *in iure*, perhaps he deliberately took this from the passage by Paulus beginning with "*Ius*," where he says in *l. pen. ff. de iust. & iur.* [Justinian, *Digest* 1, 1, 11], that *ius* is understood as a place. Nonetheless, I am not sure that this was properly said. Someone is understood to appear in *iure* just as when he is said to be summoned *in ius*. But as the Jurist says, in *ff, de in ius vocan.* [Justinian, *Digest* 2, 4, 1], "to be summoned *in ius* is to be summoned for the purpose of undergoing litigation," that is, so that the claimant suing the defendant will make trial of whether *ius* protects him. There "*ius*" is understood either as *ius* itself or as law.

The response to the second argument is that when Augustine says that justice is love serving God, he does not refer to the substance of justice. Indeed, since no one can offer God an equal return, there is no proper basis for justice between us and God. But when he says that justice is love, he means that it arises out of love for serving God and that it tends to the same end. For this reason, *fas* is the word referring to what belongs to piety and religion, namely, what is worthy of saying (*fari*) that is more exalted than what is just.

De Iustitia et Iure, IV, Q. 1, A. 1 (1553)

Whether dominium is the same as the right and faculty regarding things

The present question demands to be divided into two articles, of which one establishes the definition of *dominium*, and the other what falls under it. The question is therefore whether *dominium* is the same as the right and faculty regarding things. The argument in the affirmative is that right is the same as the faculty of disposing of things and of freely using them, and that seems to be exactly the same as *dominium*.

Secondly, because the mendicant monks have the right to make use of food, clothing, and other tools even to the point of consuming those things, they are said to be their owner, as Pope John XXII seems to conclude in *Extravagant, ad conditorem*; therefore, no difference remains between right and *dominium*.

However, the contrary position is that although owner and slave are correlative, in the *Institutes, On the Law of Persons]* [Justinian, *Institutes* 1, 3] mankind is divided into free persons and slaves. That implies that whoever has charge of free persons does not have *dominium* over them even though he has the right to order them about.

The two proposed arguments mark out the two parts of our reply. However, one must note right at the outset of this question that the word "*dominium*" is not in such frequent use among the orators and ancient Latin authors as are "absolute control" [*dominatus*] and "domination" [*dominatio*]. They use those two words more to refer frequently to something bad than to something good, for they signify an image of tyranny, that is, when someone makes use of his subjects for his own advantage. Thence Cicero in his *Tusculan Disputations*, book 5 [5, 20] says of Dionysius that "at the age of twenty-one he had seized absolute control," etc. And in *De Oratore*, Book 2 [2, 55], "Brutus freed the Roman people from the absolute control of kings." The things of which men are masters [*domini*] are called resources or substances or possessions. But it is the jurists who use this word [*dominium*] to mean that which they also call ownership [*proprietatem*] of things, which is distinguished from possession and use and usufruct. Nor is this word when used with this meaning to be considered barbarous or unusual. It is current among distinguished Latin authors, as in Varro, *de re rustica*, Book 2 [6, 3]: "they change *dominium* in trading and sale and delivery." Reference is also made to it in scripture, as in the Book of Tobias 8 [8:21]: "he made this disposition, that the remaining half should devolve to Tobias's *dominium*." And in First Maccabees 11, "King Ptolemy obtained *dominium* of the cities" **(p. 279)**. The word is used most frequently in the law. In the *Digestum Novum* Book 3 [Justinian, *Digest* 41] there are two titles: "About Acquiring *Dominium* of Things," and "About Acquiring or Losing Possession."

But more recent scholars have taken more trouble to expound this word than was necessary, for instance, Gerson in *De Potestate Ecclesiae*, considera. 13 and in his treatise *De Vita Spirituali*, lect. 3, with most of which Conrad, in book 1 of his treatise *De Contractibus* and several others agree in [comments on Peter Lombard's *Sentences*] 4. Dist. 15. First of all, these scholars say that *ius* is understood in two ways. The first is as law, the meaning according to which we say *ius civile* and *ius canonicum*. The second is as a legitimate power that someone exercises with respect to some person or thing. Then they say that *dominium* is exactly the same as *ius* understood in the second way. Therefore, they say that *dominium* is the proximate power or faculty of taking other things into one's own faculty or licit use in accordance with rationally instituted laws. That is what they say about *dominium*; whether correctly, we will consider. First, the words themselves scarcely allow the nouns "*ius*" and "*dominium*" to be used as synonyms. As was seen above, *ius* is the same as what is just [*iustum*], as Isidore says in book 5, because it is the object of justice, that is, the equity that justice establishes among people. *Dominium*, however, is the faculty of the *dominus* (as the word suggests) with respect to slaves or things that he uses as he wishes for his own benefit. It turns out, therefore, that *ius* is not interchangeable with *dominium* but is superior to it and has a broader scope. A wife has a certain *ius* against her husband; according to the famous statement of Paul in I Corinthians 7 [7:4], "it is not the husband but his wife who has power over his body." A child has a right against his parents, who are obligated to take care of their children. Slaves have a right against their masters, by whom they must be fed and sustained. For the same reason, a subject has a right against the prelate who must instruct and govern him. Yet none of these is a *dominus*, no matter how far you extend the term, or can be called his superior.

But Conrad says that at least it should not be denied that, properly speaking, whatever right a superior has against an inferior should be considered *dominium*, so that what *dominium* adds to *ius* is precisely the idea of superiority. But I would not readily concede even that. A father has a *ius* with respect to his children, but properly speaking does not likewise have *dominium*. I say that it is fair and just, and so *ius*, that a father has charge of his children for their own good, whom he loves, instructs, and educates for their sake. However, *dominium* does not signify any right whatsoever, but only that which is in respect of a thing that we can use as we wish for our own benefit and that we cherish because of ourselves. That is what the word itself evidently exhibits to our ears. The correlative of *dominus* is a slave, who whatever he is, entirely belongs to the *dominus*, just like an animal – except that a slave cannot be killed, because God alone is the *dominus* of life. Therefore, Aristotle in 1 *Politics* 3 [1 *Politics* 5, 1554b3] distinguishes civil or royal rule from despotic rule, which is the rule of a *dominus* [*dominicum*], when he says that the soul exercises the leadership of a *dominus* over the body, whereas the intellect exercises a civil and royal leadership of the appetite, which is not that of a *dominus*. And in 5 *Ethics* 6 he distinguishes the right of inheritance and paternal right: the father possesses the child before the age of majority not as a *dominus* possesses a slave, but as a part of himself, and therefore this right is not that of a *dominus*, whereas the heir possesses a slave as an instrument that he uses.

Richardus argues to the contrary. If someone were to carry off a son from his father or a wife from her husband, he would be called a thief; because, however, theft is not committed except against the will of the *dominus*, the father is the *dominus* of his son, and the husband is the *dominus* of his wife. However, on this point the reply in the following book in the question about theft is that the carrying off of a son or a wife is not, properly speaking, theft, but captivity or some other kind of injury, whereas to take another's slave is theft, properly speaking. Moreover, the basis of theft is satisfied if it happens against the will either of the *dominus* or of the person to whom the thing pertains even if he is not the *dominus* if he has some other right of possession. For this reason, in the *Institutes, On the Law of Persons* men are immediately differentiated into free persons and slaves, because the right with respect to free persons, in contrast to slaves, is not properly called *dominium*. Although the prince may be the *dominus* of cities and possessions, of citizens he is to be spoken of only as king or duke, etc. Indeed, when he acts toward his subjects with absolute control by using them for his own personal advantage, he becomes a tyrant. Because of this, even though a judge or a prelate has a right over his subjects, neither is properly said to be their *dominus*. Christ noted this in Matthew 20 [20:25]: "The princes of the nations lord it over them, etc.; it is not so among you." To now sum up: *dominium* is only the *ius* that one uses for one's own advantage; *ius*, however, signifies not only this but also includes the right that the more highly ranked person in command uses in the interest and for the good of his subjects. For this reason, *ius* is to be posited as the higher genus in the definition of *dominiun*, so far are they from being spoken of interchangeably.

Concerning the husband with respect to his wife, someone could perhaps invoke the famous verse in Genesis 3 [3:16]: "You will be under the power of your husband, and he will lord over (*dominabitur*) you." This is not a reference to civil *dominium* **(p. 280)**. Rather, Aristotle in the cited passage says that the right of a husband over his wife is innominate. But he is said to lord over the wife so far as conjugal use goes. Because nature in its perfect state was without shame or the bother of work, after the sin the woman, who would give birth in pain, was said to be under her husband's power. Moreover, because so long as innocence prevailed there was no room for the ignorance of the sort that followed the sin, thus so far as guidance is concerned the husband is said to lord over the wife, whom he must teach. As we will say below, the more cultivated must lord over the unlearned, not with legal *dominium* for the personal good of the *domini*, but with a refined rule in the interest of the very people who need instruction. Hence it follows that the definition that they ascribe to *dominium* is neither legitimate not accurately constructed. And because we grasp something directly in itself and indirectly (Aristotle 1 *De Anima* tex. 85 [402b8]), let us establish a direct definition according to our comprehension, and through that make a judgment about the other. Accordingly, if described artfully, *dominium* is each person's own faculty and right in anything at all that he can use for his own benefit with any use whatsoever permitted by law. Placed in the position of genus is faculty rather than power. The reason for this is not that given by John Gerson in Chapter 3 of his *De Vita Spirituali*, namely, that "*facultas*" derived from "*fas*" ["it is allowed"], because a robber's power to use what belongs to another is not a faculty. Faculty is not derived from "*fas*" but from "*facile*" ["easy"], as it is a facility, as it were. Faculty and difficulty are contraries. Because of this, power is a more comprehensive genus than faculty. A tyrant has the power to use the goods of citizens, but he does not have the faculty, that is the facility, to do so, because he cannot do it without the permission and faculty of the owner or a just intervening cause. For this reason, one does not have to add "proximate" because faculty means this on its own; a remote power to use what belongs to another is not a faculty. I would add "a person's *own* (*propria*) faculty and right," so that *dominium* should be distinguished from mere possession, use, and usufruct, because a person who has only use or usufruct does not have his own faculty but one dependent on the true owner or on a judge who permits it. Therefore, what not only the non-Latin jurists but even the most Latin ones regularly call "property (*proprietatem*)" is in more genuine Latin called "own faculty." Nor is there a need to add, as Gerson does, "[the faculty] of taking other things"; man through his very own will, which is the mover of all potencies, uses his very own limbs, which (as Aristotle says in the passage just cited) the soul rules as a *dominus*. Added to the definition is that *dominium* is the faculty of using for one's own benefit; in this it differs from other species of right, in which a superior governs inferiors for their own good. And then it is said that it is invariably for any use whatsoever, to distinguish *dominium* from use and usufruct. *Dominium* is a faculty not only of using and enjoying, but also of tearing it apart, giving it away, selling it, neglecting it, etc. However, the limit was applied that this use should be permitted by law, to refute an objection by which one might try to undermine the definition. Before the age of majority, the ward has the power of *dominium* over his things, but he does not have the free faculty of mastery over them, since he cannot give those goods away or sell them, because by human law he is prevented from dissipating them. Because *dominium* is based in freedom, before he has the use of reason he truly is the *dominus* in that he is truly free and not a slave; nonetheless, the use of his *dominium* is forbidden to him for his own good until the light of reason should shine forth in him. Hence Paul says [Galatians 4:1] that as long as an heir is a child, he does not differ from a slave, not as regards *dominium* but as regards use, and therefore he is under guardians. A similar argument arises concerning a person whose goods are bound by the bonds of primogeniture; although he is truly the *dominus* of those goods, he cannot alienate them for any reason because the civil law forbids it. That he truly is the *dominus* is evident from the fact that otherwise those goods would lack a *dominus*. Moreover, when the king, acceding to someone's demand, ties up in the bond of primogeniture goods that were formerly free, he does not deprive him of any *dominium*. Nor afterwards when he allows the possessor the right of alienation does he confer upon him any new property or *dominium*. He is always the *dominus* but restricted like a ward.

Far be it here to recall those incantations about whether *dominium* is the thing possessed, or the *dominus*, or rather the relation. However, I will not forego this reminder, that philosophers should beware of those barbarous locutions of the pedants. Would anyone put up with hearing that the *dominium* over a horse is either the horse or the rider? *Dominium* is that condition of things that obtains between possessor and possessed, that is, the faculty of the possessor with respect to a possessed thing. For this reason it is defined through one's act, which is the distinctive way of defining potencies. Just as sight is the potency of sensing colours and hearing is the potency of sensing sounds, so *dominium* is the faculty for using a thing, for enjoying it, and so on.

In this connection one must note that the title of *dominium* is different from *dominium* itself. Some **(p. 281)** at the University of Paris consider this matter think rather carelessly, thinking along with their Chancellor [Jean Gerson] that the same faculty that is *dominium* is also its title. Rather, title is the basis of *dominium*, like the root from which it sprouts. The title of *dominia* is either nature or law or contract or election, and so on. For example: the title of the natural *dominium* that man has with respect to things that grow from the earth is natural life, which cannot be sustained without them; for this reason God and nature gave man, along with the desire for self preservation, the right to use the food that is necessary, just as the title of the right (I will not say the *dominium*) that parents have with respect to their offspring is natural procreation. The title by which each person possesses what he owns is the law of nations (*ius gentium*) by which was made the division of things. The title of the bishop is election. The title by which someone has his house is either natural inheritance, or purchase or prescription and so on.

From the formulation of this definition of *dominium* one can infer the distinction between it and use and usufruct. *Dominium* is a faculty with regard to the substance of a thing, whereas usufruct concerns solely its qualities and accidents. I say "with regard to the substance of a thing" because if the thing is consumable by use, such as food and clothing, the *dominus* can consume it; if less, such as a house or slave, he can give it away or sell it – indeed, he can also kill it, as in the case of cattle. But usufruct is the right to use and enjoy another's things, while their substance remains unimpaired, as is said in the section on usufruct [Justinian, *Digest* 7, 1, 1] and in the *Institutes* with the same title [Justinian, *Institutes* 2, 4]. The holder of the usufruct of a field or of gardens can not only eat the fruit but also sell them and can even rent the field to another. A bare use is a right to use but not enjoy another's things, while leaving their substance unimpaired. For this reason, as is said in the *Institutes, On Use and Habitation* [Justinian, *Institutes* 2, 5, 1], there is less right in use than in usufruct. That person enjoys the thing who has full power with respect to the fruit, which he can not only eat, but also alienate in any way he wishes; the person has use of the fruit who is permitted only to eat them, or to feed his cattle, but not otherwise to distribute them. Thus, a person who has the bare use of a field can make entry into it, eat the various fruits, and feed his oxen and cattle with its hay, but not sell its fruit or rent it out. In each definition reference is made to "another's things," because the usuary or usufructuary is not said to be the true owner but the person who has a precise use or usufruct. The lessee holding the *emphyteusis* is said to have *dominium utile*, in contrast to *dominium directum*, which is unqualified *dominium*. But these matters do not pertain now to our speculation.

However, because we profess to a mendicant observance, our education advises us, concerning this established definition, to engage in some discussion of whether in the case of things consumable through use, use can be distinguished from *dominium*. Things not consumable through use are those things whose use does not consist in consumption, such as a plot of land, a house, and things of that sort. Things that are consumable through use are those whose only use is the thing's distribution or consumption, such as money, that is used by being transferred into someone else's *dominium,* and bread, that is used by being eaten. The theme of our discourse concerns things consumed in a single act (where the doubt is more serious). A garment may be worn away through use, but because it is not destroyed by being rubbed away in a single act, use of it can in some way be distinguished from *dominium*. We especially raise this doubt because of what was instituted for those who live under the holy rule of Saint Francis and those of our own order who adhere to that institution. The Friars Minor say that they have renounced all *dominium*, to the extent that they exercise *dominium* neither over money nor over bread nor over the edible things they eat in a way that they can be called (to use their own term) owners [*proprietarii*]. This issue has been disputed and contested not only among the theologians, but the popes also have also issued varied opinions about it. There is the papal bull of Nicholas III, *Exiit qui seminat, De verborum significatione* book 6, where in his explanation of the words of Gregory and other popes he clearly affirms, and with many other words confirms, that the Friars Minor have no *dominium* either in common or as individuals, over their tools and food, but they are mere usuaries, that *dominium* over their money always remains with the donors, and that *dominium* over their food and tools resides with the pope. There is an almost identical opinion of Clement; see Clement, *Exivi de paradiso*, in the same title. John XXII puts forward the opposite opinion in *Extravagantibus*, *Ad conditorem*, and *Cum inter nonnullos*, and *Quia quorundum*, *De verborum significatione*, where he asserts without doubt that in things consumable through use, use cannot be distinguished from *dominium* and cannot in any way be separated from it. The matter is certainly difficult. First – to start the counterargument from the very nature of things – it is obvious that when the use of things of this sort is their consumption, no one can use the thing except as if he were its true *dominus*. For if you look back at the definition established above, true *dominium* **(p. 282)** consists in this, that the thing can be taken up into every use; but after it is consumed, no use of it remains. Thence Saint Thomas in [*Summa Theologiae*] 2, 2, q. 78, a 1, considers it a fixed point that for wine and money and such things, the use can by no means be reckoned apart from the thing itself; whoever is given the use is given the thing, and therefore *dominium* over it. Moreover, if the use of such things is separated from *dominium*, the clear consequence would be that one could rent out the use at a price distinct from that by which the thing itself is valued, so that someone would give me so much for eating, over and above the value of the capon.

In the second place is an argument on the authority of the law. In the section *De usufructu earum rerum quae usu consumuntur*, *l.* 2 [Justinian. *Digest* 7. 6, 2] security is given, because a usufruct of money cannot be left as a legacy without the money itself, nor can other things that are consumed through use, such as wine and oil, because no one can use these things without consuming them. Because of this, insofar as one can soundly infer from that title, a usufruct of these things looks to some kind of borrowing, in that a person who receives a legacy of a usufruct of money or wheat is obligated to give security that he will restore the entire thing to the lawful heir. In the section *De usufructu, quemadmodum quis utatur, l. omnium, s. constituitur* [Justinian, *Digest* 7, 1, 3, 2], a usufruct is prevented from being perpetual so that *dominia* not become useless, because *dominium* of a thing would be in vain if the thing could never be used. From this the argument is taken that if the mendicants have use of their bread and wine, and the use is such that they are never obligated to give the thing back, it is completely obvious that they have *dominium*. They respond, however, with the following distinction in use. They say, as is contained in the aforementioned chapter *Exiit*, that the use of things is twofold, namely, the one is of right and the other is of fact. Use of right [*usus iuris*] is a concession of law, and in these things this is not separate from *dominium*; this is the use that they say the mendicants do not have. However, use of fact [*usus facti*] is the very act of eating and drinking, and only this is conceded to them. This is what Pope Nicholas says in that chapter *Exiit*. But this distinction is more easily stated than understood. The use of right is nothing other than what right permits in accordance with the will of the *dominus*: because someone gave me a usufruct of money as a legacy, the use becomes lawful for me, and if it is lawful it is conceded to me by right. Equally, if you give a mendicant bread, why will that use by the mendicants not be rightful? In addition, the Pope says in the same place that the use is conceded to them just as if they truly were *domini*. On the other hand, John XXII openly and frankly acknowledges that he has no *dominium* over the mendicants' things, and if he does have, he most willingly renounces it.

Notwithstanding these points, if the question is not a mere verbal one, the conclusion is decided in favour of the mendicants. This is the second conclusion of this article. The use of eatable things and tools is distinguished in a certain way from *dominium*, such that the mendicants can use them without any (as they say) ownership [*proprietas*]. This is the proof. It is insufficient for true *dominium* that a person is permitted to consume a thing; what is required in addition (as was posited in the definition) is that he should be able to subject it to every use, for instance, to alienate it, to claim it in court, to bequeath it, to neglect it, and so on. The Friars Minor cannot even when joined in a monastery use their things in these kinds of ways. Indeed, those who bestow money upon them can remove the money at will whenever they wish, like true *domini*. Of the other tools and of the food the pope pronounces himself the true *dominus*. Therefore, just as someone who welcomes his friends to a feast does not make them the *domini* of the foods and drinks laid out on the table and does not give them the right to take them away and bring them to their own homes, but merely lets them sit and eat, in almost the same way the pope daily invites the friars, to whom he gives only the right to eat and drink and clothe themselves and so on. If he takes those things away from them, he does them no wrong, and he is to be considered not as a thief and robber, but as a *dominus* who takes back what is his. In favour of this conclusion is the famous passage in *Acts* 2 [2:45], which says that all the believers had everything in common, which is to be understood about those who lived in Jerusalem. Everything including their food was common to them, and they conducted themselves as guests at the table of their host.

Moreover, I would add to this for following reason. The opponents of this kind of poverty admit that monks can have private property in common but not as individuals. Let us therefore make use of what they themselves admit. I as an individual monk can eat things held in common, even though I am not their individual *dominus*. Therefore, in the same way the whole monastery and the whole order can use the same goods, although they lack all *dominium*. Nor should the pronouncement of John XXII be very persuasive, when he says that he renounced such *dominium*. First, he did not do this legitimately or (if one may say this) justly, but out of hatred for Ockham and others of his order who were very hostile to him. Moreover, his successors **(p. 283)** in that position have not approved his renunciation, but on the example of his predecessors retain the same *dominium*.

The same conclusion is corroborated by the Law, *Deuteronomy* 23 [23:24], in which persons entering a neighbour's vineyard were permitted use of the grapes without *dominium*. That text says, "When you enter your neighbour's vineyard, eat as many grapes as you want, but do not carry them out with you." The text did not make the entrant the *dominus* of the grapes so as to be able to sell them or exchange them for something else, but he could eat them as if he were a guest. Likewise in *Institutes, De usu et habitatione* [Justinian, *Institutes* 2, 5, 1], a person who has the bare use of land is allowed nothing more than to use the vegetables, fruits, flowers, and so on for his daily use. It seems therefore that use is there distinguished from *dominium*. Pertaining to the same conclusion is that a person suffering extreme necessity can help himself with another's bread but cannot sell the bread, although when someone suffers from lack of bread, he could take something else that he could exchange for bread. The conjecture arises that *dominium* is not transferred in extreme necessity from the fact that otherwise a person who under that title did not assist the unfortunate person would remain liable to make restitution. For if he was obligated to transfer *dominium* to the other, his holding on to it was just like retaining what belonged to another.

Very probably these observations allow a certain clarification of what Pope Nicholas says, namely, that the Friars Minor have use of fact and not of right, that is, use in act and not in condition. Use of right or use in condition is when the *dominus* cannot prevent such a use. The kind of use does not apply to the mendicants; for them utilization consists only in the very act. Money is different; because its use is to be alienated, it is taken up into every use, and so only the *dominus* can legitimately use it.

Through these points one can reply to the contrary reasons. First it must be said that even though no other use remains after the consumption of these things, it does not immediately follow that they are taken up into every use, as the basis for *dominium* requires. But you argue more insistently: if the mendicants cannot alienate those things, it is because they are forbidden by law, like the wards or the persons bound by primogeniture, and so there is no difficulty with the mendicants being true *domini*, as those persons are. The antecedent is denied: it is not that any civil law prevents those things from being sold or given away, but because the true *dominus* does not allow them that sort of faculty. To the laws adduced above and the authority of Saint Thomas, who denied that in these things use and *dominium* can be reckoned separately, the response is that those laws establish only that a price for the use of the thing cannot be taken that is distinct from the price of the thing. But they do not deny that the *dominus* can restrict use so that the other might use it in only one particular way and not in all the ways that are required for true *dominium*.

The objections at the beginning of this question have received sufficiently clear solutions. In the first argument, the second premise is false, namely, that *dominium* and *ius* have the same force. To the contrary, the reason for *dominium* posits more than does the reason for *ius*, and therefore *ius* is the more general term. Equally, there is a response to the other point, that the *ius* of the mendicants with regard to food and tools does not suffice to make the mendicants their *domini*.

For the second argument each premise is true, as the second conclusion shows, namely, that the mendicants consume food and garments of which they are not the *domini*. From that does not follow the consequence that our definition is not legitimate. To the contrary, from that same definition one learns that they are not the *domini* of those things because they cannot alienate them.

De Iustitia et Iure, IV, Q. 3, A. 1 (1553)

Whether dominia over things were once divided by human right

After determining both who can hold *dominia* and over what, proper order demands that we deal thirdly with their division. In our usual way, the argument on the negative side goes as it did above concerning slavery. No human right can contravene natural right; however, that the goods of this world are to be held in common is a determination of natural right, as is evident from Genesis 1, where the possession of things was given to man in common. Isidore affirms the same in book 5, which is quoted in [*Decretum Gratiani*] dis. 1, c. [7] *ius naturale*. And we read the same in Genesis 9, not only when nature was intact, but also subsequently when it was already corrupted, when Noah and his sons are told to "be fruitful and multiply and enter upon the earth and fill it," where God seems not to have wanted a division.

Second, this is more explicitly confirmed in the opinion of Clement in letter 4, which is quoted in [*Decretum Gratiani*] 12, q. 1 can. *dilectissimis*, where one reads that "the use of everything in this world ought to be in common for all men, but because of iniquity one person says this thing is his and another says that thing is his, and so a division has been made among mortals;" iniquity, however, is contrary to the equity of right.

Third comes also the consideration of charity, for if everything was possessed in common, the bond of love among mortals would be much firmer. Because your heart is where your treasure is, without a division, nothing would remain to divide their souls. This is the reason that in early times the churches of Jerusalem lived in common, in order that everyone's love might be more fervently united (as is described in the Acts of the Apostles); on this example the lives of the monks were set up. For this reason Augustine in his Rule said: "You should have one soul and one heart in God, and you should not call anything your own, but everything should be common to you." He implied by this that the unity of hearts cannot be nurtured except by renouncing mine and yours. This did not escape the famous Christian poet who said: "If two pronouns were removed from our affairs, battles would cease, and peace would be without quarrels." For this reason, the saying that friends have everything in common was always most celebrated. On this basis the saying that everything should be in common was always on the lips of the holy fathers, as Augustine, *On John*, tract. 6, and is recorded in [*Decretum Gratiani*] dis. 8 can. *quo iure*. And Ambrose in [*Decretum Gratiani*] dist. 47, *sicut hi*: "No-one should call what is common his own." Chrysostom, *On Luke*, c. 6: "We received everything from God; the words mine and thine are a lie." Therefore, making a division of things was never permissible.

Against this is the statement of Christ our Saviour, Matthew 22 [22:21]: "Render unto Caesar what is Caesar's and unto God what is God's."

On this question a dispute raged even among the philosophers. Plato **(p. 296)** (to whom Aristotle attributes this form of government at the beginning of *Politics* 1) contended that everything should be in common, not only possessions but also wives and children, although Socrates (whom Plato introduces as a speaker in the *Timaeus*) is said by others to be the first inventor of this kind of republic. Aristotle himself implies the same in Chapter 4. Plato himself recollects the same thing about this sort of republic in book 5 of his dialogue *The Republic*. They tried to make this excessive form of community convincing on the very basis that we just formulated, namely, that the hearts of all would be most tightly united and joined. They, however, did not deserve to be listened to because they thought about our nature in the complete simplicity of that innocence in which it was created by God in his mercy, not knowing that it was thence thrust out of that innocence because of our father's wrong.

Therefore, the response to this question consists in five conclusions. The first is this: Just as the common possession of things was appropriate to the state of innocence (with the exception of wives, for whom the form of possession was taught by the right of nature), so also the division of *dominia* was so congruent with the condition of corrupted nature, because without a miracle the human race could not otherwise have long endured. The former part is clear on its own. At that point in time the earth, even if uncultivated, would have produced its fruit spontaneously, or it would have needed minimal cultivation, which no one would have avoided. This is what we see in Genesis 2: God took man and placed him in a paradise of pleasure, so that he should work and take care of it. Moreover, no one was then exercised by cupidity; only after the sin was it said, "By the labour of your brow shall you eat bread." That famous pagan [Ovid, *Metamorphoses* 1, 101] was smelling the flower of that age when he said: "The entire earth itself was also free, untouched by the rake, and not wounded by any ploughs, giving everything through herself, and they were satisfied with food created without any compulsion." For this reason, no danger existed either that the earth's produce would fail or that any discord would arise among those happy people.

The latter part is proved from two contrary roots. The Socratic or Platonic community of wives and children does not require lengthy refutation, as its absurdity is evident. First, the very love that such community was supposed to support is undermined by it. Those philosophers said that all men would call any woman "my wife," and all children "my sons," and youths would call any older man "my father." This was best refuted by Aristotle. If they understood the word "all" collectively, it would be true, for all the older men would in combination be the fathers of those children. But this has very little to do with love. Such love would be thin and diluted in the entire republic, just as a little bit of honey in a large quantity of water is unable to sweeten it. Indeed, love would weaken all the more quickly because no one would recognize his own child or father. But if they understood the word "all" distributively as dealing with individuals, that is, that each individual child is the child of an individual parent, that certainly would conduce to greater love. But this is impossible, because one can be the child of only one mother and one father. There might even be neglect of children, because rarely would anyone recognize his own. Moreover, one can often discern who the father is from the lines on a child's face, and because of this, that person's heart would be more inclined to his own children than to others'. Accordingly, nature itself protested against that confused holding in common. In addition, after the collapse of nature, quarrels would inevitably arise, and among the undetermined fathers and children there would repeatedly be both impious murders and unspeakable loves and couplings. In sum, so natural is the identification of wives and children, that even in intact nature, where there was no opportunity for such evil inclinations, that absurd mixing of wives would not have been admitted but each would have his own. For they will be, it says [Genesis 2:24; Matthew 19:5; Mark 10:8]], two in one flesh. It was advantageous even then that each person should know by what kinship and tie of blood he was connected to others. And although the old law dispensed with this in order to propagate the special people of God, it was never to the effect that one wife might be married to two men. This was to take precautions against there being an unidentified throng of children.

Therefore, setting aside this silly form of holding in common, we return to demonstrating how congruent the division of possessions is with corrupted nature. This is from two corrupted roots: negligence and cupidity. On one side the earth, rebelling against man because of man's own rebellion, began to produce thorns and thistles and to need the sweat of the human brow in order to feed man. On the other side, after eating from the forbidden tree, man was stuffed with many desires. That form of possessing things was necessary that would most advantageously deal with both issues, cultivating the earth so that crops would not fail, and curbing scarcely satiable human avarice **(p. 297)**. Such possession could not be in common. Therefore, a division was necessary. This last conclusion is proved. For (as Aristotle says in the cited place), we can understand this possession in common in three ways: the fields should be private, but the produce should be common; or on the contrary, the fields should be common, and the produce divided; or both the fields and the produce should be common. If you allow the first, you provide an occasion for discord, because the labours are unequal; for whoever has more land puts in more labour, but the produce comes to all equally in accordance with each person's need. No one would lightly bear not getting produce commensurate with his labour. However, if they wanted the fields to be common, men would create the opportunity for laziness and indolence; for one cannot express how ardent is the love for one's own things, and how inert and languid it is for things in common, just as service is worse when there are many servants, because each one waits for others to do what he was going to do. The same thing happens in this kind of republic. On this basis the produce would turn out badly. The same misfortune would follow if both the produce and the fields were in common. In view of the human thirst for things, everyone would repeatedly strive on his own behalf to snatch up as much as he could. In this way the peace and tranquility of the citizens, and the friendship favoured by those philosophers, would inevitably be disturbed.

The second reason stems from the order that a republic must have if it is to be honourably preserved. Diverse orders and diverse classes of men are necessary, as Socrates himself recognized. He established three orders: farmers (among whom artisans are to be counted), and guardians, namely, soldiers and nobles who are assigned to defend the republic. The third order is the that of the jurists, who set out what the law is and respond to cases in doubt. The argument proceeds from this. If everything was in common, any person might refuse the burden of being a farmer and might desire to be a soldier. But when war is imminent, unless proper incentives were established, everyone would withdraw from the danger, and as many as possible would long to be among the governors. Next, when the highest class would have need of more members, it would follow that greater burdens would be given to some and greater honours to others. Unless *dominia* were divided, the republic could not avoid serious disturbance.

Thirdly, the same conclusion is evident. Just as allowing community of wives destroys the virtue of temperance by which one abstains from another's bed, so allowing community of possessions destroys the virtue of liberality, which is a firm adornment for a republic. For if one does not have something as one's own, one cannot be liberal; and if one has everything, one does not need another's liberality. And so would perish the virtue of providing hospitality for guests and pilgrims and of assisting the unfortunate, and with it would perish a grateful spirit for benefits received. Therefore, the assertion that things should be divided is so certain that its denial is heretical, as Augustine says in his book *On Heresies*. There in Chapter 40 he refers to the heresy of the Apostolici, who flaunted that title, because they did not admit into their communion those who had wives and possessed things of their own. For this John Hus, who denied that clergy can have anything of their own, was condemned at the Council of Constance.

One might argue that the division of things does not go far enough against the evils and inconveniences to the republic. Even now lands lie uncultivated because of man's laziness, and out of ambition and thirst for things men encroach on others' rights, and there are all the other evils of that sort. The answer is that it is not necessary for a law's equity that it achieve its end perfectly; it is sufficient that in accordance with its capability it establishes those things that are suitable to its end, for man's unbridled freedom cannot be totally restrained by any reins.

Second conclusion: although it is advantageous that possession of things be divided so far as property and *dominium* are concerned, so that a person might know what is his by the law of justice and keep his hands off what is another's, nonetheless so far as use is concerned things should be common through the benignity of mercy and liberality. The person with an abundance should give to the needy, and the needy should be grateful to him. On this basis friendship among men is more easily consolidated than if everything was possessed in a common *dominium*. From this is drawn the saying that friends have everything in common.

Third conclusion: the first division of external things was made by the right of nations (*ius gentium*), although later many other divisions were added by civil right (*ius civile*). Already in Book 1, q. 5, human right (*ius humanum*) was partitioned into these two. The conclusion is evident for this reason. *Dominium* began with the creation of the world (as was said above). Then God began to have objects of dominion, and similarly both angels and men by their own nature and right began to be masters of their own actions (*domini suarum actionum*), so that they might serve their creator with that liberty. Thus, a certain division of *dominia* was made by natural right, namely, *dominium* over one actions and (**p. 298**) man's having his own honour and reputation. For each one owns these not by the right of nations but by natural right. However (as the first conclusion shows), the distribution of possessions was made not before the sin but immediately after, for then (as we said) was born the reason for the division. Because of this we read that goods were at once divided between the two brothers, in that Cain offered from the produce of the earth and Abel from the best of his flock. For if these were not the private property of each, Abel would not have deserved praise nor Cain criticism.

The division is said to have been made not by natural right but by the right of nations, because natural right needs no reasoning but is written in the hearts (as the joining of male and female), but the right of nations is that which each person's reason infers from a comparison of principles. That is why it is called the right of nations, that is, of mankind, to whom belongs the ability to reason. For from the principles of corrupted nature the family of Adam immediately was taught — and subsequently nations in general — that each person should possess his own.

If you ask who first made this division, some respond that it was Adam. Others argue against this, on the grounds that he did not have regal power or coercive public authority, but he was only the paterfamilias, who could not distribute to his children anything but his own goods. This argument, however, is not very compelling. Perhaps (although this is nowhere stated) he had the authority of a prince by the very right of being the first and only parent of the human race. For it is not plausible that at some time the world lacked a human prince who could punish crimes; then by paternal right he could distribute to his children the wealth that he had in abundance. Indeed, it would not be absurd to say that he was the master of the whole world, because the world was made for man, and he was the only one. Nor was the world so crowded with people that he could not rule them through his agents. However, with respect to division by the right of nations, we need not be hemmed in by these difficulties. What is established by such right needs neither a prince nor the agreement of any republic, for the right of nations differs from civil right in this respect, that reason itself teaches the right of nations separately to individual persons. Because of this, the individual brothers by agreement, and then the grandchildren and great-grandchildren, could have occupied individual lands and fields and increased their goods, instructed by reason itself that unowned things go to the first occupier and that others abstain from them, as is held in Inst. *De iure pers, s. ferae* [Justinian, *Institutes* 2, 1, 12]. It says: "What previously belonged to no one is by natural reason allowed to the occupier." What he calls "natural reason" he understands as the right of nations, who infer it from natural principles. Thus, we read that Cain built a city, and in Genesis 10 that Noah's descendants were dispersed to the various regions and islands of the world; and thus immediately in chapter 11 that Nimrod's progeny and the multitude of those who had conspired with him to erect a tower were scattered. And thus immediately we read in Genesis 13 that a division was made between Abraham and Lot by agreement: "Behold the entire earth is before you. I beseech you to separate from me. If you go to the left, I will hold what is on the right, and if you choose the right, I will go to the left." From this it follows that not only is division in general by the right of nations, but also that certain nations possess this region and others another. Cajetan's opinion on [*Summa Theologiae*] 2, 2, q. 66, a. 2 was contrary to this. Because Saint Thomas says in the solution to the first objection that the division of things belongs to positive right (*ius positivum*), and nonetheless in [*Summa Theologiae* II-II] q. 57 had said that it was under the right of nations, Cajetan thought that these statements differed. He accordingly inferred that division in general was under the right of nations, but that appropriation in particular cases was under positive right, which is civil right. However, Saint Thomas extends the positive right to all human right, so that it includes the right of nations.

The second part of the conclusion, namely, that subsequently many particular *dominia* were assigned by civil right, that is, by the right of particular states and kingdoms, is very clear. For with the passage of time, states transferred to kings their power of command and the kingdom's *dominia*, as is recorded in *l. Quod principi placuit ff. de const. princip* [Justinian, *Digest* 1, 4, 1]. And by the *lex agraria* common fields were distributed. And by divine positive right (as we said above) the region of the Canaanites was promised and given to the Israelites, and the kingship to Saul and David. And later tithes to the Levites and now to the clergy.

Fourth conclusion: many things whose *dominia* the right of nations could not disperse, remain in common, for example, the place (as Aristotle says there), that is, the state, roads, etc., and (as is mentioned in the same place in the *Institutes*) the elements such as air and water, shores and harbours, fish, wild animals, birds, etc. By natural right and by allowance of the right of nations, fishing and hunting are common, although later they were excessively restricted by civil laws, perhaps more out of arbitrariness and custom than out of equity.

Fifth conclusion: the fifth conclusion is similarly easy **(p. 299)**. *Dominia* can be transferred by every kind of right. First, on the supposition that that *dominia* and possessions belong to particular persons through the division of things, by the natural right of liberty through which he is free the owner transfers *dominium* of his own goods to another, whether by voluntary gift or by some other free transaction, such as by selling or exchanging it and so on, as we noted in the previous book and will be more fully developed in the subsequent ones. Moreover, I think that the inherited succession of children to their father's goods has been established by the right of nations. Natural reason immediately taught this to all nations, that somehow or other the father's essence and name and right to goods continue in the children. Then the civil law of particular regions applied the rights of primogeniture and prescription and the other rights by which *dominia* are transferred. Moreover, *dominia* are transferred against the will of the owner in order to avenge and punish crimes, for men are deprived of their goods for the impiety of heresy, for the crime of treason, and for many other crimes of that sort. And similarly for the sake of cutting off lawsuits, as in the case of prescription.

Various ways exist for responding to the first argument. Some people understand the saying that "by natural right everything is in common" not universally but restrictively, for instance, in extreme necessity or among friends. This interpretation is supported neither by the matter itself nor by the jurists, for they understand the saying to be about common possession in general, which subsequently was divided by the right of nations. This is evident from the cited passage of Isidore and from Gratian dist. 8, cap. *differ*. Scotus, however in [*Ordinatio*] 4. dist. 15, q. 2. cleverly accepts the saying as universal, but says that after nature was corrupted, there was a derogation from this right of nature. But with all respect to the authority of that doctor, this seems less consistent with reason. This is because, first, natural right does not change, as is evident from Isidore in [*Decretum Gratiani*] dist. 6. Can. *Non est peccatum*, for he concluded that the precepts of the Decalogue are immutable because they belong to the right of nature.

Likewise, either there was a precept of the right of nature that things were possessed in common or there was no such precept. If you grant the first alternative, then either that precept was universal for every condition, which no one of sound mind would admit, for it would be a mistake to insist that in collapsed nature the same mode of possession would persist; or it was particular to that state of innocence, and no derogation from it was made, for the fact that the division was made in our condition does not derogate from its equity, inasmuch as if the state of innocence had continued, common possession would have continued. Therefore, the correct response is found in Saint Thomas [*Summa Theologiae* II-II] q. 66, ar. 2, though I will formulate this response more acutely through a distinction. With respect to things, one should consider both *dominium* and use. With respect to *dominium*, the right of nature never prevented a division of things by a precept that would have made a contrary law into a derogation from it. Common possession is said to belong to the right of nature only in the negative sense that the natural law never required that division, but permitted possession to be in whatever way was more convenient and advantageous to the different conditions of man. Therefore, it was not natural right that was changed but the thing. The statement in Augustine's *Confessions,* book one [Augustine, *On True Religion* XVII, 34] clarifies this with an excellent example. There is a medical rule, he says, that wine is suitable for men. There is no derogation from this rule if a sick person is forbidden to drink wine. The change is in the person for whom that continuing rule is not suitable. But with respect to use, the right of nature can in a certain way be affirmed as requiring all things to be in common in a condition of necessity.

As for the second objection, taken from the words of Clement in [*Decretum Gratiani*] 12, q. 1] can. *Dilectissimus*, the exposition of the gloss of John Teutonicus is wonderful. The text says that the use of all things should have been in common, but that because of iniquity one person says this thing is his and another says that thing is his. The gloss says: because of iniquity, that is because of the custom introduced by the right of nations, contrary to natural equity. But if the right of nations was an iniquity, it would never have been thought of under the designation of right. The plain sense, therefore, is that "because of iniquity" means "because of the original sin," by which dissolute liberty could not be restrained except by a division of things.

With respect to the third objection, it is not true that once nature was corrupted, the bonds of love between mortals would have been stronger if things were possessed in common, as is sufficiently clear in a series of conclusions. A small number of monks enclosed in the cloisters of monasteries can live peacefully in common, but that is not the case with vast republics of mortals who avidly long for secular things. We sincerely acknowledge the saying of the poet that two pronouns, mine and thine, are the seed and kindling of lawsuits and battles, but many more would arise if everything was possessed in common. The saints speak of the use of things when poor neighbours are in need; for then we have already said that use should be in common to the extent that suffices to free the unfortunate from poverty.

De Iustitia et Iure, V, 5, Q. 3, A. 4 (1553)

Is it permissible for a person pressed by indigence to steal?

After the iniquity of stealing has been made so clear by strict right, it is convenient to discuss whether some exception is to be made, at least when extreme necessity comes upon one. And it is argued in the negative *first*, from the chapter cited above *si quis extra de furt* [*Decretales Gregorii IX*, Lib V, tit. XVIII], which says that that if anyone out of the necessity of hunger has stolen a garment or food or cattle, he should do penance for three weeks, which would not be ordered unless theft was then impermissible. *Second*, it is argued from Aristotle's *Ethics* book 2, [1107a11] where he says that there are certain things which immediately on being named are tied up with wickedness, and he gives the example of theft, which signifies something inherently wicked, and therefore by no end and no cause can be made permissible, in which it is similar to lying. *Third*, a person ought to love another as himself; no one, however, is permitted to assist another through alms by stealing, as Augustine admonishes in his book against lying. Therefore, neither can one help oneself in this way.

To the contrary, however, in necessity (as the popular saying goes) everything is held in common **(p. 428)**.

The reply to the question is with three conclusions. *First*, things that are superfluous for a person are by the right of nature owed to the sustenance of the poor. The authority for this is Ambrose, quoted in *Decretum*, distin. 47: "the bread that you possess belongs to the hungry, the clothes in which you are clad to the naked, the money that you bury in the earth is the redemption and absolution of the miserable." Natural reason implies this. No right of nations or human right can derogate from natural or divine right, since these latter are superior. By the right of nature and by divine providence it has been instituted that inferior things are subservient to the necessity of men, for whom they were established. Therefore, when superfluous things of this sort do not serve their possessor, no human right can preclude them from coming into the use of the indigent.

Second conclusion: nonetheless, no one who does not suffer extreme necessity can snatch goods from one who has them in abundance. The proof: because even if the rich person is obligated to disperse those goods, there are many indigent people who happen to encounter him in different places and times, for whom the possessor can fittingly perform that act of charitable giving.

Third conclusion: in extreme necessity, that is, when it is evident and urgent, then that unfortunate person can help himself with someone else's goods, removing them whether in secret or in the open. The conclusion has often been adduced by us, that so innate in man is the right to save himself that everything else yields to it.

You should not understand in the *first* of these conclusions an obligation that sounds in justice but only in mercy, as we have noted in the fourth book in the question about the division of things. For after things were divided, each person is the owner of his goods. Nonetheless, the natural right in common continues to the extent that whoever has too much ought to be beneficent to the indigent. By this reason arises the truth of the *second* conclusion, that no person no matter how gravely he suffers can steal from the rich. Nor is the argument valid that in such a case (that is, in a case of grave necessity) a wealthy person is obligated to give to the indigent, in accordance with what John says in his canonical work [I John 3:17] that "Whoever sees his brother in need and closes his heart to him, how can the love of God remain in him?" and that therefore he can on his own authority snatch it away. This argument is not valid because that obligation is not of justice but of charity, to which no one can unwillingly be compelled. But this topic on the obligation of almsgiving is not to the present point. For Saint Thomas deals with it in the [*Summa Theologiae*] *Secunda Secundae*, question 32.

However, with respect to the *third* conclusion which pertains to the present issue, there is uncertainty as to what must be adjudged to be extreme necessity. Is it only when someone is right on the verge of being choked by hunger or by cold or is being consumed by some other calamity? For the very word "extreme" seems to designate that. The response, however, is that one should not wait until that point as is popularly thought. For there are those who call that necessity extreme which it is impossible at that time to remedy. Therefore, what is considered to be the moment of extreme necessity is when you see your brother being approached by a danger of incurable illness or of some other misery that usually kills people. That moment, I say, is when the greatest misery could be prevented and guarded against. Necessity that places a person's honour in danger, although it is not considered extreme, is certainly grave; it obligates the person who has the opportunity to provide help to do so or be guilty of mortal sin.

What if a girl is placed in danger of losing her shame because of lack of food? That too seems to be considered extreme because not only is her honour endangered but also the safety of her soul. It is responded that although there is a notable duty of this sort of compassion to assist the miserable orphans who are in danger, it is not considered extreme necessity such that the girl can seize what belongs to another, because there is no necessity that can compel her to make herself available to another. Otherwise, consent to this would not be a sin; but she should rather perish than be delinquent. However, there are civil laws that command that a person suffering extreme necessity should have recourse to the magistrates before taking what belongs to another on his own. This is understandable when it can be done conveniently.

To be sure, there will perhaps be no lack of objection to the present conclusions. For we have said both often elsewhere and just now that no one can be compelled to do what charity alone obligates, but only what justice obligates. In the case of extreme necessity, one is obligated to assist only out of charity. For if it was an obligation of justice, anyone who then did not assist would be bound to make restitution – which is not conceded; therefore, neither public power can then rightly compel anyone, nor can anyone in danger privately take anything belonging to someone else. The response is that it makes little difference whether you say in such necessity that some reason of injustice intervenes; indeed, properly speaking it is nothing but compassion that nonetheless strictly obliges. That compulsion then plays a role because of the singular right accruing to everyone of saving one's own life (**p. 429**).

Here should be appended the discussion of whether a person who in the moment of necessity takes what belongs to another is obligated to restore it when fortune later smiles more happily upon him. But I have already sufficiently resolved this in the preceding book under the title of restitution.

Accordingly, with regard to the rule adduced in the *first* argument the response is that it must be understood as being about necessity that is not extreme, where stealing has some fault. With respect to the *second*, we sincerely concede that theft is an action of intrinsic wickedness, indeed such that, as we said in Book 2, God as enactor of the natural law, cannot give a dispensation from it. And yet just as we said regarding the prohibition against murder, that by the generality of "Thou shalt not kill," which is a natural precept, are not included the cases which nature itself cannot include, nor in that precept not to swear, neither by the prohibition on theft can be precluded the taking of someone else's goods that nature itself allows. Therefore, that kind of taking is not theft but the taking of something allowed by nature.

Finally, the response to the *third* is that anyone is permitted the equal right in that necessity of taking what belongs to another in order to assist an indigent person. But short of that necessity Augustine prohibits alms that come from takings.

De Iustitia et Iure, IV, Q. 7, A. 1 (1553)

It remains to decide whether a person pressed by extreme necessity who has taken something that he previously owed to another or that he has then seized is absolved from the debt, or whether, if he subsequently becomes more prosperous, he is nonetheless obliged to pay it. The argument that he is immediately absolved [in the first of those situations] is that if he were then seizing something from the other, he would not be obligated. To this Scotus in the cited passage [*Ordinatio* IV, d. 15, q. 2, n. 203] elegantly **(p. 366)** responds with the following distinction. If he owed that thing by virtue of some other action before he was in a situation of extreme necessity, he does not become immune to restitution; but if he took it then [when in extreme necessity], he does not become subject to restitution. The reason is obvious: because in extreme necessity everything is held in common, the person who then takes something contracts no debt. However, if the debt had already been contracted, there is no reason for the pre-existing obligation to be dissolved, and therefore it will remain.

However, Adrian [*Quaestiones de sacramentis in quartum Sententiarum librum* 4] on the topic *de restitutione* does not admit this distinction, but holds absolutely that the person who, when subjected to extreme necessity, takes another's goods is obligated to make restitution when fortune smiles more favorably upon him. He has no lack of followers, who support his view. The weight of their argument depends on this, that in extreme necessity everything is not in common with respect to ownership. For otherwise a person who failed to assist the indigent would subsequently be liable to make restitution, which is not a credible position, because the precept of assistance belongs not to justice but to charity. Therefore, things are in common only with respect to use, with the result that once the use is complete one is obligated to restore the thing.

Secondly, it is argued that the person in extreme need is sufficiently assisted by the loan of a thing, and so no one is obligated simply to give; for this reason, the person who consumes the thing remains subject to restitution. Thirdly, a physician is not obligated to give his services free to the person in need, nor is a pharmacist obligated to make a gift of his drugs. It is enough if they expect repayment. To this is added tex. can. *Si quis de furt* [*Decretales Gregorii IX*, Lib V, tit. XVIII], which says that the person who seized another's goods because of the necessity of hunger or nakedness and then subsequently returns what is taken is not compelled to fast. Thence the inference from the converse is that if he did not return them, he would be compelled to fast.

Nonetheless one should persist in the former view, provided it be rightly explained. First, everyone acknowledges that no obligation to make restitution remains when the thing is of small value. But when the thing for which the need is extreme is of greater value, one must consider whether the person is needy without qualification, that is, whether he does not have the means of payment anywhere, or whether he does not have it here but has it elsewhere, or whether it is owed to him. Such a person should not be considered needy without qualification, and for that reason it is sufficient to give what would relieve him of his necessity as a loan to be repaid. For only his absolute necessity creates the right to get someone else's goods in such a case. However, if he is needy without qualification, it should be beyond controversy that he does not remain liable to make restitution for taking what he needs. For although it is the case that then everything is held in common only with respect to use, nonetheless for things that are consumed by use, ownership follows use by natural law; for example, the person who takes food or drink or money becomes its owner. In this matter, if we are not mistaken, the contrary opinion deceives its adherents. For the fact that everything is in common with respect to use means that to that extent the needy person could take another's goods as if they were his own. Therefore, he is not obligated to accept them as something to be repaid, but the other is obligated to give them for nothing. But if the thing is something that is not consumed by use, then when the necessity passed, he would be obligated to return them, for example, if someone uses another's horse to escape the danger of death, or if he needed a bed while ill. On this basis one can respond to the argument about the physician or the pharmacist. Certainly, if the other person was in extreme need of his services or his medicine, he would be obligated on pain of mortal sin, although bystanders would no less be subject to the same obligation to contribute, if the thing was so expensive. And yet fault does not so frequently occur in removing medicine as in food and other things. Nor does the bond of mercy oblige that so expensive a medicine counteract the threat of a pauper's death, or that a physician be so skilful.

With respect to what is adduced from cap. *si quis de furt.*, this is not relevant, because clearly what is mentioned there is not an extreme necessity but a less serious one, as the gloss rightly says. The text *Si quis propter necessitatem occupaverit* etc. [*Decretales Gregorii IX*, Lib V, tit. XVIII, c. 3] says that he should do penance for three weeks, and it is clear that since one is not at fault when seizing another's property in extreme necessity, no penance would be imposed.

Note on the Texts Translated

The following are the sources of the texts by Domingo de Soto translated in this volume:

In Causa Pauperum Deliberatio. In Domingo de Soto, *Relecciones y Opúsculos* II-2, edited by Jaime Brufau Prats, 204–361. Salamanca: Editorial San Estaban, 2011). The version of the book in the Biblioteca Virtual del Patrimonio Bibliográfico was also consulted.

Relección De Dominio. In Domingo de Soto, *Relecciones y Opusćulos* I, edited by Jaime Brufau Prats, 98–191. Salamanca: Editorial San Estaban, 1995.

Commentarium in II. II. q. 32 De eleemosyna (anno 1539–40). In Karl Deuringer, *Probleme der Caritas in der Schule von Salamanca*, 143–58. Freiburg: Verlag Herder, 1959.

De Iustitia et Iure. In *The School of Salamanca, A Digital Collection of Sources*. Accessed 3 September 2024. https://id.salamanca.school/texts/W0011. The page numbers in parentheses refer to the pagination in the text on this site.

Throughout the translations material that appears in square brackets is not explicit in the Latin text.

Bibliography

Primary Sources

Adrian. *Quaestiones de sacramentis in quartum Sententiarum librum*. 1522.

Ambrose. *De Officiis*. Edited J. Davidson. Oxford: Oxford University Press, 2001.

Aquinas, Thomas. *The Epiphany and Ante-Lenten Homilies*. Translated by John M. Ashley. Church Press Company. 1867.

— *Summa Theologiae*. In *Opera Omnia*, t. 4–12. Leonine Edition. Rome: Typographia Polyglotta. 1888–1906.

Aristotle. *Analytica Priora et Posteriora*. Edited by David Ross and L. Minio-Paluello. Oxford: Oxford University Press, 1981.

— *Politica*. Edited by David Ross. Oxford: Oxford University Press, 1957.

Augustine. *Homilies on the Gospel of John 1-40*. Translated by Edmund Hill. Hyde Park, NY: New City Press. 2009.

Azor, Juan. *Institutionum Moralium, in quibus universae quaestiones ad conscientiam recte aut prave factorum pertinentes breviter tractantur*. 1600.

Azpilcueta, Martin de (Doctor Navarrus). *Libri de Reditibus Ecclesiasticis*. 1571.

— *Manuel de Confessoribus*. 1549.

Banez, Domingo. *De Iure et Iustitia Decisiones*. 1595.

Biel, Gabriel. *Collectorium Sententiarum*. 1501

Cajetan, Thomas. *Commentaria ad Aquinas, Summa Theologiae*. In *Aquinas, Opera Omnia*. Leonine Edition, t. 4–12. 1888–1906.

Cicero, Marcus Tullius. *De Officiis*. Edited by M. Winterbottom. Oxford: Oxford University Press, 1994. https://doi.org/10.1093/actrade /9780198146735.book.1.

Covarrubias y Leyva, *Diego de. Regulae, Peccatum*. 1553.

Duns Scotus, John. Ordinatio. in *Omnia Opera*. Vatican edition, volume 13. Vatican City: Typis Polyglottis Vaticanis, 1990

— *Selected Writings on Ethic*. Edited by Thomas Williams. Oxford: Oxford University Press. 2017.

Erasmus, Desiderius. *The Collected Works of Erasmus: Colloquies*. Translated by Craig R. Thompson. Toronto: University of Toronto Press, 1997.

Friedberg, Emil, ed. *Decretum Magistri Gratiani*. Vol. 1 of *Corpus Iuris Canonici*. Leipzig: Bernhard Tauchnitz, 1879; reprint, Graz: Akademische Druck- und Verlagsanstalt, 1959.

Gli Scritti di S. Francesco d'Assisi. Edited by Kajetan Esser. Padua: O.F.M. Edizioni Messagero, 1982.

Grotius, Hugo. *Commentary on the Law of Prize and Booty*. Edited by Martine Julia van Ittersum. Carmel, IN: Liberty Fund, 2006.

— *De Jure Belli Ac Pacis*. Edited by B.J.A. de Kanter-van Hettinga Tromp. Aalen: Scientia Verlag Aalen, 1993.

Kant, Immanuel. *The Metaphysics of Morals*. Edited by Lara Denis. Translated by Mary Gregor. Cambridge: Cambridge University Press, 2017.

Krueger, Paulus, and Theodorus Mommsen, eds. *Corpus Iuris Civilis, Volumen Primum: Institutiones, Digesta*. Dublin/Zurich: Weidmann, 1966.

Lactantius, Lucius Caecilius Firminianus. *The Divine Institutes: Books I–VII*. Translated by Mary Francis McDonald. Washington, DC: Catholic University of America Press, 1964.

Lessius, Leonardus. *De Iustitia et Iure Ceterisque Virtutibus Cardinalibus*. 1605.

Lugo, Juan de. *De Iustitia et Iure*. 1642.

Molina, Luis de. *De Iustitia et Iure, Tomus Tertius (De Restitutione)*. Geneva: Marc Michel & C. Bosanquet, 1733.

Molina, Luis de., *De Iustitia et Iure/Über Gerechtigkeit und Recht, Teil I*. Edited by Matthias Kaufmann and Danaë Simmermacher. Stuttgart: Frommann-Holzboog, 2019. https://doi.org/10.5771/9783772831096.

Ockham, William of. *A Letter to the Friars Minor and Other Writings*. Edited by Arthur Stephen McGrade and John Kilkullen. Translated by John Kilcullen. Cambridge: Cambridge University Press, 1995.

— *Opus Nonaginta Dierum*, in *Guillelmi de Ockham Opera Politica II*. Edited by G.J. Sikes. Manchester: University of Manchester Press, 1963.

Plato. *Respublica*. Edited by S.R. Slings. Oxford: Oxford University Press, 2003.

Robles, Juan de. *De la orden que en algunos pueblos de España se ha puesto en la limnosa para remedio de la verdaderos pobres*. (1545). In Alonso Seco, Juan de Robles, Anexo.

Sanchez, Thomas. *Consilia Seu Opuscula Moralia*. 1640.

Soto, Domingo de. *De Iustitia et Iure*. 1553.

— *Relecciones y Opusculos I*. Edited by Jaime Brufau Prats. Salamanca: Editorial San Estaban, 1995.

— *Relecciones y Opúsculos. II-2*. Edited by Jaime Brufau Prats. Salamanca: Editorial San Estaban, 2011.

Vásquez, Gabriel. *Tractatus de Eleemosyna*. 1617.

Vasquius Menchacensis, Fernandus. *Controversiae*. 1564.

Vitoria, Francisco de. *Commentarios de la Secunda Secundae de Santo Tomás*. *T. III*. Edited by Vicente Beltran de Heredia. 1934.

– *De Iustitia/Über die Gerechtigkeit, Teil 2.* Edited by Joachim Stüben. Stuttgart: Frommann-Holzboog, 2017.

– *Political Writing.* Edited by Anthony Pagden and Jeremy Lawrence. Cambridge: Cambridge University Press, 1991.

Secondary Sources

Adams, David M. "Hohfeld on Rights and Privileges." *ARSP: Archiv für Rechts- und Sozialphilosophie/Archives for Philosophy of Law and Social Philosophy* 71, no. 1 (1985): 84–95. http://www.jstor.org/stable/23679529.

Alonso Seco, José María. *Juan de Robles: Un reformador social en* época *de crisis.* Madrid: Tirant Humanidades, 2012.

Badian, Ernst. *Foreign Clientelae.* Oxford: Oxford University Press, 1958.

Barak, Aharon. *Proportionality: Constitutional Rights and Their Limitations.* Cambridge: Cambridge University Press, 2012. https://doi.org/10.1017/CBO9781139035293.

Birks, Peter. *The Roman Law of Obligations.* Edited by Eric Descheemaeker. Oxford: Oxford University Press, 2014. https://doi.org/10.1093/acprof:oso/9780198719274.001.0001.

Blank, Andreas. "Domingo de Soto on Justice to the Poor." *Intellectual History Review* 25, no. 2 (2014): 133–46. doi:10.1080/17496977.2014.971499.

Brett, Annabel S. *Changes of State: Nature and the Limits of the City in Early Modern Natural Law.* Princeton, NJ: Princeton University Press, 2011.

– *Liberty, Right and Nature: Individual Rights in Later Scholastic Thought.* Cambridge: Cambridge University Press, 1997.

Cavallar, Georg. *The Rights of Strangers: Theories of International Hospitality, The Global Community and Political Justice Since Vitoria.* Aldershot: Routledge, 2002.

Chung-Kim, Esther. *Economics of Faith: Reforming Poverty in Early Modern Europe.* Oxford: Oxford: Oxford University Press, 2021. https://doi.org/10.1093/oso/9780197537732.001.0001.

Coccoli, Lorenzo. "Il conflitto sulla mobilità alle soglie dell'età moderna. Riforma dell'assistenza ai poveri e ius migrandi." *Jura Gentium* 11, no. 1 (2014): 40–57.

Deuringer, Karl. *Probleme der Caritas in der Schule von Salamanca.* Freiburg: Verlag Herder, 1959.

Doyle, John P. "Soto, Domingo de (1494–1560)." In *Routledge Encyclopedia of Philosophy.* London: Taylor and Francis, 1998. https://www.rep.routledge.com/articles/biographical/soto-domingo-de-1494-1560/v-1.

du Bois, François. "Punishment, Reparation and the Evolution of Private Law: The *Actio Iniuriarum* in a Changing World." *Acta Juridica*, no. 1 (2019): 229–82. https://journals.co.za/content/journal/10520/EJC-1a7573ac74.

Dyck, Andrew R. *A Commentary on Cicero, De Officiis.* Ann Arbor: University of Michigan Press, 1996.

Fantazzi, Charles. "Vives and the *emarginati.*" In *A Companion to Juan Luis Vives*, edited by Charles Fantazzi, 65–112. Leiden: Brill, 2008. https://doi.org/10.1163/ej.9789004168541.i-431.

Flynn, Maureen. *Sacred Charity.* Ithaca, NY: Cornell University Press, 1989. https://doi.org/10.1007/978-1-349-09043-3.

Folgado, Avalino. *Evolucion Historica del Concepto del Derecho Subjectivo: Estudio especial de los teólogosjuristas españoles del siglo XVI.* San Lorenzo de El Escorial, 1960.

Fouto, Ana Caldeira. "Revisiting 'Subjectivity' in Rights Theories: The (Re)Creation of the 'Legal Subject' in Second Scholastics Juridical Discourse." *Revista Portuguesa de Filosofia* 75, no. 2 (2019): 1103–24. https://www.jstor.org /stable/26678102.

Geltner, Guy. "Eden Regained: William of Ockham and the Franciscan Return to Terrestrial Paradise." *Franciscan Studies* 59 (2001): 63–89. https://doi .org/10.1353/frc.2001.0023.

Gordley, James. *The Jurists: A Critical History.* Oxford: Oxford University Press, 2013. https://doi.org/10.1093/acprof:oso/9780199689392.001.0001.

Grice-Hutchinson, Marjorie. *The School of Salamanca: Readings in Spanish Monetary Theory, 1544–1605.* Auburn, AL: Mises Institute, 2009.

Grimm, Harold J. "Luther's Contributions to Sixteenth-Century Organization of Poor Relief." *Archiv* für *Reformationsgeschichte – Archive for Reformation History* 61, no. jg (1970): 222–34. https://doi.org/10.14315/arg -1970-jg11.

Hohfeld, Wesley Newcomb. "Some Fundamental Legal Conceptions as Applied in Judicial Reasoning." *Yale Law Journal* 23, no. 1 (1913): 16–59. https://doi .org/10.2307/785533.

Holmes, Oliver Wendell. *The Common Law.* Boston: Little, Brown, 1881.

Hubeñak, Florencio. "Domingo de Soto en el contexto de su época." In *La ley natural como fundamento moral y jurídico en Domingo de Soto*, edited by Juan Cruz Cruz. Barañáin: EUNSA, 2007.

Izbicki, Thomas, and Matthias Kaufmann. "The School of Salamanca." In *The Stanford Encyclopedia of Philosophy.* 2019. https://plato.stanford.edu/archives/sum2019 /entries/school-salamanca/.

Kahl, Sigrun. "The Religious Roots of Modern Poverty Policy: Catholic, Lutheran, and Reformed Protestant Traditions Compared." *European Journal of Sociology/Archives Européennes de Sociologie / Europäisches Archiv Für Soziologie* 46, no. 1 (2005): 91–126. http://www.jstor.org/stable/23998794.

Klimchuk, Dennis. "Grotius on Property and the Right of Necessity." *Journal of the History of Philosophy* 56, no. 2 (2018): 239–60. https://doi.org/10.1353 /hph.2018.0022.

Lawson, F.H., and B.S. Markesinis. *Tortious Liability for Unintentional Harm in the Common Law and the Civil Law.* Cambridge: Cambridge University Press, 1982.

Lindberg, Carter. "Reformation Initiatives for Social Welfare: Luther's Influence at Leisnig." *Annual of the Society of Christian Ethics* 7 (1987): 79–99. http://www.jstor.org/stable/23559472.

Martz, Linda. *Poverty and Welfare in Hapsburg Spain.* Cambridge: Cambridge University Press, 1983. https://doi.org/10.1017/CBO9780511897979.

Moon, Donald. "The Idea of the Welfare State." In *The Oxford Handbook of the History of Political Philosophy*, edited by George Klosko, 660–72. Oxford: Oxford University Press, 2011.

Nicholas, Barry. *An Introduction to Roman Law.* Oxford: Oxford University Press, 1962.

Nicols, John. "Hospitality among the Romans." In *Social Relations in the Roman World*, edited Michael Peachin, 422–37. Oxford: Oxford University Press, 2011. https://doi .org/10.1093/oxfordhb/9780195188004.013.0020.

Nolf, J. *La Réforme de la Bienfaisance Publique* à Ypres au *XVIe siècle.* Ghent: E. van Goethem, 1915.

Salamanca, Beatriz E. "Domingo de Soto and Itinerant Poverty: A Mobile Concept." In *Do Good unto All: Charity and Poor Relief across Christian Europe, 1400–1800*, edited by Timothy G. Fehler and Jared B. Thomley, 25–43. Manchester: Manchester University Press, 2023. https://doi.org/10.7765/9781526162489.

Sampson, Joe. *The Historical Foundations of Grotius' Analysis of Delict.* Leiden: Brill, 2018. https://doi.org/10.1163/9789004344372.

Scattola, Merio. "La virtud de la justicia en la doctrina de Domingo de Soto." *Anuario Filosófico* 45, no. 2 (2017): 313–41. https://doi.org/10.15581/009.45.1209.

— "Natural Law Part I: The Catholic Tradition." In Henrik Lagerlund and Benjamin Hill, *The Routledge Companion to Sixteenth Century Philosophy*, no pp. Routledge, 2017.

Schermaier, Martin. "Res Communes Omnium: The History of an Idea from Greek Philosophy to Grotian Jurisprudence." *Grotiana* 30, no. 1 (2009): 20–48. doi: https://doi.org/10.1163/016738309X12537002674204.

Schwartz, Daniel. *The Political Morality of the Late Scholastics.* Cambridge: Cambridge University Press, 2019. https://doi.org/10.1017/9781108591522.

Spicker, Paul, ed. *The Origins of Modern Welfare*, Volume I. Verlag Peter Lang, 2010. https://doi.org/10.3726/978-3-0353-0017-8.

Spindler, Anselm. "Vernunft, Gesetz und Recht bei Francisco de Vitoria." In *Die Normativität des Rechts bei Francisco de Vitoria*, edited by Kirstin Bunge, Anselm Spindler, and Andreas Wagner, 41–70. Stuttgart: Frommann-Holzboog, 2011. https://doi.org/10.5771/9783772830563.

Steinbicker, Carl Richard. *Poor Relief in the Sixteenth Century.* Washington, DC: Catholic University of America, 1937.

Swift, Louis J. "*Iustitia* and *Ius Privatum*: Ambrose on Private Property." *American Journal of Philology* 100, no. 1 (1979): 176–87. https://doi.org/10.2307/294237.

Tierney, Brian. "Hohfeld on Ockham: A Canonistic Text in the *Opus nonaginta dierum*." In *Medieval Church Law and the Origins of the Western Legal Tradition*, edited by Wolfgang P. Müller and Mary Summar, 365–74. Washington, DC: Catholic University of America Press, 2006.

— *The Idea of Natural Rights: Studies on Natural Rights, Natural Law, and Church Law 1150–1165*. Atlanta: Scholars Press, 1997.

Tuck, Richard. *Natural Rights Theories: Their Origin and Development*. Cambridge: Cambridge University Press, 1979. https://doi.org/10.1017/CBO9781139163569.

Varkemaa, Jussi. *Conrad Summenhart's Theory of Individual Rights*. Leiden: Brill, 2012. https://doi.org/10.1163/9789004225565.

Weinrib, Ernest J. *Corrective Justice*. Oxford: Oxford University Press, 2012. https://doi.org/10.1093/acprof:oso/9780199660643.001.0001.

— "Defending the Juridical." *Canadian Journal of Law and Jurisprudence*, published online 3 October 2025. https://doi.org/10.1017/cjlj.2025.10044.

— *Reciprocal Freedom: Private Law and Public Right*. Oxford: Oxford University Press, 2022. https://doi.org/10.1093/oso/9780198754183.001.0001.

Weinrib, Jacob. *The Impasse of Constitutional Rights*. Cambridge: Cambridge University Press, 2025. https://doi.org/10.1017/9781009010078.

Zimmermann, Reinhard. *The Law of Obligations: Roman Foundations of the Civilian Tradition*. Oxford: Oxford University Press, 1996. https://doi.org/10.1093/acprof:oso/9780198764267.001.0001.

Index

able-bodied beggars: expulsion of, 122,
135, 145; law concerning, 101, 119;
right to beg, 119; treatment of, 121–2
Abraham: dispute between Lot and, 60,
106, 167, 190; hospitality of, 23, 123,
124, 125, 126
actio iniuriarum of Roman law, 51, 52
Adrian VI, Pope, 81, 151, 196
Alexander of Hales, 149–50, 151
Alexius of Rome, 143
alms: diminishing and loss of, 129, 135,
137; effect on the condition of the
poor, 146; meaning of, 123; provision
of, 114
almsgiving: Christian view of, 114–17,
129; compassion and, 5, 76, 88–9,
90; enforcement of, 104; in extreme
necessity, 16–19, 20, 42, 150, 151–2,
153, 154; failure of, 77, 148; in grave
necessity, 16, 19, 20, 26, 42; laws
on, 53, 136–7; by a loan, 83, 153;
as a matter of counsel, 149, 150; as
a matter of natural right, 15, 193; as
a matter of personal choice, 42–3; as
a matter of precept, 13–20, 42, 148,
149, 150, 152, 155; from necessities
of nature, 150; from necessities of
status, 150, 151, 152, 155; obligation
of, 12–13, 14, 15, 17–20, 42, 77, 78,
79, 91, 104, 114–17, 157; observation
of, 128; preaching on, 130; precept
of mercy and, 77; *quod superest*
("regarding what is left"), 154–5;
registration for, 136–7; right to beg
and, 26–7; to sinners, 126; *superfluum
date* ("give what is superfluous"),
154; theological debates on, 104;
Thomistic view on, 14, 15, 17–18,
115, 148–9; traditional practices of,
12; uncertainties about, 153–4
Ambrose, Bishop of Milan: on acquisition
of *dominium*, 165; on almsgiving, 17–
18, 115, 116–17, 124, 128, 140, 151–
2, 156; on common possession, 58,
186; *De Officiis*, 151; on hospitality,
26; on laws on the poor, 112; *Liber
de Nabuthi*, 124; *On Luke*, 116; on
obligation of mercy, 116, 154; parable
of rich man, 116; on possession of
superfluous things, 193
Antoninus, archbishop of Florence:
Summa Rosellae, 149
Apostolici, 62, 63, 188
appropriation of innocent goods, 166–7,
168
Aquilian liability, 45, 46
Aristotle: Buridan's critique of, 171–2;
on civil vs. despotic rule, 177; on

Toronto Studies in Medieval Law